URBAN HORTICULTURE
Ecology, Landscape, and Agriculture

URBAN HORTICULTURE
Ecology, Landscape, and Agriculture

Edited by
J. Blum, PhD

Apple Academic Press Inc.
3333 Mistwell Crescent
Oakville, ON L6L 0A2
Canada

Apple Academic Press Inc.
9 Spinnaker Way
Waretown, NJ 08758
USA

©2016 by Apple Academic Press, Inc.
Exclusive worldwide distribution by CRC Press, a member of Taylor & Francis Group
No claim to original U.S. Government works
Printed in the United States of America on acid-free paper
International Standard Book Number-13: 978-1-77188-423-5 (Hardcover)
International Standard Book Number-13: 978-1-77188-424-2 (eBook)

This book contains information obtained from authentic and highly regarded sources. Reprinted material is quoted with permission and sources are indicated. Copyright for individual articles remains with the authors as indicated. A wide variety of references are listed. Reasonable efforts have been made to publish reliable data and information, but the authors, editors, and the publisher cannot assume responsibility for the validity of all materials or the consequences of their use. The authors, editors, and the publisher have attempted to trace the copyright holders of all material reproduced in this publication and apologize to copyright holders if permission to publish in this form has not been obtained. If any copyright material has not been acknowledged, please write and let us know so we may rectify in any future reprint.

Trademark Notice: Registered trademark of products or corporate names are used only for explanation and identification without intent to infringe.

Library and Archives Canada Cataloguing in Publication

Urban horticulture : ecology, landscape, and agriculture / edited by J. Blum, PhD.

Includes bibliographical references and index.
Issued in print and electronic formats.
ISBN 978-1-77188-423-5 (hardcover).--ISBN 978-1-77188-424-2 (pdf)

1. Urban agriculture. 2. Horticulture. 3. Urban gardening. 4. Community gardens.
5. Urban soils. 6. Sustainable agriculture. 7. Human ecology. I. Blum, Janaki, editor

S494.5.U72U73 2016   635.09173'2   C2016-901477-0   C2016-901478-9

Library of Congress Cataloging-in-Publication Data

Names: Blum, Janaki, editor.
Title: Urban horticulture : ecology, landscape, and agriculture / editor: J. Blum.
Description: Oakville, Ont. ; Waretown, NJ : Apple Academic Press, 2016. | Includes bibliographical references and index.
Identifiers: LCCN 2016009303 | ISBN 9781771884235 (hardcover : alk. paper)
Subjects: LCSH: Urban gardening. | Horticulture. | Ecological landscape design.
Classification: LCC SB453 .U73 2016 | DDC 635.09173/2--dc23
LC record available at http://lccn.loc.gov/2016009303

Apple Academic Press also publishes its books in a variety of electronic formats. Some content that appears in print may not be available in electronic format. For information about Apple Academic Press products, visit our website at **www.appleacademicpress.com** and the CRC Press website at **www.crcpress.com**

ABOUT THE EDITOR

J. BLUM, PhD

J. Blum, PhD, has a background in biology as well as urban and environmental policy and planning. Her experience in education, field work, research, evaluation, and project coordination is diverse, and includes biotechnology, food systems and urban agriculture, affordable housing policy, and small-scale economic development. She has studied or worked in educational, non-profit and for-profit environments in the USA, Europe, and Asia.

CONTENTS

Acknowledgment and How to Cite ix
List of Contributors xi
Introduction xv

Part I: Urban Horticulture and Ecological Landscaping

1. **Introduction to Ecological Landscaping: A Holistic Description and Framework to Guide the Study and Management of Urban Landscape Parcels** 3

   Loren B. Byrne and Parwinder Grewal

2. **New Approaches to Ecologically Based, Designed Urban Plant Communities in Britain: Do These Have Any Relevance in the United States?** 33

   James Hitchmough

3. **Urban Cultivation in Allotments Maintains Soil Qualities Adversely Affected by Conventional Agriculture** 55

   Jill L. Edmondson, Zoe G. Davies, Kevin J. Gaston, and Jonathan R. Leak

4. **Lead Levels in Urban Gardens** 79

   Annie King, Peter Green, Guadalupe Pena, Wendy Chen, and Louis Schuetter

Part II: Urban Soil and Water

5. **Urban Community Gardeners' Knowledge and Perceptions of Soil Contaminant Risks** 103

   Brent F. Kim, Melissa N. Poulsen, Jared D. Margulies, Katie L. Dix, Anne M. Palmer, and Keeve E. Nachman

6. **Sustainable Water Management for Urban Agriculture, Gardens and Public Open Space Irrigation: A Case Study in Perth** 129

   Raju Sharma Dhakal, Geoff Syme, Edward Andre, and Charles Sabato

7. **Where Is the UK's Pollinator Biodiversity? The Importance of Urban Areas for Flower-Visiting Insects** 149

   Katherine C. R. Baldock, Mark A. Goddard, Damien M. Hicks, William E. Kunin, Nadine Mitschunas, Lynne M. Osgathorpe, Simon G. Potts, Kirsty M. Robertson, Anna V. Scott, Graham N. Stone, Ian P. Vaughan, and Jane Memmott

8. The Influence of Garden Size and Floral Cover on Pollen
   Deposition in Urban Community Gardens 173
   Peter A. Werrell, Gail A. Langellotto, Shannon U. Morath, and Kevin C. Matteson

Part III: Urban Pollination

9. Bumble Bee Abundance in New York City Community Gardens:
   Implications for Urban Agriculture 193
   Kevin C. Matteson and Gail A. Langellotto

10. Modification of a Community Garden to Attract Native Bee
    Pollinators in Urban San Luis Obispo, California 211
    Jaime C. Pawelek, Gordon W. Frankie, Robbin W. Thorp, and Maggie Przybylski

Part IV: Urban Home and Community Gardening

11. Urban Home Gardens in the Global North: A Mixed Methods
    Study of Ethnic and Migrant Home Gardens in Chicago, IL.............. 241
    John R. Taylor and Sarah Taylor Lovell

12. Community Gardens as Contexts for Science, Stewardship,
    and Civic Action Learning 267
    Marianne E. Krasny and Keith G. Tidball

Author Notes.. 291
Index... 297

ACKNOWLEDGMENT AND HOW TO CITE

The editor and publisher thank each of the authors who contributed to this book. The chapters in this book were previously published elsewhere. To cite the work contained in this book and to view the individual permissions, please refer to the citation at the beginning of each chapter. Each chapter was read individually and carefully selected by the editor; the result is a book that provides a multiperspective look at research into many elements of urban horticulture. The chapters included examine the following topics:

- Written as an introduction to a conference, Byrne (chapter 1) grounds the rest of the papers as it uses the term "landscape" as an umbrella for all urban horticultural practices, presenting a holistic ecological framework for understanding urban landscapes. It also suggests design guidelines that help mitigate the potentially negative effects of built-up areas on the environment.
- The Hitchmough article (chapter 2) provides an approach to sustainable urban landscape design that emphasize more mixed plantings of both native and exotic species that fit particular, frequently extreme, soil and water conditions found in urban areas.
- Contrary to common wisdom, Edmondson et al. (chapter 3) demonstrate that urban soil quality in general tends to be higher than that of areas depleted by industrial agricultural practices, and may be maintained by sustainable gardening methods.
- Their hypothesis that poor soil quality is associated with extreme anthropogenic disturbance is borne out by King (chapter 4) who gives a detailed account of a major soil contaminant on former housing or industrial areas that can cause ill health in humans.
- Kim et al. (chapter 5) reveal that urban gardeners' awareness of soil contaminants and associated health risks is not as developed compared to that of other issues such as pesticide use. They stress the need for balanced educational messaging to further the practice of safe gardening.
- Johnson et al (chapter 6) deal with the very critical issue of irrigation under conditions of shading found in densely built cities, using a modelling system to determine agricultural potential of an urban area with respect to water demand.

- Dhakal et al. (chapter 7) pursue this topic further by examining a particular sustainable water management system in Australia, to highlight continuing issues and good practices. However, I shall have to explain some of the terminology in the introduction
- Werrell et al. (chapter 8) hypothesize that floral cover positively impacts conspecific pollen deposition by attracting a greater number of pollinators into an urban garden, and that total cucumber area positively impacts conspecific pollen deposition when pollinators are locally foraging within a garden, and they suggest that the arrangement of plants within a garden can positively influence yield in fruit and vegetable-producing plants within urban community gardens.
- Matteson and Langellotto (chapter 9) suggest that *B. impatiens* may be an especially important pollinator of several common crops grown within community gardens and other urban green spaces that are used for agricultural production.
- Pawelek et al. (chapter 10) discuss ways to attract native bee pollinators by planting known bee-attractive plants.
- Taylor and Lovell (chapter 11) demonstrate the oft neglected significance of urban home gardens to urban horticulture, particularly agriculture, but also warn of the persistence of faulty practices that contribute to ecosystem disservices, indicating the need for educational outreach.
- The article on community gardens continues the theme of education in urban agriculture. Krasny and Tidball (chapter 12) deliver a fascinating article based on their youth-oriented education program which suggests that community gardens may provide opportunities for multi-layered learning that could apply to larger urban social-ecological systems.

LIST OF CONTRIBUTORS

Edward Andre
Centre for Planning, Edith Cowan University, Perth, Australia.

Katherine C. R. Baldock
School of Biological Sciences, University of Bristol, Life Sciences Building, Bristol BS8 1TQ, UK; Cabot Institute, University of Bristol, Bristol BS8 1UJ, UK

Loren B. Byrne
Assistant Professor of Biology, Department of Biology, Marine Biology and Environmental Science, Roger Williams University, Bristol, RI 02809

Wendy Chen
Department of Animal Science, Law Office of Brian C. McCarthy, Peachtree Street Northwest, Atlanta, GA, USA

Zoe G. Davies
Durrell Institute of Conservation and Ecology (DICE), School of Anthropology and Conservation, University of Kent, Canterbury, Kent, UK

Raju Sharma Dhakal
Centre for Planning, Edith Cowan University, Perth, Australia.

Katie L. Dix
Community Greening Resource Network, Parks & People Foundation, Baltimore, Maryland, United States of America

Jill L. Edmondson
Department of Animal and Plant Sciences, University of Sheffield, Sheffield, UK

G. W. Frankie
Professor, Department of Environmental Science, Policy and Management, University of California, Berkeley, CA 94720 USA

Kevin J. Gaston
Environment and Sustainability Institute, University of Exeter, Penryn, Cornwall, UK

Mark A. Goddard
School of Biology, University of Leeds, Leeds LS2 9JT, UK; School of Civil Engineering and Geosciences, Newcastle University, Newcastle upon Tyne NE1 7RU, UK

Peter Green

Department of Animal Science, Law Office of Brian C. McCarthy, Peachtree Street Northwest, Atlanta, GA, USA

Parwinder Grewal
Professor of Entomology, Department of Entomology, OARDC/The Ohio State University, Wooster, OH 44691

Damien M. Hicks
Institute of Evolutionary Biology, University of Edinburgh, Kings Buildings, Edinburgh EH9 3JT, UK

James D. Hitchmough
Professor of Horticultural Ecology, Department of Landscape Architecture, Arts Tower, University of Sheffield, S10 2TN, United Kingdom

Brent F. Kim
Johns Hopkins Center for a Livable Future, Baltimore, Maryland, United States of America, Department of Environmental Health Sciences, Johns Hopkins Bloomberg School of Public Health, Baltimore, Maryland, United States of America.

Annie King
Department of Animal Science, Law Office of Brian C. McCarthy, Peachtree Street Northwest, Atlanta, GA, USA

Marianne E. Krasny
Professor and Chair, Department of Natural Resources, 118 Fernow Hall, Cornell University, Ithaca, NY 14853 USA

William E. Kunin
School of Biology, University of Leeds, Leeds LS2 9JT, UK

Gail A. Langellotto
Assistant Professor, Department of Horticulture, 4017 Agriculture and Life Sciences Building, Oregon State University, Corvallis, OR 97331, USA.

Jonathan R. Leake
Department of Animal and Plant Sciences, University of Sheffield, Sheffield, UK

Sarah Taylor Lovell
University of Illinois at Urbana-Champaign, Department of Crop Sciences, Urbana, Illinois, USA

Kevin C. Matteson
Postdoctoral Teaching Fellow, Department of Biological Sciences, Fordham University, Rose Hill Campus, Bronx, NY 10458, USA.

Jared D. Margulies
Johns Hopkins Center for a Livable Future, Baltimore, Maryland, United States of America, Department of Environmental Health Sciences, Johns Hopkins Bloomberg School of Public Health, Baltimore, Maryland, United States of America, Department of Geography and Environmental Systems, University of Maryland, Baltimore, Maryland, United States of America

Jane Memmott
School of Biological Sciences, University of Bristol, Life Sciences Building, Bristol BS8 1TQ, UK; Cabot Institute, University of Bristol, Bristol BS8 1UJ, UK

List of Contributors

Nadine Mitschunas
School of Biological Sciences, University of Bristol, Life Sciences Building, Bristol BS8 1TQ, UK; School of Agriculture, Policy and Development, University of Reading, Reading RG6 6AR, UK

Shannon U. Morath
Graduate Student, Department of Biological Sciences, Fordham University, Rose Hill Campus, Bronx, NY 10458, USA.

Keeve E. Nachman
Johns Hopkins Center for a Livable Future, Baltimore, Maryland, United States of America, Department of Environmental Health Sciences, Johns Hopkins Bloomberg School of Public Health, Baltimore, Maryland, United States of America, Department of Health Policy and Management, Johns Hopkins Bloomberg School of Public Health, Baltimore, Maryland, United States of America

Lynne M. Osgathorpe
School of Biological Sciences, University of Bristol, Life Sciences Building, Bristol BS8 1TQ, UK

Anne M. Palmer
Johns Hopkins Center for a Livable Future, Baltimore, Maryland, United States of America, Department of Environmental Health Sciences, Johns Hopkins Bloomberg School of Public Health, Baltimore, Maryland, United States of America, Department of Health, Behavior and Society, Johns Hopkins Bloomberg School of Public Health, Baltimore, Maryland, United States of America

Jaime Pawelek
Research Assistant, Department of Environmental Science, Policy and Management, University of California, Berkeley, CA 94720 USA

Guadalupe Pena
Department of Animal Science, Law Office of Brian C. McCarthy, Peachtree Street Northwest, Atlanta, GA, USA

Simon G. Potts
School of Agriculture, Policy and Development, University of Reading, Reading RG6 6AR, UK

Melissa N. Poulsen
CLF-Lerner Fellow, Johns Hopkins Center for a Livable Future, Baltimore, Maryland, United States of America, Department of International Health, Johns Hopkins Bloomberg School of Public Health, Baltimore, Maryland, United States of America

Maggie Przybylski
Research Associate, California Department of Parks and Recreation

Kirsty M. Robertson
School of Biology, University of Leeds, Leeds LS2 9JT, UK

Charles Sabato
Water Corporation, Perth, Australia.

Louis Schuetter
Department of Animal Science, Law Office of Brian C. McCarthy, Peachtree Street Northwest, Atlanta, GA, USA

Anna V. Scott
School of Agriculture, Policy and Development, University of Reading, Reading RG6 6AR, UK

Graham N. Stone
Institute of Evolutionary Biology, University of Edinburgh, Kings Buildings, Edinburgh EH9 3JT, UK

Geoff Syme
Centre for Planning, Edith Cowan University, Perth, Australia.

John R. Taylor
University of Illinois at Urbana-Champaign, Department of Crop Sciences, 1105 Plant Sciences Lab, Urbana, Illinois, USA;

Robbin W. Thorp
Professor Emeritus, Department of Entomology, University of California, Davis, CA 95616 USA

Keith G. Tidball
Extension Associate, Department of Natural Resources, 101A Rice Hall, Cornell University, Ithaca, NY 14853 USA.

Ian P. Vaughan
Cardiff School of Biosciences, Cardiff University, Museum Avenue, Cardiff CF10 3AX, UK

Peter A. Werrell
Former Undergraduate Honors Student, Department of Biological Sciences, Fordham University, Rose Hill Campus, Bronx, NY 10458, USA.

INTRODUCTION

Urban Horticulture, referring to the study and cultivation of vegetation in built environments, is gaining more attention as the world rapidly urbanizes and cities expand. While plants have been grown in urban areas for millennia, it is now recognized that they not only provide food, ornament, and recreation, but also supply invaluable ecological services that help mitigate potentially negative impacts of urban ecosystems, and thus increase the livability of cities.

The field of Urban Horticulture is complex and extensive. The articles in this volume, "Urban Horticulture: Ecology, Landscape and Agriculture" provide background on key issues. The first section introduces ecological landscaping, providing a holistic framework for understanding urban landscapes and horticultural practices, both ornamental and agricultural. The complexity of the field is further illustrated by two different approaches to sustainable ornamental landscape design. The second section examines urban soil and its essential role in regulating and supporting horticultural ecosystem services on which urban populations depend. The third part focuses on pollination, and the importance of urban areas and horticultural practice to this vital service. The fourth section concerns the often overlooked area of domestic gardens and their influence on urban horticulture, while the final part employs community gardens to explore the multi-faceted educational experience they provide and its adaptability to other socio-ecological contexts.

—J. Blum

Urbanized ecosystems and urban human populations are expanding around the world with potentially negative environmental outcomes. A challenge for achieving sustainable urban social-ecological systems is understanding how urbanized landscapes can be designed and managed to minimize negative effects. To this end, an interdisciplinary ecological landscaping conference was organized to examine the interacting sociocultural and ecological causes and consequences of landscaping practices and products. A theme of the conference was that scientific principles are important for guiding the development of sustainable landscaping practices and the public policies. Chapter 1 is the introductory article for this conference.

The essence of ecological landscaping is a holistic systems-thinking perspective for understanding the interrelationships among many physical-ecological and sociocultural variables that give rise to the patterns and processes of biodiversity, abiotic conditions and ecosystem processes in urbanized ecosystems. This perspective suggests that 1) variables not considered part of traditional landscaping and 2) the effects of landscaping within an individual parcel on variables outside of it must both be considered when making design and management decisions. To illustrate how these points help create a more holistic, ecological approach to landscaping, an ecosystem model is used in chapter 1 to create a framework for discussing how sociocultural and physical-ecological inputs to a landscape parcel affect its characteristics and the outputs leaving it. Byrne and Grewal conclude their paper by discussing the challenges for the future of ecological landscaping research and practice and a list of preliminary ecological landscaping guidelines.

Chapter 2 discusses the reasoning behind the development of a new approach to designed urban planting with grasses, forbs and geophytes that has been undertaken at the University of Sheffield over the past 15 years. The resulting plant communities are the result of applying contemporary ecological science to planting design, to maximize their sustainability while at the same time meeting the aesthetic and functional needs of the users of urban public landscapes. The geographical origin of the plants used in these communities varies according to the physical, ecological, and cultural context in which they are to be used. In some cases species are entirely native, in others entirely non- native. In many cases, a mixture of both is used. In discussing the rationale for the development of this approach in the United Kingdom context, the paper raises important issues about increasing the capacity of urban landscapes to support a greater diversity of native animals and to engage ordinary citizens in these activities at a time of dramatic climatic and social change. The approach Hitchmough outlines addresses some of these issues in the United

Kingdom context, but he acknowledges that he is uncertain whether there is merit in these approaches in the context of American towns and cities.

Modern agriculture, in seeking to maximize yields to meet growing global food demand, has caused loss of soil organic carbon (SOC) and compaction, impairing critical regulating and supporting ecosystem services upon which humans also depend. Own-growing makes an important contribution to food security in urban areas globally, but its effects on soil qualities that underpin ecosystem service provision are currently unknown. In chapter 3, Edmondson et al. compare the main indicators of soil quality; SOC storage, total nitrogen (TN), C : N ratio and bulk density (BD) in urban allotments to soils from the surrounding agricultural region, and between the allotments and other urban greenspaces in a typical UK city. A questionnaire was used to investigate allotment management practices that influence soil properties. They found that allotment soils had 32% higher SOC concentrations and 36% higher C : N ratios than pastures and arable fields and 25% higher TN and 10% lower BD than arable soils. There was no significant difference between SOC concentration in allotments and urban non-domestic greenspaces, but it was higher in domestic gardens beneath woody vegetation. Allotment soil C : N ratio exceeded that in non-domestic greenspaces, but was lower than that in garden soil. Three-quarters of surveyed allotment plot holders added manure, 95% composted biomass on-site, and many added organic-based fertilizers and commercial composts. The authors indicate that this may explain the maintenance of SOC, C : N ratios, TN and low BD, which are positively associated with soil functioning. Maintenance and protection of the quality of our soil resource is essential for sustainable food production and for regulating and supporting ecosystem services upon which we depend. The authors' study establishes that small-scale urban food production can occur without the penalty of soil degradation seen in conventional agriculture, and maintains the high soil quality seen in urban greenspaces. Given the involvement of over 800 million people in urban agriculture globally, and its important contribution to food security, their findings suggest that to better protect soil functions, local, national, and international urban planning and policy making should promote more urban own-growing in preference to further intensification of conventional agriculture to meet increasing food demand.

In chapter 4 turn to a historical perspective. In the early 1890s during the Depression, land was donated for gardening by the unemployed. By the early 1920s, civic beautification campaigns in many parts of the country included gardens on vacant lots and at school sites. War gardens became popular first as the US School Garden Army during WWI (1917–1919) and as Victory Gardens during WWII (1941–1945). The popularity of urban gardens have subsided and reoccurred many times since the 1950s and are popular once more. Presently, school and community gardens are used as resources to inform students and the general population about nutritious food choices and for providing fresh produce for home use and food banks. Students in the UC Davis chapters of a national organization are involved in development of community gardens for the homeless in Sacramento, CA. Understanding that lead content may be a major concern in potential gardens sites that once had homes built during an earlier era, the first concern for members of the organization was to analyze the soil for specific metal contaminants, especially lead.

Although urban community gardening can offer health, social, environmental, and economic benefits, these benefits must be weighed against the potential health risks stemming from exposure to contaminants such as heavy metals and organic chemicals that may be present in urban soils. Individuals who garden at or eat food grown in contaminated urban garden sites may be at risk of exposure to such contaminants. Gardeners may be unaware of these risks and how to manage them. In chapter 5, Kim et al. used a mixed quantitative/qualitative research approach to characterize urban community gardeners' knowledge and perceptions of risks related to soil contaminant exposure. The authors conducted surveys with 70 gardeners from 15 community gardens in Baltimore, Maryland, and semi-structured interviews with 18 key informants knowledgeable about community gardening and soil contamination in Baltimore. The authors identified a range of factors, challenges, and needs related to Baltimore community gardeners' perceptions of risk related to soil contamination, including low levels of concern and inconsistent levels of knowledge about heavy metal and organic chemical contaminants, barriers to investigating a garden site's history and conducting soil tests, limited knowledge of best practices for reducing exposure, and a need for clear and concise information on how best to prevent and manage soil contamination. Key informants discussed various strategies for developing and disseminating educational materials to gardeners. For some challenges, such as barriers to conducting site history and soil tests, some informants recommended city-wide interventions that bypass the need for gardener knowledge altogether.

Urban agriculture has been increasingly popular as a form of modern agriculture in urban settings. It includes community gardens, fruit orchards, home gardens, veggie patches, public open spaces, reserves, urban forest, and recreational landscaping. However, irrigation using urban water supply has been identified as a major constraints for the development of urban agriculture. The study in chapter 6 presents a sustainable water management trial at Butler, a northern sub-urban development in Perth, Western Australia, for urban irrigation. The trial system consists of a number of water saving features including untreated fit-for-purpose groundwater supplied via a third pipe network, drip irrigation, local weather station, soil moisture sensors connected with a local weather station, night time irrigation, soil enhancement with conditioning and mulching, and use of native plants and vegetation. The trial outcome was compared against controlled areas in terms of irrigation efficiency and sustainable water management for urban agriculture. The study demonstrated that a fit-for-purpose irrigation along with water sensitive land management could be a sustainable alternative for urban agriculture that would achieve a significant water saving and irrigation efficiency at urban settings. However, quality of untreated groundwater can be an issue while utilizing it for irrigation, but the research has shown that it can be managed with innovative irrigation techniques. This indicates that the fit-for-purpose irrigation system with water sensitive land management practices would be highly supportive in sustainable development of urban agriculture, vegetation and recreational landscaping.

Insect pollinators provide a crucial ecosystem service, but are under threat. Urban areas could be important for pollinators, though their value relative to other habitats is poorly known. In chapter 7, Baldock et al. compared pollinator communities using quantified flower-visitation networks in 36 sites (each 1 km^2) in three landscapes: urban, farmland and nature reserves. Overall, flower-visitor abundance and species richness did not differ significantly between the three landscape types. Bee abundance did not differ between landscapes, but bee species richness was higher in urban areas than farmland. Hoverfly abundance was higher in farmland and nature reserves than urban sites, but species richness did not differ significantly. While urban pollinator assemblages were more homogeneous across space than those in farmland or nature reserves, there was no significant difference in the numbers of rarer species between the three landscapes. Network-level specialization was higher in farmland than urban sites. Relative to other habitats, urban visitors foraged from a greater number of plant species (higher generality) but also visited a lower proportion of available plant species (higher specialization), both possibly driven by higher urban plant richness. Urban areas are growing, and improving their value for pollinators should be part of any national strategy to conserve and restore pollinators.

Many cucurbits, such as cucumbers, squashes and pumpkins, depend on pollinating bees in order to set fruit. However, fruit yield and progeny vigor in these plants generally decreases as heterospecific pollen deposition increases. In chapter 8, Werrell et al. studied how the spatial area dedicated to cucumbers (Cucumis sativis), versus other flowering plants, influenced the deposition of conspecific and heterospecific pollen on cucumber plants in New York City community gardens. They also examined the effect of garden size on conspecific and heterospecific pollen deposition on cucumber plants. Female flowers were collected from potted cucumber plants that had been experimentally placed into the gardens, specifically for this study, or that were established in raised beds by members of the community garden. In the laboratory, pollen grains were isolated from the flower by acetolysis, and the number of heterospecific and conspecific cucumber pollen grains were quantified. Conspecific pollen deposition was positively and significantly associated with the size of a community garden, as well as with the area of each garden dedicated to non-cucumber, flowering plants (i.e. floral cover) and the area of each garden dedicated to cucumber plants (i.e. cucumber cover). Although floral cover explained a greater proportion of the variance, cucumber cover had the strongest effect on conspecific pollen deposition. Heterospecific pollen deposition was positively and significantly related to garden area. However, no significant relationship was found between heterospecific pollen deposition and floral cover or cucumber cover. Based upon these results, the authors hypothesize that floral cover positively impacts conspecific pollen deposition by attracting a greater number of pollinators into an urban garden, and that total cucumber area positively impacts conspecific pollen deposition when pollinators are locally foraging within a garden. The authors suggest that the arrangement of plants within a garden can positively influence yield in fruit and vegetable-producing plants within urban community gardens. Due to the low availability of fruits and vegetables within the stores of the neighborhoods where this study was conducted, developing a better understanding of those factors that constrain or foster fruit and vegetable production are important to increasing food security and public health.

A variety of crops are grown in New York City community gardens. Although the production of many crops benefits from pollination by bees, little is known about bee abundance in urban community gardens or which crops are specifically dependent on bee pollination. In 2005, Matteson and Longellotto compiled a list of crop plants grown within 19 community gardens in New York City and classified these plants according to their dependence on bee pollination. In addition, using mark-recapture methods, they estimated the abundance of a potentially important pollinator within New York City urban gardens, the common eastern bumble bee (*Bombus impatiens*). This species is currently recognized as a valuable commercial pollinator of greenhouse crops. However, wild populations of *B. impatiens* are abundant throughout its range, including in New York City community gardens, where it is the most abundant native bee species present and where it has been observed visiting a variety of crop flowers. Matteson and Longellotto conservatively counted 25 species of crop plants in 19 surveyed gardens. The literature suggests that 92% of these crops are dependent, to some degree, on bee pollination in order to set fruit or seed. *Bombus impatiens* workers were observed visiting flowers of 78% of these pollination-dependent crops. Estimates of the number of *B. impatiens* workers visiting individual gardens during the study period ranged from 3 to 15 bees per 100m^2 of total garden area and 6 to 29 bees per 100m^2 of garden floral area. Of 229 *B. impatiens* workers marked, all recaptured individuals (45%) were found in gardens where they were initially marked. In chapter 9, the authors' results indicate an abundance of *B. impatiens* workers within New York City community gardens and suggest that, at least for certain time periods, many individual workers forage within single gardens. Both findings suggest that *B. impatiens* may be an especially important pollinator of several common crops grown within community gardens and other urban green spaces that are used for agricultural production. Studies of other pollinating insect species in urban habitats as well as the relationship between pollen movement and seed or fruit set will complement the findings of this study.

Gardens have become increasingly important places for growing nutritional food, for conserving biodiversity, for biological and ecological research and education, and for community gathering. In chapter 10, Pawelek et al. discuss the ways in which gardens can also be designed with the goal of attracting aesthetically pleasing wildlife and pollinators, like birds and butterflies, and remind us that other important garden visitors, like bees, can also be drawn to specially planned and modified gardens. A community garden in San Luis Obispo, California provided the setting for modification with the goal of attracting native bee pollinators by planting known bee-attractive plants. The local gardeners participated in a survey questionnaire and focused interviews to provide their input and interest in such a project. Presentations on the authors' work with native bees in urban environments and gardening to attract bees were also given to interested gardeners. Work of this type also benefited from a lead gardener who managed donated bee plants and kept up momentum of the project. Modification of the garden and monitoring of native bees started in 2007 and continued through the growing season of 2009. Diversity of collected and observed native bees has increased each year since 2007. To date, 40 species in 17 genera of mostly native bees have been recorded from the garden, and this number is expected to increase through time.

In the United States, interest in urban farms and community gardens is flourishing, yet the urban home food garden (UHFG) and its contributions to urban systems have been overlooked and understudied. To begin to address this gap, in chapter 11, Taylor and Lovell conducted a mixed methods study of African American, Chinese-origin and Mexican-origin households with home gardens in Chicago, IL. Study methods include in-depth interviews, participant observation, ethnobotanical surveys and analysis of the chemical and physical properties of garden soils. Their findings indicate that home gardening has an array of beneficial effects, contributing to household food budgets and community food systems, the reproduction of cultural identity and urban biodiversity. The majority of informants in the study were internal or international migrants. For these individuals, gardening, culture-specific food plant assemblages and the foodways they support represent a continuation of cultural practices and traditional agroecological knowledge associated with their place of origin. The gardens of some migrant households also harbor urban agrobiodiversity with roots in the Global South. At the same time, gardens may have less salubrious effects on urban systems and populations. A lack of knowledge of safe gardening practices may expose vulnerable populations to environmental hazards such as soil contaminants. Gardeners in this study reported using synthetic chemical fertilizers and pesticides, sometimes indiscriminately, and the repeated application of synthetic fertilizers and compost may contribute to the nutrient loading of urban stormwater runoff. These effects may be moderated by the relatively low bulk density and high porosity of garden soils due to tillage and the application of organic matter, which can be expected to enhance stormwater infiltration. While the UHFG's potential contributions to urban systems are significant, outreach and research are needed to help gardeners grow food safely and sustainably in ways that contribute to overall ecosystem health.

Community gardens are heterogeneous environments that integrate environmental restoration, community activism, social interactions, cultural expression, and food security. As such, they provide a context for learning that addresses multiple societal goals, including a populace that is scientifically literate, practices environmental stewardship, and participates in civic life. Several theories are useful in describing the learning that occurs in community gardens, including those focusing on learning as acquisition of content by individuals, learning as interaction with other individuals and the environment and as increasingly skilled levels of participation in a community of practice, and social learning among groups of stakeholders leading to concerted action to enhance natural resources. In the final chapter of this compendium, Krasny and Tidball use preliminary evidence from the Garden Mosaics intergenerational education program to suggest the potential for community gardens to foster multiple types of learning.

PART I

WHAT IS GREEN INFRASTRUCTURE?

CHAPTER 1

Introduction to Ecological Landscaping: A Holistic Description and Framework to Guide the Study and Management of Urban Landscape Parcels

LOREN B. BYRNE AND PARWINDER GREWAL

1.1 INTRODUCTION

In the U.S., more than 80% of the population resides, works, and plays in environments intentionally created and managed by humans (United Nations 2007). These human-dominated urbanized environments are characterized by horizontal and vertical impervious surfaces surrounded by lawns, scattered trees, and other ornamental vegetation. Management of urbanized landscapes is mostly aimed at maintaining roads, plants, and other structures in desired forms and spatial patterns. Although these points may be self evident, probably few of us reflect on them critically; instead, for most people, continued urbanization and typical landscape management practices are unquestioned social norms, to be accepted at face value rather than critiqued. It is only when something out of the

---

© Byrne, L.B. and Grewal, P. 2008. Introduction to Ecological Landscaping: A Holistic Description and Framework to Guide the Study and Management of Urban Landscape Parcels. Cities and the Environment. 1(2):article 3. Creative Commons Attribution license (http://creativecommons.org/licenses/by/3.0/).

"norm" occurs—a new type of residential development appears or a suburban lawn is replaced with a prairie—that people tend to reflect on their expectations about how urbanized landscapes should look and function, both socioculturally and ecologically.

In recent years, however, the design, management, and social-ecological dynamics of urbanized environments have been examined more critically by scientists, landscape architects, engineers, planners, policy makers, and concerned citizens. As a result, knowledge and awareness are increasing about the unintended, often negative, environmental effects caused by urbanization and certain landscape management practices (Grimm et al. 2008). To reduce or mitigate these negative effects, efforts have been made to develop new perspectives and strategies for more ecologically-informed approaches to urban landscape design and management (Smith et al. 2007; Tallamy 2007; Ecological Landscaping Association 2008; National Wildlife Federation 2008; Sustainable Sites Initiative 2008).

A guiding theme is a focus on smaller-scale (meters to 10^2 meters) parcels of land (or patches) defined by, e.g., legal property boundaries that are directly or indirectly managed by the properties' owners (as for residential households, apartment complexes and commercial properties) or other institutions (as for government agencies managing public lands). This focus complements other efforts to examine larger-scale ($\geq 10^3$ m) dynamics and planning of urbanized regions (Forman 2008; Grimm et al. 2008). However, larger-scale urban patterns and dynamics ultimately emerge from the combination of smaller-scale parcel management decisions and effects (Odum 1982; Pouyat et al. 2006; Grimm et al. 2008). Thus, understanding the emergent properties of larger urban regions (sensu Kaye et al. 2004)—the scale at which many environmental planning and management policies are targeted—depends on examination of patterns and relationships among social and ecological variables at the scale of landscape parcels (e.g., a yard around a single-family home). Although an exclusive focus on individual parcels may not alone contribute to a full understanding of urbanized ecosystems, it provides an essential complement to a larger-scale perspective.

Additionally, individual landscape parcels represent the scale at which people readily think about the urban environment and, therefore, where landscaping choices, activities, and environmental consequences are most apparent, comprehendible, intimate, and immediately made. Thus, parcels provide a personal human-scale focus useful for engaging parcel owners and managers in thinking—in a "down-to-earth" way—about how their individual landscaping choices affect environmental variables, both positively and negatively. Such engagement can be made more meaningful by discussing information from a growing, but incomplete, body of research which reveals some of the important sociocultural variables that interactively affect human landscape design and management choices and activities within a parcel, including income, aesthetic preferences, advertising, public policies, and peer pressure (Jenkins 1994; Hope et al. 2003; Byrne 2005; Larsen and Harlan 2006; Clayton, 2007; Robbins 2007; Baker et al. 2007). Helping people understand the underlying reasons for their landscaping choices and the effects of those choices on environmental variables should be essential foci for educational outreach programs that seek to positively transform the social norms, behaviors, and public policies associated with urban landscape design and management. A major challenge for increasing the overall sustainability and environmental quality of urbanized societies and ecosystems is developing effective educational messages about the methods of ecological landscaping and the importance of adopting them.

In the remainder of this introductory paper, we define our use of the phrase ecological landscaping and develop a conceptual framework to illustrate the interdisciplinary complexity associated with the causes and consequences of urban landscape management practices. This framework is then used as a lens through which to summarize important points from each of this issue's articles. We conclude by suggesting key questions, challenges, and future directions for ecological landscaping research and practice. Our hope is that ideas raised here will contribute to increased interest in and research about this increasingly important topic.

1.2 WHAT IS ECOLOGICAL LANDSCAPING?

Because it may have various meanings to different people, it is necessary to clarify our use of the phrase "ecological landscaping." First, "landscaping" refers to either 1) the set of design and maintenance activities associated with landscape manipulation or 2) the collection of biotic and abiotic physical structures within a given area produced and maintained by those activities. In colloquial use, as in landscaping companies or landscaping a yard, the word connotes both the practices and products of common lawn and garden management such as choosing and installing ornamental vegetation, mowing lawns, weeding, and watering. We adopt the word to bring forth these two meanings which help focus attention on the on-the-ground, parcel scale of urbanized landscapes; indeed, many of the characteristics of a landscape parcel are ultimately determined by the landscaping activities carried out within it.

In addition, because "landscaping" suggests many practices rather than focusing on one activity over others, its use provides an opening for simultaneously examining diverse aspects of the urban landscaping endeavor. As such, it serves as an inclusive, neutral, umbrella word that can foster interdisciplinary discussion about the scholarly study and everyday practices of landscape management. For instance, within a discussion about landscaping, information and perspectives from ecology, horticulture, and the social sciences, among other fields, should be included and synthesized. However, ideas from landscape managers must also be considered because, as the ones actively shaping the physical structure of urbanized environments, they may have different insights and concerns than scholars. We propose that the word landscaping has well-established, colloquial appeal and can thus help bring landscape managers (including industry professionals and private homeowners) and their ideas into discussions that might otherwise become overly academic and removed from everyday situations. In this way, landscaping is an integrative word that links scholarly theories with on-the-ground application, an essential outcome for effecting positive changes to landscaping norms and practices.

In many ways, all landscaping has an ecological dimension because both landscaping practices and products affect, and are affected by, environmental variables within a parcel. (For example, irrigation practices affect plant growth and are affected by local precipitation and a soil's water holding capacity.) However, this does not presuppose that all landscaping is properly called ecological in a strict sense because many activities are carried out without regard for their broader environmental effects. In most cases, urban landscaping activities are guided by a focus on maintaining the health and appearance of ornamental plants and desired state of other landscaping elements (e.g., walls, paths). Certainly, this focus is relevant and makes sense as it is the *raison d'être* for many urban landscaping practices. However, with this ecologically-limited perspective, landscape managers may view landscaping elements in isolation from their environment and inadvertently exclude, or deliberately ignore, other relevant factors that can—and arguably should—guide socially and environmentally responsible landscaping decisions. As such, the ubiquitous plant/structure-centered landscaping perspective and the landscaping designs and activities associated with it should not be called "ecological" because their purview is too focused on certain variables while possibly excluding others completely.

Instead, use of the word ecological to describe landscaping should be reserved for specific instances when landscaping practices and products are influenced by a broader, more holistic perspective. The essence of this perspective, as informed by an understanding of contemporary ecological science (Odum and Barrett 2005; Cary Institute of Ecosystem Studies 2008), is a synthetic approach for examining the interconnected relationships among organisms, abiotic conditions and resources, and environmental patterns and processes (especially the transformations and flow of matter and energy) both within and outside of an individual landscape parcel. This ecological science view is related to what Fritjof Capra (1996, 2002) has called "systems thinking" because, with it, our focus shifts from individual parts (i.e., a reductionist view) to the patterns and dynamics of relationships among all parts comprising a system (Cary Institute of Ecosystem Studies 2008). In addition, a more holistic, ecosystems view emphasizes that all individual landscape parcels lie within the environmental context of larger landscapes that affect the embedded parcels. Likewise, what occurs in parcels can affect the larger ecosystems and landscapes of which they are a part, possibly leading to feedback loops and indirect effects across spatial scales and among seemingly unrelated variables (Grimm et al. 2008; Cadenasso and Pickett 2008). This ecological, systems worldview is reflected in the colloquialism that nothing can be understood in isolation because everything is connected to everything else. Indeed, sayings such as this might provide effective, colloquial talking-points for educational outreach programs that seek to engage the public in thinking about the ecology and sociology of urban landscaping. Capra (1996, 2002) provides additional discussion and details about systems thinking and ecological literacy.

Compared to the plant/structure-focused landscaping perspective, a more ecological, systemsoriented viewpoint shifts attention from individual, managed organisms (plants, pests) and structures to interactions among all parts (variables) of the landscape, including unmanaged ones, with each other and those of surrounding ecosystems. Two important points follow from this perspective. First, variables not usually considered within the urban landscaping endeavor are recognized as integral parts of a larger system that may have relationships to focal managed elements within a parcel. For example, birds and spiders are not direct targets of many landscaping activities but are important consumers of pests; thus, an ecological landscaping approach considers how landscaping practices (e.g., plant selection, pesticide applications, mulching) and products (e.g., density and composition of trees and shrubs) might positively or negatively affect the abundance and predation rates of these natural enemies (Rebek et al. 2005; Byrne 2007). In addition, with an ecosystem perspective, potential consequences of landscaping activities for variables outside the managed parcel must be considered to avoid what Odum (1982) called "the tyranny of small decisions:" the aggregation of individual choices that cause large-scale environmental problems. These two points have important implications for decisions about how to design and manage landscapes more efficiently and sustainably. For instance, realization that chemical applications could have negative effects on beneficial organisms, nearby waterways, and human health might effect a reduction or elimination of their use (Potter et al. 1990; Nishioka et al, 1999; Bormann et al. 2001; Robbins 2007).

Another dimension of contemporary ecological science that bears on the ecological landscaping perspective is the objective of integrating humans and sociocultural variables into the study of environmental patterns and processes (Redman et al. 2004), a goal exemplified by the field of urban ecology (Pickett et al. 1997, 2008; Grimm et al. 2008). Results of urban ecology studies indicate complex and sometimes surprising relationships between sociocultural and environmental variables within urbanized ecosystems (Pickett et al. 2008). For example, household income, advertising, environmental ethics, and aesthetic values, among other factors, have been found to influence urban ecological patterns, especially of plant communities, more than traditional physical-ecological variables because these sociocultural variables drive human landscaping choices and activities that dictate vegetation patterns (Hope et al. 2003; Larsen and Harlon 2006; Clayton 2007; Robbins 2007). In addition, surveys have found that although over half of U.S. households use landscaping chemicals (Law et al. 2004; National Gardening Association 2004), many people do not readily connect their personal landscaping activities to broader environmental concerns such as water pollution and the potential for indoor pollution (Nishioka et al. 1999; Robbins 2007). Such information is needed to understand how and why people design and manage urbanized environments. This understanding also provides a foundation for developing education programs that seek to help people appreciate relationships between parcels and "big-picture" environmental issues and, in turn, make more informed landscaping choices (Baker et al. 2008). To encourage such reflection, landscape parcels could be referred to as "social-ecological systems" (sensu Redman et al. 2004) and the phrase "social-ecological landscaping" could be used in certain contexts. For simplicity however, we suggest that "ecological landscaping" can, by definition, include examination of sociocultural variables as drivers of urban landscape practices and products.

We readily acknowledge that the phrase *ecological landscaping* has been used by others and that the concepts it embodies draw from a rich history of scholarly work (especially within the field of landscape architecture, a review of which is outside the scope of this paper). Certainly, the goals of the Cleveland Ecological Landscaping conference and this special issue were to build on and advance the efforts of others. For example, the Ecological Landscaping Association, based in Framingham, Massachusetts, was formed in 1992 to promote "change in landscaping practices through educating landscape professionals and the public" (Ecological Landscaping Association 2008). Some landscape architects and landscaping companies have also adopted the phrase to describe their work (e.g., Terra Nova 2004; Four Dimensions 2008). In addition, the word *ecological* has been used to create other phrases that have meaning similar to ecological landscaping but with slightly different emphasis on spatial scale or management foci, including ecological horticulture (Stewart 2008) and ecological planning (Thompson and Steiner 1997). Other organizations (Wild Ones 2008; National Wildlife Federation 2008), projects (Sustainable Sites Initiative 2008), and scholars (Smith et al. 2007) are also actively advancing the ideas and practices of sustainable urban landscaping. Regardless of the phrase used, a commonality among these efforts is the explicit embracement of a "green" or "environmentally friendly" ethic to guide urban landscaping for improving environmental quality. In our use of the phrase *ecological landscaping*, we also hope to bring forth a set of ecocentric values.

1.3 A SOCIAL-ECOLOGICAL FRAMEWORK FOR ECOLOGICAL LANDSCAPING

Conceptual frameworks are important tools that help organize ideas into systematic relationships and provide insights into new research topics and questions (Pickett et al. 2007). They have been particularly useful in the field of urban ecology for describing interdisciplinary relationships among sociocultural and ecological variables (Pickett et al. 1997; 2008, Pouyat et al. 2006; Grimm et al. 2008). Drawing from other ecosystem and urban ecology frameworks and content of papers in this issue, we constructed a conceptual framework to help organize and advance the study of ecological landscaping (Fig. 1). Although the content and organization of this framework shares some broad similarities with others, it is differentiated by its focus on individual landscape parcels (Fig. 1A). This focus provides an appropriate starting point from which to develop an interdisciplinary ecological landscaping framework because parcels are the discrete units about which landscape managers make landscaping decisions and within which they carry out landscaping activities, a point echoed by Cadenasso and Pickett 2008. Therefore, each individual parcel is a unique social-ecological system that, for research purposes, is amenable to fine-scale examination of relationships among sociocultural and ecological variables. In addition, parcels provide tangible, personal foci for ecological landscaping education programs.

To reflect the holistic, systems-thinking perspective needed for a rigorous approach to ecological landscaping, the framework is developed in two ways. First, a traditional input-output ecosystem model (sensu Likens 1992 and Odum; Barrett 2005) is employed to emphasize how an individual landscape parcel is connected to its broader environmental context through the flow of materials and energy across its boundaries. Second, the framework explicitly incorporates many sociocultural and physical-ecological components which are not usually considered within a plant/structure-centered view (in addition to those that are) and shows how they are interrelated as inputs, internal parcel characteristics, and outputs. Although not illustrated in the figure, many direct and indirect relationships exist among the sociocultural and ecological variables, giving rise to a synthetic, complex social-ecological framework for examining the causes, dynamics, and consequences of ecological landscaping practices and products.

A landscape parcel can be described by a set of physical-ecological (including landscaping products) and management characteristics. The physical ecological characteristics (Fig. 1B) are the biotic and abiotic structures including vegetation, walls, and sidewalks; the abiotic conditions; spatial patterns of these three variables; and ecological processes associated with population dynamics, food webs, and transformations of energy, matter, and nutrients within the parcel (Cary Institute of Ecosystem Studies 2008). These variables relate directly and indirectly to human management decisions and practices which help characterize the sociocultural characteristics of a parcel (Fig. 1C). Management decisions lead to management activities that directly affect many of a parcel's physical-ecological characteristics, especially the composition and spatial patterns of structures. Management practices may also indirectly affect unmanaged variables through changes in managed variables (e.g., mulch applications impact earthworm populations that change soil properties; Byrne et al. 2008). In some instances, changes in physical-ecological variables not directly caused by human activities can spur management decisions and practices as when pest outbreaks catalyze pesticide applications. Many common landscape management practices, like mowing, weeding, and mulching, are used specifically in response to undesired structural changes

Table 1. Fundamental questions that can guide research about the practice of ecological landscaping.

- How should sustainable urbanized landscapes function and what should they look like?
- What is the quantity and quality of previous research that is available to provide a foundation for understanding the ecological and social characteristics of urbanized environments?
- What are the key research gaps and needs that need to be resolved to make future progress in developing sound scientific principles and sustainable practices for ecological landscaping?
- What are the positive and negative environmental, health, social and economic effects of common urban landscape management practices?
- How can we most efficiently create and maintain urbanized landscapes that are environmentally, economically and socially sustainable over long timescales?
- What sociocultural, economic, policy and political factors influence the ways in which people design and manage urbanized landscapes?
- How can we bring about positive changes in public attitudes for adopting more sustainable urban landscaping norms and practices?
- How can changes to public policies be effected to guide people toward more sustainable urban landscape design and management?
- Can educational programs about scientific principles change people's perspectives about appropriate and sustainable urban landscaping practices?

of plants or other materials. The dynamic feedback relationship between changes in physical-ecological characteristics and management decisions and practices is probably a universal characteristic of urban landscape parcels (Cadenasso and Pickett 2008). Although the nature of these dynamics may be intuitive, this explicit description of landscape parcels as social-ecological systems (Fig. 1A, B, C) is an essential foundation for a rigorous ecological landscaping framework.

Management decisions about a parcel are not made solely on the basis of characteristics within the parcel; rather, a wide range of external variables, both physical-ecological and sociocultural, also influence landscaping decisions. Within a traditional ecosystem model, these can be conceptualized as inputs to the landscape parcel (Fig 1D). Many physical-ecological inputs enter without human regulation including animals, plant seeds, precipitation, sunlight, and gases. The effects of these environmentallyderived inputs (Fig. 1E) on a landscape parcel depend on many factors including the amount and timing of the input and a parcel's internal characteristics. For example, both beneficial (e.g., predatory) and harmful, pest organisms enter parcels in varying numbers over the seasons; whether they establish populations will depend on the availability of favorable habitat and human management responses. Although the entry of environmentally-derived physical-ecological inputs into a parcel is, for the most part, uncontrollable, these variables should be considered when management decisions are made because some of the parcel's characteristics can be manipulated to affect how these inputs influence the parcel's other characteristics and the outputs leaving it (e.g., precipitation inputs leave as runoff; Baker et al. 2008, Shuster et al. 2008).

Other physical-ecological inputs to a landscape parcel are directly controlled by humans (Fig. 1F). These include, among other things, purchased plants and their packaging; the irrigation water, pesticides, fertilizers, and tools used for managing the health and growth of plants; mulches; materials for creating and managing abiotic structures; and the electricity and fossil fuels needed to operate tools. Unlike environmentally-derived inputs, the timing, amount, and frequency of human-controlled inputs depend on a manager's landscaping decisions. These are influenced by a combination of many factors including the processing rates of inputs in the parcel (e.g., water and fertilizer uptake by plants), their durability and disposability (e.g., lifespan of tools and plants), and, for many inputs, a diversity of sociocultural variables.

Sociocultural variables (Fig. 1G) that affect landscaping decisions and practices (Fig. 1C) can also be envisioned as inputs to a landscape parcel. They affect the physical-ecological characteristics of a parcel (Fig. 1A) by influencing the human-controlled physical-ecological inputs (Fig. 1F) and what happens to them in the parcel (Fig. 1C). In addition, sociocultural variables also affect choices about how to manage some environmentally-derived inputs such as pests (Fig. 1E). The personal aesthetic, environmental, and social-responsibility values of a landscape manager play a central role in decisions about landscaping (Larsen and Harlan 2006; Clayton 2007; Hitchmough 2008) as does the manager's financial abilities to purchase desired inputs (i.e., a luxury effect; Hope et al. 2003). In addition, a certain amount of "peer pressure" is exerted on landscape managers via neighborhood covenants (Martin et al. 2003), local "weed laws" (Rappaport 1993; Sandberg and Foster 2005), historical cultural legacies, and advertising by the landscaping industry (Jenkins 1994; Larsen and Harlan 2006; Robbins 2007). These external social factors interact to generate social norms (or standards) about "proper" landscaping practices and products that responsible citizens are expected to follow (Byrne 2005; see below). However, scientific information about effective landscaping methods (e.g., leaving lawn clippings in place as a nutrient source; Kopp and Guilliard 2002) are also externally-derived inputs transmitted via various educational routes that can also impact landscaping decisions and characteristics of a parcel. Thus, for a holistic approach to ecological landscaping, understanding is needed about how sociocultural variables act as inputs that affect a manager's monetary and informational resource bases and his/her personal values regarding landscaping which in turn affect a parcel's physical-ecological characteristics through management activities.

Increased understanding of relationships among the sociocultural and physical-ecological variables in individual parcels is critically important for future study because these relationships ultimately determine the emergent sustainability of larger urbanized regions (Odum 1982; Grimm et al. 2008). In particular, the spatial and temporal dynamics of urbanized regions are affected by the physical-ecological and sociocultural outputs leaving individual parcels (Fig. 1H). Physical-ecological outputs (Fig. 1I) consist of biotic and abiotic solids, liquids, and gases as well as thermal energy generated by energy transformations in the parcel or reradiated from solar inputs. The thermal characteristics of a parcel (as affected by its physical-ecological properties) partially affect its microclimate conditions and may contribute to the urban heat-island effect (Byrne et al. 2008). Inorganic solid outputs include unwanted and/or unusable wastes such as packaging from plants and landscaping materials, broken or unwanted tools, and other garbage. Biotic wastes include plant materials that leave a parcel as garbage or materials for local composting programs.

While solid outputs are usually managed directly by humans, other outputs are indirectly affected via management activities' effects on a parcel's physical-ecological characteristics. These outputs include dispersing organisms (e.g., weed seeds); gases produced by organisms and fossil fuel combustion; and water leaving a parcel through evaporation, percolation to ground-water, and run-off, the latter two of which may contain other chemicals (e.g., pesticides, fertilizers). The amount and composition of outputs are determined directly or indirectly by those of the inputs as well as how the inputs are managed, transformed, and retained within a parcel (Baker et al. 2008). In many cases, outputs (like blowing seeds or leaves) are likely to become inputs to another parcel. A common output that readily crosses parcel boundaries is the noise generated by landscaping tools such as lawn mowers and leaf blowers; while certainly noticeable by humans, the collective noise created in urbanized environments has also been found to affect the songs of urban birds (Slabbekoorn and Margriet 2003; Wood and Yezerinac 2006). Although other research has been conducted on the physical-ecological outputs from urbanized landscapes (e.g., gases: Kaye et al. 2004; Byrne et al. 2008; water and nutrients: Easton and Petrovic 2004; Frank et al. 2006), this aspect of the ecological landscaping framework remains a relatively unexplored area of study in need of future study.

Also contributing to the total physical-ecological outputs associated with a landscape parcel are the solid waste, greenhouse gases, and waste water generated during the manufacturing and transport of materials used as landscaping inputs (Fig. 1E, J). Even though these indirect outputs occur offsite and out of a landscape manager's sight, they are important to consider because they may be large and have significant local and broad-scale environmental effects (e.g., as contributions to climate change). Few studies have quantified the indirect outputs associated with landscaping materials (Parker 1982). However, given that the U.S. landscaping industry generates an estimated $147.8 billion in annual economic activity (Hall et al. 2006), it is reasonable to assume that the total amount of these by-products will also be large. Further investigation of this topic presents a challenging objective for future research.

In addition to physical-ecological outputs, a landscape parcel also produces sociocultural outputs (Fig. 1K). A central concern for most landscape managers is how the appearance of physical-ecological elements in a parcel communicates information to others (i.e., visual aesthetic outputs). As proposed by Nassauer (1988), "cues to care"—including pruned shrubs, weeded flower beds, mowed lawns and wellmaintained structures such as fences and paths—are socioculturally important because they help show that a land owner and/or manager is adhering to widely held social norms or legal requirements about acceptable landscaping (Piekielek 2003,;Robbins 2007). Therefore, landscaping products are also "costly signals" because they require resource inputs to maintain the physical-ecological communication signals that symbolize that the parcel's owner and/or manager is respectable and responsible member of the community (Piekielek 2003; Larsen and Harlan 2006). In turn, a kind of sociocultural feedback among landscape parcels can be generated when conformity to landscaping norms within one parcel (an output) serves a sociocultural peer pressure input to other parcels (Fig. 1L; Byrne 2005). Indeed, studies have found that adjacent parcels are more likely to have similar landscaping than those farther apart due to this "keeping up with the Jones's" effect (Zmyslony and Gagnon 1998). Pickett et al. (2008) suggest that this pattern (especially regarding lawn management) helps build social capital within communities that contributes to the overall sustainability of urbanized ecosystems. In addition, urban landscaping practices and products have been documented to have beneficial effects on people's physiological, psychological, and social well-being (Kaplan et al. 1998). Increasing such sociocultural ecosystem service outputs should be an important goal of ecological landscaping.

Although some beneficial ecosystem services may arise from urban landscaping, certain lawn and garden design and management approaches have been increasingly questioned in recent years because of their negative effects on human health, biodiversity and the overall environmental quality and sustainability of urbanized ecosystems (Stein 1993; Bormann et al. 2001; Waskowski and Waskowski 2002; Robbins 2007; Tallamy 2007). These negative effects, which may be called "ecosystem disservices" (Byrne et al. 2008), include generation of air, water, and soil pollution, inefficient use of energy, and negative effects on biodiversity and food webs that increase the possibility of pest outbreaks (Zenger and Gibb 2001; Baker et al. 2008). Some ecosystem disservices generated in urbanized regions may result from the collective outputs from many landscape parcels and thus appear outside of and distant from each parcel that contributes to them. In turn, information about these negative effects can be used as educational inputs of information to landscape parcels that might catalyze landscaping changes (Fig. 1L) as well as lead to public policy changes such as bans on pesticide use (Sandberg and Foster 2005). Emphasis of systematic feedback relationships among landscaping inputs, parcel characteristics and outputs within the framework presented here (Fig. 1) highlights its utility as a tool for analyzing and promoting more integrated, socio-ecological and systems-thinking approaches to designing and managing urbanized landscapes.

1.4 URBAN ECOLOGY

The study of ecological landscaping falls under the broader heading of urban ecology. Thus, it is not surprising that the structure and content of the ecological landscaping framework (Fig. 1) reflects many themes in the paper by Cadenasso and Pickett (2008), who propose five scientific principles to form a general theory of urban ecology. Collectively, four of these principles describe urbanized areas as dynamic, spatially and temporally heterogeneous, integrated ecosystems whose emergent characteristics arise from interactions among social (including information) and biophysical variables. Although urbanized ecosystems are often viewed as human-dominated, Cadenasso and Pickett (2008) emphasize in their fifth principle that basic physical-ecological processes are still important for determining many of their basic properties, as is also emphasized in our framework (Fig 1B, E, J). In addition, they provide a thoughtful summative, discussion about a central aspect of the ecological landscaping conference's theme (Fig. 1): how scientific principles can be translated into ecological landscape design and management practices that help increase the sustainability of urbanized ecosystems.

In his paper, Martin (2008) also utilizes scientific information to develop a set of landscape design and management guidelines. His focus is on the urbanized arid region around Phoenix, Arizona and, thus, the dynamics of water usage within landscape parcels. In the context of ecosystem services and resilience, he reviews ecological landscaping research to show how socio-ecological variables such as economic status and preferences influence landscape managers' decisions and activities, specifically for plant selection and management. In terms of the ecological landscaping framework (Fig. 2), Martin (2008) highlights the need for large irrigation water inputs to sustain the desired physical-ecological characteristics of lawns and other "oasis" vegetation within this desert biome. Although such water use may seem wasteful, he points out that greener landscape parcels provide cooler microclimates by mitigating the effects of solar radiation inputs. In conclusion, he proposes that, within each landscape parcel, a balance should be sought among practices that minimize water inputs and those that increase the value of ecosystem service outputs (including aesthetic value). Resolving trade-offs is a challenge that requires integration of scientific and design principles. In addition, elucidating general guidelines that are applicable to all, or many, individual parcels of a region may be a central problem for the study and practice of ecological landscaping (Byrne et al. 2008).

While Martin's (2008) focus is mainly vegetation, Marzluff and Rodewald (2008) draw attention to how human manipulation of plant communities and landscape patterns impact animal, especially bird, populations. Drawing from general ecological theories and numerous studies, they discuss scientificallyinformed guidelines for designing and managing urbanized regions and individual parcels in ways that support a higher diversity of animal species (e.g., by providing favorable nesting and food resources). In particular, two of their points exemplify an ecological approach to landscaping. First, they note that human provision of bird feeders can significantly affect the abundance and distribution of various bird species across urbanized areas. By affecting the inputs of an important environmentally-derived input (birds) to a parcel, this activity may affect other physical-ecological characteristics of a parcel in ways that affect landscaping practices (e.g., birds feed on pests that reduce the need for pesticides; Fig. 1E; Tallamy 2007). Second, they emphasize the need for a large-scale approach to thinking about relationships between landscape and biodiversity patterns because the ability of one landscape parcel to support wildlife is affected by—and in turn will affect—the ability of surrounding parcels to do so since many animals move readily among human-defined parcels. These points emphasize two central aspects of the ecological landscaping framework: the importance of considering variables not traditionally defined as landscaping practices (feeding birds), and the value in examining relationships between individual parcels and the environment surrounding them. As Marzluff and Rodewald (2008) suggest, such insights can help guide management and restoration activities in urbanized areas that lead to more successful biodiversity conservation.

Three papers in this issue discuss the management of a parcel's inputs and outputs of water. The focus of Baker et al. (2008) is the nutrient load carried with runoff from lawns that can contribute to the pollution of water bodies. They hypothesize that, in a given urbanized area, a large proportion of polluting nutrients (nitrogen and phosphorous) are likely derived from a small subset of all the parcels (i.e., a "tyranny of small decisions" effect; Odum 1982). Baker et al. (2008) develop a disproportionality framework that can be used to indicate which parcels have the physical-ecological (e.g., soil), sociocultural (e.g., managers' attitudes), and management (e.g., fertilizer application) characteristics that would, alone or in combination, generate a higher likelihood of producing excessive, polluting runoff. They argue that such a framework can lead to the development of more personalized educational outreach messages targeting the owners and managers of higher-polluting lawns. As an example of the type of cross-disciplinary integration needed in ecological landscaping studies, they discuss how social science theories (especially those of reasoned action and planned behavior) can inform the content and approaches of more effective educational programs that help decrease water pollution by effecting changes in parcel managers' knowledge, attitudes, and landscaping decisions and behaviors.

Another conclusion suggested by the Baker et al. (2008) paper is the importance of analyzing the site-specific characteristics of a landscape parcel to guide effective management of its water outputs. This point is also emphasized by Shuster et al. (2008) in their discussion of methods for altering the internal characteristics of landscape parcels to reduce runoff. Using two case studies, they describe approaches for engaging stakeholders (homeowners, local governments) in the processes of adopting landscaping practices that help process and/or retain storm water at its source (e.g., removing impervious surface, installing rain gardens and barrels), thus preventing it from entering sewers and nearby bodies of water. Their approach exemplifies a large-scale social-ecological systems perspective for landscaping because they emphasize the value of 1) including many stakeholders in the landscaping decision-making, design and management processes and 2) considering urbanized regions as integrated systems whose emergent hydrological patterns are affected by the collective processing and outputs of water in individual landscape parcels. In addition, Shuster et al. (2008) emphasize the important role of public policies and incentives to encourage and facilitate landscaping that generates ecosystem services regarding the desirable flow of water through urbanized ecosystems.

In an additional analysis of urban hydrological dynamics, Carter and Butler (2008) draw our attention up from the ground-level with their studies about the physical-ecological characteristics of green roofs. In the context of ecological landscaping, green roofs may help increase the overall sustainability of urban landscape parcels by replacing the ecosystem disservice of increased runoff from impervious roofs with the service of increased storm water retention. Data provided by Carter and Butler (2008) support this conclusion with storm water retention rates in vegetated roof parcels of ~30 to 85%, depending on the total precipitation volume per storm. In addition, they present data about the ability of green roofs to increase the energy efficiency of buildings and the effects of weather conditions on growth rates of different plant species on roofs. Such data contribute to the development of scientific principles to guide green roof landscaping practices and the policies that support their creation.

The theme of using scientific principles to guide ecological landscaping also appears in Hitchmough's (2008) thought-provoking essay. Specifically, he draws from 15 years of his own research about the ecology of designed plant communities to develop a new philosophical view about the ecological and sociological meanings and functions of urban green spaces. In part, this integrated view emphasizes the importance of allowing for a landscape parcel's specific physical-ecological contextual and internal conditions to dictate how it is designed and managed. This contrasts with situations in which sociocultural factors lead to landscaping practices that try to "force" plants to survive in locations where they otherwise would not (e.g., turfgrasses in the desert; Larsen and Harlan 2006, Martin 2008). As he discusses, an implication of this view is that the use of non-native species and novel combinations of plants may be needed to create long-lasting, low maintenance landscapes in locations where the physicalecological conditions do not allow native plants and communities to persist (a conclusion relevant to green roofs as supported by data in Carter and Butler 2008). In addition, he proposes that the sustainability of plant communities which are products of landscaping depend on how local human inhabitants respond to the sociocultural informational outputs (e.g., seasonal color, cues to care) that emerge from them. In this way, Hitchmough's essay suggests an important sociocultural metric for assessing the overall sustainability of landscaping products: those that are appreciated by the public are sustainable; those which are disliked are not. However, a challenge for widespread adoption of ecological landscaping may be reconciling the, perhaps conflicting, sociocultural and physical-ecological aspects of what determines acceptable sustainable urban landscaping (as when intensive lawn management is socioculturally desired but generates negative outputs; Martin 2008, Baker et al. 2008).

When conflicts arise between the sociocultural and physical-ecological desires for landscaping, engaging community members in the discussion, analysis, and design of alternative ecological landscaping strategies may be essential for reaching solutions (as is exemplified by the case studies described by Shuster et al. 2008 and implied in the discussions of Baker et al. 2008 and Marzluff and Rodewald 2008; see also McKenzie-Mohr and Smith 1999). One model for community engagement is a citizen science program in which non-scientists participate in a study that has real-world relevance (Bäckstrand 2003). In their paper, Taylor et al. (2008) describe an innovative high-school education program in which students are being trained as citizen scientists who collect data about the physical-ecological characteristics of their local urbanized ecosystems. Although still in its initial stages, Taylor et al. (2008) report encouraging evidence of positive outcomes from this program including increased student interest in learning and conducting science. Thus, this program—and especially its exemplary use of educational theory and technology to guide the curriculum—can inform the development of others that seek to engage students of all ages in learning and collecting data about the unique social-ecological characteristics of their neighborhood environments. Such public engagement may go a long way toward increasing citizens' interest in understanding—and concern for—how the landscaping practices they engage in affect the ecosystems in which they reside while remedying the effects of "nature-deficit disorder" on urban residents, especially children (Louv 2008).

1.5 CONCLUSIONS, CHALLENGES AND FUTURE DIRECTIONS

For the first time in history, more humans now live in urbanized than rural environments; the growth trends of urbanized areas and populations are expected to continue into the foreseeable future (Pouyat et al. 2006; United Nations 2007; Grimm et al. 2008). Thus, the overall well-being of most people is, and will increasingly be, intimately linked to the environmental quality of urbanized environments. Thus, a major challenge to ensuring the long-term sustainability of human societies is creating and maintaining urbanized ecosystems in which the ecosystem services and biodiversity that support human well-being are conserved and, where needed, restored (Millennium Ecosystem Assessment 2005). In addition, sustainable environments are those that humans wish to maintain because they find them aesthetically pleasing, an important sociocultural dimension of sustainability (Kaplan et al. 1998; Hitchmough 2008). To help guide the creation of sustainable urbanized societies and ecosystems, this paper has presented a description of, and conceptual framework for, ecological landscaping that connote a holistic, integrated sociocultural-ecological and systems-thinking perspective and approach for designing and managing urbanized landscapes. However, real-world creation of ecological landscapes may be challenged by a lack of four supporting factors: 1) sufficient scientific information about the causes, characteristics, and consequences of different landscaping practices and products, 2) ecological landscaping guidelines, 3) widespread public understanding of ecological science and systems thinking, and 4) sociocultural norms and public policies that embrace ecological landscaping practices. For ecological landscaping to become widely valued and adopted, further progress must be made in all these areas simultaneously. In this section, we conclude by briefly discussing these four challenges with an eye toward possible future directions in the study, practice, and public education about ecological landscaping.

Certainly, scientific research and principles should play a central role in shaping ecological landscaping practices and products (Byrne 2008). Although much research has been conducted in many fields that has relevance to this topic, a coherent body of ecological landscaping research has not yet emerged. Possible questions to guide such research (Table 1) cross many traditional disciplinary boundaries, including the natural and social sciences, education, and design and planning fields. Thus, development of an integrated scholarly study of ecological landscaping depends on dissolution of these boundaries to facilitate collaborative, inter- and transdisciplinary research. In this effort, a challenge will be discussing and reconciling differences in paradigms and vocabularies underlying the disciplines. This became clear during the review and editing of papers for this special issue because authors, reviewers, and editors occasionally had conflicting views about the meaning of words and concepts used in different ways across different fields. The ecological landscaping framework (Fig. 1) could help resolve disciplinary communication problems and provide a guide for future interdisciplinary, collaborative work to address important ecological landscaping questions (Table 1).

Another challenge for progress in ecological landscaping is elucidation of general guidelines for the practices involved in designing and managing sustainable urbanized landscapes. In this issue, Martin (2008) and Marzluff and Rodewald (2008) suggest possible guidelines for ecological desert landscaping and successful conservation of urban vertebrate wildlife, respectively. Although they drew from extensive scientific research, their guidelines might be limited by the specific organismal, geographic, and sociocultural contexts in which the reviewed research was conducted; thus, it is uncertain how applicable these guidelines are to other organisms and geographical areas. Examining how the causes, consequences and interpretation of certain landscaping practices and products vary in different contexts represents an exciting challenge for future work that calls for large-scale, cross-biome collaborations (Byrne et al. 2008).

Others have also made progress toward listing guidelines for ecological landscaping (a review of which is outside the scope of this paper but see: Kaplan et al. 1998; Smith et al. 2007; Ecological Landscaping Association 2008; Sustainable Sites Initiative 2008). In the spirit of contributing to this discussion, we suggest here a short list of general, summative guidelines for sustainable, ecological landscaping within an individual landscape parcel by drawing from the framework presented above (Fig. 1). At this point, these guidelines are by necessity very general, preliminary and in need of supporting research to provide more specific insights about how the guidelines should be implemented in different contexts. Nonetheless, their presentation here may help guide future research. These ecological landscaping guidelines are:

1. Examine relationships among as many physical-ecological variables in and outside the parcel as possible (especially those not traditionally considered part of the landscaping endeavor) to uncover potentially unexpected indirect relationships and unintended effects;
2. Minimize material and energy inputs (collectively resource use) and direct and indirect negative outputs (generation of solid waste and pollution) associated with an individual parcel;
3. Use energy and materials within a parcel as responsibly and efficiently as possible, in particular by reusing and recycling as much as possible;
4. Drawing from the best available scientific data and principles, design and manage landscapes in ways that maximize the conservation of ecosystem services (including sociocultural ones) and associated beneficial biodiversity while minimizing ecosystem disservices (Millennium Ecosystem Assessment 2005; Tallamy 2007; Byrne et al. 2008);
5. Reflect on the sociocultural factors that influence landscaping decisions and question their importance and relevance in context of the guidelines listed above and the societal objective of creating sustainable, healthy urbanized ecosystems.

In addition to being very general, these guidelines require a certain level of familiarity with ecological science and systems thinking to comprehend their broader context, meaning, and relevance. Thus, two additional challenging tasks emerge for taking scientific principles and ecological landscaping guidelines into the "real world" of urbanized environments. First, scholars familiar with the ideas underlying the essential framework and guidelines of ecological landscaping should increase efforts toward translating them into less-technical language and materials for other audiences, especially professional landscape managers and public policy makers. (Although the content of this paper could be used for this purpose, such translation was outside its scope.) In concert with these efforts, new environmental education programs need to be developed to increase societal understanding about why anyone should care about ecological landscaping in the first place. Ecological landscaping educational programs will overlap with broader science and environmental literacy programs already established, including citizen scientist efforts (Capra 1996, 2002; Bäckstrand 2003; Taylor et al. 2008). For school children especially, the value of using urbanized landscapes for environmental education programs is obvious given their accessibility and relevance to people's daily lives (Louv 2008; National Wildlife Federation 2008).

It is reasonable to assume that widespread, sustained outreach efforts about the practices and value of ecological landscaping are essential to bring about large-scale changes in social landscaping norms, given the enormous inertia and feedback loops in place that maintain the predominant aestheticsdriven, plant/structure-centered view (Jenkins 1994; Byrne 2005; Robbins 2007). In turn, effective outreach programs—perhaps taking the form of public service and social marketing campaigns—could "nudge" (sensu Thaler and Sunstein 2008) people toward sustainable changes in attitudes, decisions and behaviors related to landscaping (McKenzie-Mohr and Smith 1999; Baker et al. 2008). This may be very difficult in some instances because some common landscaping norms are in direct opposition to what ecological landscaping guidelines suggest are more sustainable practices (e.g., the desire for high-input "perfect" lawns versus more ecologically sustainable low-input or "freedom" lawns; Bormann et al. 2001). As highlighted by some of the papers in this issue, reconciling opposing socioculturally- and ecologically-derived expectations for sustainable landscapes may be the greatest challenge that needs to be overcome for achieving more widespread adoption of ecological landscaping practices and products (Hitchmough 2008; Martin 2008). However, increased study of these challenges, along with development of strategies for and case studies documenting successful changes, provide insights into future directions for initiating positive changes in urban

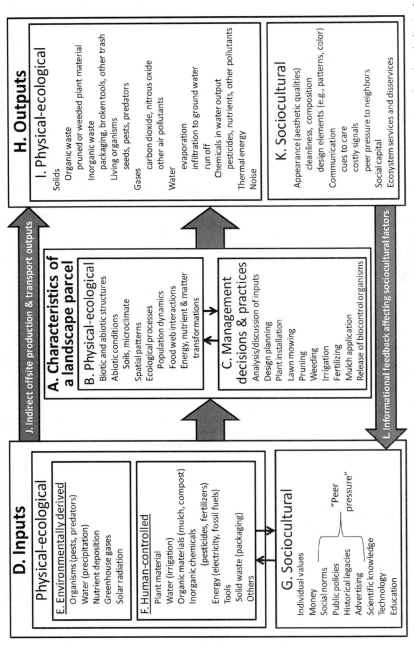

FIGURE 1: This synthetic, holistic conceptual framework illustrates the interconnected relationships among sociocultural and physical-ecological variables that affect the characteristics of an individual landscape parcel. A traditional inputs-outputs ecosystem model (Likens 1992, Odum and Barrett 2005) provides the central organization of the framework. Detailed description of the framework's components is provided in the text.

landscape design and management practices and public policies (Rappaport 1993; McKenzie-Mohr and Smith 1999; Martin et al. 2003; Sandberg and Foster 2005; Shuster et al. 2008). We suggest that greater appreciation for scientific principles in general and specifically for those related to ecological landscaping will underlie increased success for such efforts. Our hope is that this paper and others in this special issue help catalyze greater visibility, understanding, research, and adoption of ecological landscaping perspectives, practices, and policies that lead to more sustainable urbanized societies and ecosystems.

REFERENCES

1. Bäckstrand, K. 2003. Civic Science for Sustainability: Reframing the Role of Experts, Policy-Makers and Citizens in Environmental Governance. Global Environmental Politics 3: 24-41.
2. Baker, L., A. Brazel, L. Byrne, A. Felson, J.M. Grove, K. Hill, K.C. Nelson, J. Walker, V.Shandas. 2007. Effects of human choices on characteristics of urban ecosystems. Bulletin of the Ecological Society of America, October: 404-409.
3. Baker, L.A., B. Wilson, D. Fulton, and B. Horgan. 2008. Disproportionality as a framework to target pollution reduction from urban landscapes. Cities in the Environment 1(2):article 6, 14pp. http://escholarship.bc.edu/cate/vol1/iss2/6 (accessed 12/10/2008).
4. Bormann, F.H., D. Balmori, and G.T. Geballe. 2001. Redesigning the American Lawn: A Search for Environmental Harmony. Second edition. Yale University Press, New Haven. pp. 178.
5. Byrne, L.B. 2005. Of looks, laws and lawns: How human aesthetic preferences influence landscape management, public policies and urban ecosystems, pp. 42-46. In Laband, D. (Ed.). Emerging Issues Along Urban-Rural Interfaces: Linking Science and Society. Auburn University, Auburn, GA.
6. ———. 2007. Habitat structure: a fundamental concept and framework for urban soil ecology. Urban Ecosystems 10: 255-274.
7. ——— 2008. Ecological landscaping: From scientific principles to public policies and practices. Cities and the Environment 1(2):article 2, 3 pp. http://escholarship.bc.edu/cate/vol1/iss2/2 (accessed 12/10/2008).
8. Byrne, L.B., M.A. Bruns, and K.C. Kim. 2008. Ecosystem properties of urban land covers at the aboveground-belowground interface. Ecosystems 11: 1065-1077.
9. Cadenasso, M. L. and S. T. A. Pickett. 2008. Urban Principles for Ecological Landscape Design and Management: Scientific Fundamentals. Cities in the Environment 1(2):article 4, 16 pp. http://escholarship.bc.edu/cate/vol1/iss2/4 (accessed 12/10/2008).
10. Capra, F. 1996. The Web of Life. Anchor Books, New York. 347 pp.

11. Capra, F. 2002. The Hidden Connections. Doubleday, New York.. 320 pp.
12. Carter, T. and C. Butler. 2008. Ecological impacts of replacing traditional roofs with green roofs in two urban areas. Cities and the Environment 1(2):article 9, 17 pp. http://escholarship.bc.edu/cate/vol1/iss2/9 (accessed 12/10/2008).
13. Cary Institute of Ecosystem Studies. 2008. Defining ecology. http://www.ecostudies.org/definition_ecology.html (accessed 10/28/2008).
14. Clayton, S. 2007. Domesticated nature: Motivations for gardening and perceptions of environmental impact. Journal of Environmental Psychology 27: 215-224.
15. Easton, Z.M., and A.M. Petrovic. 2004. Fertilizer source effect on ground and surface water quality in drainage from turfgrass. Journal of Environmental Quality 33: 645-655.
16. Ecological Landscaping Association. 2008. About ELA. http://www.ecolandscaping.org/about.html (accessed 10/28/2008)
17. Forman, R. T. 2008. Urban Regions: Ecology and Planning Beyond the City. Cambridge University Press, New York. 422 pp.
18. Four Dimensions Landscape Company. 2008. http://www.fourdimensionslandscape.com/content.html?page=9 (accessed 10/28/2008).
19. Frank, K.W., K.M. O'Reilly, J.R. Crum, and R.N. Calhoun. 2006. The fate of nitrogen applied to a mature Kentucky bluegrass turf. Crop Science: 46: 209-215.
20. Grimm, N.B., D. Foster, P. Groffman, J.M.Grove, C.S. Hopkinson, K.J. Nadelhoffer, D.E. Pataki, and - D.P.C. Peters. 2008. The changing landscape: ecosystem responses to urbanization and pollution across climatic and societal gradients. Frontiers in Ecology and the Environment 6: 264-272.
21. Hall, C.R., A.W. Hodges, and J.J. Haydu. 2006. The economic impact of the green industry in the United States. HortTechnology 16: 345-353.
22. Hitchmough, J. 2008. New approaches to ecologically based, designed urban plant communities in Britain: do these have any relevance in the USA? Cities and the Environment 1(2):article 10, 15 pp. http://escholarship.bc.edu/cate/vol1/iss2/10 (accessed 12/10/2008).
23. Hope D., C. Gries, W. Zhu, W.F. Fagan, C.L. Redman, N.B. Grimm, A.L. Nelson, C. Martin and A.
24. Kinzig. 2003. Socioeconmics drives urban plant diversity. Proceedings of the National Academy of Sciences 100: 8788-8792.
25. Jenkins, V.S. 1994. The Lawn: A History of an American Obsession. Smithsonian Institution Press, Washington, DC. 246 pp.
26. Kaplan, R., S. Kaplan, and R.L. Ryan. 1998. With People in Mind: Design and Management of Everyday Nature. Island Press, Washington, DC. 225 pp.
27. Kaye, J.P., I.C. Burke, A.R. Mosier, and J.P. Guerschman. 2004. Methane and nitrous oxide flues from urban soils to the atmosphere. Ecological Applications 14: 975-981.
28. Kopp, K.L., and K. Guillard. 2002. Clipping management and nitrogen fertilization of turfgrass: growth, nitrogen utilization and quality. Crop Science 42: 1225-1231.
29. Larsen, L., and S.L. Harlan. 2006. Desert dreamscapes: Residential landscape preference and behavior. Landscape and Urban Planning 78: 85-100.

30. Law, N.L., L.E. Band, and J.M. Grove. 2004. Nitrogen input from residential lawn care practices in suburban neighborhoods in Baltimore County, Maryland, Journal of Environmental Management 47: 737-755.
31. Likens, G.E. 1992. The Ecosystem Approach: Its Use and Abuse. The Ecology Institute, Oldendorf/Luhe, Germany. 166 pp.
32. Louv, R. 2008. Last Child in the Woods: Saving Our Children from Nature-Deficit Disorder. Algonquin Books, Chapel Hill, NC. 390 pp.
33. McKenzie-Mohr, D., and W. Smith. 1999. Fostering Sustainable Behavior: An Introduction to Community-Based Social Marketing. New Society Publishers, Gabriola Island, B.C. Canada. 160 pp.
34. Martin, C.A. 2008. Landscape Sustainability in a Sonoran Desert City. Cities in the Environment 1(2):article 5, 16 pp. http://escholarship.bc.edu/cate/vol1/iss2/5..(accessed 12/10/2008).
35. Martin, C.A., K.A. Peterson, and L.B. Stabler. 2003. Residential landscaping in Phoenix, Arizona, U.S.: Practices and preferences relative to covenants, codes, and restrictions. Journal of Arboriculture 29: 9-16.
36. Marzluff, J.M. and A.D. Rodewald. 2008. Conserving biodiversity in urbanizing areas: nontraditional views from a bird's perspective. Cities and the Environment 1(2):article 6, 27 pp. http://escholarship.bc.edu/cate/vol1/iss2/6. (accessed 12/10/2008).
37. Millennium Ecosystem Assessment. 2005. Ecosystems and Human Well-Being: Synthesis. Island Press, Washington, DC. 137 pp.
38. Nassauer, J.I. 1988. The aesthetics of horticulture: neatness as a form of care. HortScience 23: 973-977.
39. National Gardening Association. 2004. Environmental Lawn and Garden Survey. South Burlington, Vermont.
40. Nishioka,[, M.G., H.M. Burkholder, M.C. Brinkman, and R.G. Lewis. 1999. Distribution of 2,4- Dischlorophenoxyacetic acid in floor dust through homes following homeowner and commercial lawn applications: Quantitative effects of children, pets and shoes. Environmental Science and Technology 33: 1359-1365.
41. National Wildlife Federation. 2008. Gardening in an environmentally friendly way. http://www.nwf.org/backyard/resourceconservation.cfm (accessed 10/28/2008).
42. Odum, W.E. 1982. Environmental degradation and the tyranny of small decisions. BioScience 32: 728- 729.
43. Odum, E.P., and G.W.Barrett. 2005. Fundamentals of Ecology. Fifth edition. Thomson, Brooks/Cole, Belmont, CA. 598 pp.
44. Parker, J.H. 1982. An energy and economic analysis of alternative residential landscapes. Journal of Environmental Systems 11: 271-287.
45. Pickett, S.T.A., W.R. Burch, S.E. Dalton, T.W. Foresman, J.M. Grove, and R. Rowntree. 1997. A conceptual framework for the study of human ecosystems in urban areas. Urban Ecosystems 1: 185-199.
46. Pickett, S.T.A., J. Kolasa, C.G. Jones. 2007. Ecological Understanding. Second Edition. Academic Press, London. 233 pp.

47. Pickett, S.T.A., M.L. Cadenasso, J.M. Grove, P.M. Groffman, L.E. Band, C.G. Boone, W.R. Burch, C. Grimmond, C.S.B., J.J. Hom, J.C. Jenkins, N.L. Law, C.H. Nilon, R.V Pouyat, K. Szlavecz, P.S. Warren, M.A. Wilson. 2008. Beyond urban legends: An Emerging Framework of Urban Ecology, as Illustrated by the Baltimore Ecosystem Study. BioScience 58: 139-150.
48. Piekielek, N.B. 2003. Suburban dynamics of lawn care. Master's thesis. University of Georgia, Athens, GA.
49. Potter, D.A., M.C. Buxton, C.T. Redmond, C.G. Patterson, and A.J. Powell. 1990. Toxicity of pesticides to earthworms (Oligochaeta: Lumbricidae) and effect on thatch degradation in Kentucky bluegrass turf. Journal of Economic Entomology 83: 2362-2369.
50. Pouyat, R.V., K. Belt, D. Pataki, P.M. Groffman, J. Hom, and L. Band. 2006. Effects of urban land-use change on biogeochemical cycles. Pp 55-78. In Canadell, P., D. Pataki, and L. Pitelka, eds. Terrestrial Ecosystems in a Changing World. Springer, Canberra, Australia.
51. Rappaport, B. 1993. The John Marshall Law Review. Volume 26, Summer 1993, Number 4. http://www.epa.gov/greenacres/weedlaws/. (accessed 10/28/2008).
52. Rebek, E. J., C. S. Sadof, and L.M. Hanks. 2005. Manipulating the abundance of natural enemies in ornamental landscapes with floral resource plants. Biological Control 33: 203-216.
53. Redman, C.L., J.M Grove, L.H. Kuby. 2004. Integrating social science into the Long-Term Ecological
54. Research (LTER) network: Social dimensions of ecological change and ecological dimensions of social change. Ecosystems 7: 161-171.
55. Robbins, P. 2007. Lawn People: How Grasses, Weeds and Chemicals Make Us who We Are. Temple University Press, Philadelphia. 186 pp.
56. Sandberg, LA. and J. Foster. 2005. Challenging lawn and order: Environmental discourse and lawn care reform in Canada. Environmental Politics 14: 478-494.
57. Shuster, W.D., M.A. Morrison and R. Webb. 2008. Front-loading urban stormwater management for success – a perspective incorporating current studies on the implementation of retrofit low-impact development. Cities and the Environment 1(2):article 8, 15 pp. http://escholarship.bc.edu/cate/vol1/iss2/8. (accessed 12/10/2008).
58. Slabbekoorn, H. and P. Margriet. 2003. Birds sing at a higher pitch in urban noise. Nature 424: 267.
59. Smith, C., A. Clayden, and N. Dunnett. 2007. Residential Landscape Sustainability: A Checklist Tool. Blackwell Publishing, Malden, MA. 197 pp.
60. Sustainable Sites Initiative. 2008. http://www.sustainablesites.org/ (accessed 10/28/2008).
61. Stein, S. 1993. Noah's Garden: Restoring the Ecology of our Backyards. Houghton-Mifflin Co., Boston. 294 pp.
62. Stewart, J.R. 2008. http://ecohort.nres.uiuc.edu/index.htm (accessed 10/28/2008).
63. Tallamy, D. 2007. Bringing Nature Home: How Native Plants Sustain Wildlife in our Gardens. Timber Press, Portland, OR. 288 pp.
64. Taylor, D., M.L. Holly, and S. Zachariah. 2008. Landscaping locally: Fostering stewardship with real science in high school curricula. Cities and the Environment

1(2):article 11, 12 pp. http://escholarship.bc.edu/cate/vol1/iss2/11. (accessed 2/12/2009).
65. Terra Nova. 2004. http://www.terranovalandscaping.com/ (accessed 10/28/2008).
66. Thaler, R.H., and C.R. Sunstein. 2008. Nudge: Improving Decisions about Health, Wealth and Happiness. Yale University Press, New Haven, CT. 293 pp.
67. Thompson, G.F., and F.R Steiner, editors. 1997. Ecological Design and Planning. John Wiley and Sons, Inc. New York. 348 pp.
68. United Nations, Population Division of the Department of Economic and Social Affairs of the United Nations Secretariat. 2007. World Urbanization Prospects: The 2007 Revision Population Database. http://esa.un.org/unup (accessed 2/17/2009).
69. Waskowski, A., and S. Waskowski. 2002. The Landscaping Revolution: Gardening with Mother, Nature not Against Her. McGraw-Hill, New York. 176 pp.
70. Wild Ones. 2008. http://www.for-wild.org/aboutsit.html (accessed 10/28/2008).
71. Wood, W.E. and S.M. Yezerinac. 2006. Song sparrow (Melospiza melodia) song varies with urban noise. The Auk 123: 650-659.
72. Zenger. J.T., and T.J. Gibb. 2001. Impact of four insecticides on Japanese beetle (Coleoptera: Scarabaeidae) egg predators and white grubs in turfgrass. Journal of Economic Entomology 94: 145-149.
73. Zmyslony, J., and D. Gagnon. 1998. Residential management of urban front-yard landscape: A random process? Landscape and Urban Planning 40: 295-307.

CHAPTER 2

New Approaches to Ecologically Based, Designed Urban Plant Communities in Britain: Do These Have Any Relevance in the United States?

JAMES HITCHMOUGH

2.1 THE NEED FOR NEW APPROACHES TO DESIGNED URBAN PLANTING

Over the past 15 years a program of research undertaken by the author, his colleague Dr Nigel Dunnett, and numerous postgraduate students has led to the creation of new paradigms as to how public and in some cases private urban spaces (gardens) could be designed and planted. This research was conceived as a response to two long-term problems affecting urban parks and green space in Britain: a significant decline in the funding of maintenance programs and the erosion of horticultural vegetation maintenance and management skills within urban park authorities (Dunnett et al. 2002). These two factors had resulted in an ongoing simplification of urban parks and green spaces into mown grass and trees, as plantings of herbaceous plants and shrubs were "edited out" in both existing landscapes

---

© Hitchmough, J. 2008. New approaches to ecologically based, designed urban plant communities in Britain:do these have any relevance in the United States? Cities and the Environment 1(2):article 10. Creative Commons Attribution license (http://creativecommons.org/licenses/by/3.0/). Used with the permission of the authors.

and new developments. The challenge was to develop new types of vegetation that were inexpensive to install and could be maintained within a minimal resources environment, while meeting human aspirations for color and seasonal change, and providing a valuable habitat for native animal biodiversity.

Our research is not derived from, or based upon, any one particular theory or model, but is a pragmatic approach that draws upon a variety of interdisciplinary perspectives, as is discussed in greater detail in Dunnett and Hitchmough (2004). The central thrust in this work has been to take the understanding derived from contemporary ecological science (e.g., Grime 2001; Grime et al. 2007) and restoration ecology (e.g., Luken 1990; Pywell et al. 2003) and apply this to the design of plant communities, and in particular, those composed of herbaceous plants (grasses, forbs, and geophytes) for use in urban landscapes. There is a long European tradition of creating (or more commonly wishing to create) naturalistic or "wild-looking" herbaceous vegetation in designed landscapes (e.g., Robinson 1870; Jager 1877). In practice these plantings were often difficult to sustain given the limited historical understanding of the mechanics of competition between plants and other ecological processes.

In terms of urban ecology perspectives, our research is grounded in recognition of human created urban environments as habitats in the tradition of Gilbert (1989). This view interprets urban ecology in *laissez-faire* terms of understanding the outcome (positive and negative) of interactions between human beings, environments, and natural processes, rather than focusing mainly on surviving remnant native plant communities in urban areas and seeing everything else as a degraded landscape.

In terms of semi-natural plant communities, urban ecosystems often have peculiar, sometimes extreme characteristics. This is particularly true for potential vegetation productivity in the case of landscapes that are the product of past industrial processes and practices. When new environmental design initiatives, such as Sustainable Urban Drainage (SUDS) Schemes (Dunnett and Clayden 2007) and the development of green/brown roofs on large buildings (Dunnett and Kingsbury 2008) are overlaid across existing post-industrial urban landscape, the result is a huge diversity of new planting opportunities, many of which lie outside the canon of traditional designed plantings. Some of these planting environments are extremely unproductive, for example, a 50 mm layer of crushed brick substrate on a roof; others are extremely productive, as in a SUDS scheme on urban soils subject to past and ongoing eutrophification. When confronted by these types of sites, most landscape architects and other urban designers have sought firstly to amend or ameliorate these sites to take them back into the "normative" range associated with a horticultural–agricultural perspective.

Our work has deliberately chosen not to do this, but rather has sought to develop designed vegetation that is capable of responding positively to the specific ecological conditions of the site largely as found. This approach results in unique, site-specific plant communities that lie outside of conventional phytosociology frameworks, as the combination of site and management generates natural selection pressures on the plant community originally established on the site. The purpose of this paper is to explore whether our approach has any relevance to thought and practice of designing and managing urban landscapes in urban North America.

2.1.1 NATIVE VERSUS NON-NATIVE PLANT USE IN NATURALISTIC PLANTING

Where our work deviates from "ecological practice" norms is that we do not restrict ourselves solely to plants native to the British Isles; indeed often we create plant communities that contain no native species whatsoever and yet still involve the ecological processes that are often seen to be the prerogative of native species. We do not prefer exotics over natives or viceversa, other than when the ecological and social-cultural context suggests that this is the appropriate thing to do. Native species are, however, widely used in landscape architecture in Britain, and indeed they are the norm within rural and urban fringe landscapes and in major green infrastructure projects irrespective of location, as woodland, scrub, and various meadow communities. When it is sensible to do so, we are as keen to conserve and expand the territory of remnant native vegetation as are ecological practitioners in the United States.

My experiences of the United States as a regular visitor and one time resident, plus host to numerous American visiting scholars and students, is that there is a widely held perspective that non-native species lie outside of ecology, like souls separated from their physical body (the native habitat). While this view is understandable, it is clearly nonsensical; alien species have physiological and ecological niche ranges in the same way that native species do, and like native species, they interact with the biotic world in that they form relationships with other organisms, and provide habitat opportunities for herbivores, predators, decomposers, and indirectly for parasites. From a purely objective perspective, alien species have ecology. In an urban context it is sensible to recognize this, as by doing so it is possible to use them in ways that allow them to fit well enough to maximize benefits for the minimum resource input possible, but not so well that they colonize beyond the planting site.

But why do we use alien species? Why not restrict ourselves entirely to native species? There are a number of issues here. Firstly we respond strongly to context. Where extant seminatural vegetation is the dominant character around or next to a site, or where there are areas of significant remnant native vegetation, we would tend to use predominantly native species. In contrast, on a green roof in a city center we would potentially use no native species at all as the potentially extreme conditions may lie beyond the physiological and ecological niche ranges of otherwise desirable native species.

A second factor that encourages our use of exotic species is that the native flora of the British Isles is extremely small. Due to post-ice age sea level rises that isolated the United Kingdom from the European mainland, the flora consists of only 1140 truly native species (i.e., species that re-colonized post the last ice age without obvious human agency), plus approximately 300 archaeophytes (introduced pre-AD 1500) and neophytes (post-AD 1500) (Preston et al. 2002). Native plant species richness in the United Kingdom is approximately half that of, for example, Ohio, United States on an equivalent area basis. As only a percentage (experience suggests typically <20%) of this flora is judged sufficiently attractive to be used in designed contexts, in Britain designers soon run out of species that are well enough suited to the conditions as found (i.e., to be used in a sustainable way) and that do things such as flower at the desired time of year. In most of our native forbs, flowering is restricted to late spring-early summer. In rural contexts where human expectation of landscape content is reduced, and vegetation viewed far less closely and intensively as a component of "scenery", having no flowers in late summer is not a problem. These are, however, potentially significant issues of choice in some "pressurecooker" urban contexts, such as public parks that are heavily visited during the summer months. North America has a much richer flora, both in total and regionally, than Britain, and hence it is much easier to achieve visually acceptable results by relying on the native and in some cases regionally native flora. Of course even in America there are situations when the use of nonnative, or politically native but geographically "exotic" species, is extremely helpful in urban design.

We are fortunate in Britain, in that we have extremely detailed, long term records at a 10 km grid scale, of naturalization of non-native species (Preston et al. 2002). Since most of the species we use are long and widely cultivated in millions of gardens across the land, generally for periods in excess of 100 years, there are strong cues to species that have high dominance potential or are invasive, and we avoid these. During the 10 years or so it takes to develop a new designed plant community, we continue to assess likely invasive potential. A major factor restricting alien forb invasiveness in Britain is intense slug and snail predation; seedlings of palatable species are quickly eliminated beyond the management regime of the designed planting that allows them to persist. Many widely naturalized herbaceous species are highly unpalatable as seedlings and adults. This is one of the factors we screen for in developing new communities, together with assessments of seed production and dispersal capacity, relative growth rates of seedlings and adults, and capacity to spread by rhizomes and other colonizing structures. In general we operate within the guidelines developed in the United States to identify species with a high risk of becoming invasive (e.g., Widrlechner et al. 2004).

2.1.2 THE AESTHETIC CHARACTERISTICS OF NATURALISTIC URBAN VEGETATION

The herbaceous vegetation that we design and create (be it native, nonnative or a mixture) has a strongly naturalistic appearance. As most species are established by sowing *in situ*, in a visual sense, distribution is strongly random, although of course in many cases there are patterns that the informed viewer can perceive, and these tend to increase through time as natural selection pressures are imposed, and species move around through recruitment and mortality. This is a very different aesthetic to the public herbaceous plantings of in-vogue designers in the United States, such as Oudolf (Oudolf and Kingsbury 2005), and Oehme and Van Sweden (2002), where species are planted in groups or blocks. This form of arrangement makes it clear to viewers that the plantings are intentional and probably cared for; some of the requirements of the "Cues to Care" hypothesis (Nassauer 1995) are therefore satisfied.

In our work this is not the case, and likewise this is also true of the habitat and perhaps most specifically prairie restoration movement in the United States Layperson appreciation of naturalistic herbaceous, and particularly tall herbaceous vegetation in urban contexts is therefore potentially problematic. The creators of a tall-grass prairie in the United States are engaged with its appearance because they see it as ecologically and ethically worthy, but urban vegetation generally has to stand or fall on its immediate visual interpretation by laypeople without deciphering coded messages regarding its goodness. This has been a major challenge for us in the United Kingdom, even though I would suggest that as a culture we are more attuned to accept the disordered appearance of naturalistic vegetation in urban contexts than are Americans. The landscape fabric of British suburbia is far more heterogeneous than its United States equivalent; it is relatively messy, there are many shrubs and tall herbaceous plantings in the 0-2.0 m above ground level zone, many boundary walls, fences and hedges, fewer large trees, and lawn is much less cared for. There are no "weed" ordnances that dictate the composition and height of vegetation as there are in the United States (Rappaport 1993). Despite this British cultural preconditioning to accept difference and disorder in the private and public landscapes adjacent to where they live, in public spaces attempts to gain acceptance of naturalistic herbaceous vegetation have often struggled except where that vegetation has included colorful, visually dramatic species. This latter approach has been developed for native meadows and woodland understory vegetation by urban based, socially focused agencies in Britain such as Landlife/National Wildflower Centre, as part of their "Creative Conservation Agenda" (Luscombe and Scott 2004) but is largely absent from the "rural founded" thinking of many ecological practitioners. The author is currently directing a United Kingdom Economic and Social Research Council funded study into how color and other drivers affect attitudes of the public and grounds maintenance staff towards wildflower meadows in urban parks.

Our experience to date suggests that in order to make naturalistic (irrespective of where the species come from) urban herbaceous vegetation acceptable to laypeople, it must be designed and managed to be visually dramatic at some point in its annual growth cycle. This often means increasing forb density and reducing grass density, and within the forbs increasing the density of the most dramatic, long flowering species. If this means a designed native plant community looks substantially different to the wild occurring stereotype, so be it. Within the United States this approach has been championed within restored prairie plant communities in urban contexts by Neil Diboll of Prairie Nursery, Wisconsin and Carol Franklin of Andropogon Associates (Kingsbury 2004). By doing this, a bridge is provided that some people will be able to cross over to allow them to gradually value the latent ecological worthiness of naturalistic urban vegetation.

2.1.3 AMATEUR GARDENING AS A SHAPER OF ATTITUDES TO NATURE IN A CULTURAL CONTEXT

Another reason why we use non-native plants extensively is that they are an extremely important part of our urban cultural tradition. Discussions about the (de)merits of non-native cultivated species within conservation biology and even the popular media rarely reflect the fact that many of these species are strongly culturally valued commodities, in the same way as opera, sport, cooking, literature, and art. In Britain these notions of value and meaning are particularly highly developed within the people who own and use the country's 16 million private gardens, and make millions of day visits per year to the huge number of public and institutional gardens (Dunnett et al. 2007). To the British, the American vernacular for the garden ("yard") suggests a disturbingly utilitarian relationship with this space. The rear (and often front) garden in Britain is generally a highly gardened space, a dialogue between the creativeness of (or absence of) householder and nature. Gardening is an extremely important recreational activity within Britain and is often pursued with vigor, passion, and even intellect. Although participation in gardening is also high in the United States as evidenced by National Gardening Association (2004) surveys, I suggest that there is, however, a discernible qualitative difference between the intensity and degree of engagement in gardening between the two countries. This in turn explains why our work in Britain has developed such strong connections with this aspect of popular mass culture.

The capacity to grow a diversity of colorful herbaceous plants in parks and public green space that are highly valued in private gardens has been diminished in the late 20th century by declining green space budgets. Our work has sought to turn this around by using plants valued by the public, but reorganized into naturalistic designed communities that are managed at very low resource levels using the tools of nature conservation management, often cutting and burning. We value the meaning and richness these plants and plantings give to urban life, and we challenge the notion that valuing non-native plants limits the capacity to do the same for native plants and native plant habitats. We would argue that the converse is true; developing an interest in cultivated plants, predisposes people to value vegetation of nature-conservation significance. Michael Pollan's seminal text "Second Nature" (Pollan 1991) suggests that this may also be true in an American context.

2.1.4 SUSTAINABILITY AND NON-NATIVE PLANTS

At the Ohio Ecological Landscaping Conference from which this paper is derived, a number of speakers and members of the audience articulated the view that only native plants could be sustainable. Native plants can be very sustainable, but they can also be extremely unsustainable; it is all a question of the context in which they are used. In terms of plant use in landscapes, sustainability is largely determined by the degree of fit of a species to the environment in which it is to be cultivated. In more technical terms, it is whether the environment falls within the niche range for all the key factors that determine the survival of a given species, for both juveniles and adults: soil moisture regime, minimum and maximum air temperature, solar radiation, predation regime, soil potential productivity, competition with neighboring plants and so on. Because urbanization often radically changes these factors one cannot assume that what vegetation once occurred on a site will be well-fitted post-urbanization. Indeed experience from around the world shows that attempts to re-establish the original native flora of a now urban environment often struggle, and require large inputs of resources to facilitate this (Brown and Bugg 2001). Most often this is because eutrophication from urban processes and changed disturbance regimes have made sites far more productive than they originally were, making the original lower productivity plant communities poorly fitted. They frequently need ongoing management to restrict colonization by more productive native or non-native species not part of the original plant community.

On urban sites in Britain we use North American tall grass prairie for a variety of reasons, but one of the most important is that many of the component species are able to compete and persist at productivity levels that would lead to competitive exclusion of much less productive native forbs of species-rich meadow communities.

This idea of an organism placed outside of its original climatic, geological and biotic context by urbanization is a really important one to the sustainability debate. To illustrate this point I will draw on a paper given at the conference on using Northeastern United States species on un-irrigated green roofs in that region. The summer soil moisture regime in 100 mm of crushed brick substrate on a building in New Jersey is not of that place; urbanization has created a highly xeric habitat that has more in common with montane Colorado than New Jersey. Sustainability requires this to be recognized in plant selection; plants need to come from somewhere in the world where these summer soil moisture conditions naturally occur. If native plants evolved to these conditions can be found locally this is good; however if not, sustainable planting may have to utilize species from Grand Mesa in Colorado or the Roggeveld Plateau in South Africa. You could, of course, irrigate to pretend the green roof is not a green roof to allow you to grow the local mesic native species that occurred on this site pre-urbanization, but in most cases this is not a sustainable path and mirrors the cultural construct underpinning the idealized American lawn.

The latter involves applying a near universal standard of greenness, freedom from broadleaved forbs, and the absences of pest and disease symptoms, irrespective of precipitation and temperature regime, which is then achieved through the intensive application of energy and other resources. Whatever its merits as a ubiquitous, and highly valued cultural landscape that potentially sequesters carbon (Milesi et al. 2005), overall the idealized lawn is not a model for more sustainable urban landscapes (National Gardening Association 2004; Robbins 2007).

In the case of the conference paper I previously referred to, the Northeastern American species planted on the roof performed very badly or died, as one would have expected given their evolutionary selection for mesic environments. One could have used more xeric genotypes of some of the more widely distributed species used, for example Colorado populations of *Asclepias tuberosa*, however, this might be seen as inappropriate in terms of current sustainability debates on local populations (Jones 2003). Native plants can, like exotic plants, be either sustainable or non-sustainable, it all depends on context.

Climate change is going to have a major impact on these considerations. In Britain the Climatic Models suggest that Southern England is going to experience a climate similar to present day Southwest France (Met Office 2005). Severe winter frosts are already increasingly infrequent in our major cities. As a result of these climatic changes exotic species that historically were seen as transients in the garden-landscape flora, for example, many South African species, are increasingly perennial and correspondingly more widely planted. Within 50 years many of the semi-natural native plant communities of South England will also be significantly changed, and as an island with no physical connections with the European mainland, many of the currently alien Southern European species that could and should colonize these new habitats will be unable to do so, unless introduced through deliberate human agency or allowed to colonize from cultivated plants in gardens. The United State's contiguous north-south landmass will buffer some of these changes, although habitat fragmentation through agriculture and urbanization will raise similar issues to those discussed above for the United Kingdom. A fluid rather than dogmatic, approach to native and non-native plantings is going to be required together with the publication of new regional floras. Fighting over what is native at the state border will become ever more fatuous.

2.1.5 DESIGNED "CULTURAL" VEGETATION AS A HABITAT FOR NATIVE ANIMAL BIODIVERSITY

The fifteen years of our vegetation research has coincided with growing interest in the capacity of designed garden-like vegetation to support the native invertebrate fauna of Britain. This started with the seminal work of Owen (1991) on investigating the flora of a typical suburban garden in the city of Leicester over a 15 year period. This revealed extraordinary invertebrate richness across a wide range of taxa, even though much of the garden vegetation was composed of exotic species and not in the least bit "wild". Owen's work put the potential of garden vegetation for urban invertebrate conservation on the map, and led indirectly to the Biodiversity in Urban Gardens Study (BUGS), coordinated through the University of Sheffield and funded by NERC (BUGS 2007). This is the most extensive study of the plant and invertebrate biodiversity of urban gardens yet undertaken anywhere in the world and to date has resulted in a large number of published papers in international journals (e.g., Loram et al. 2007).

BUGS has confirmed that Owen's findings were not anomalous. The 60 study gardens in Sheffield also show extremely high invertebrate diversity, and this is also seen in other cities in the United Kingdom. Far from being a biological desert simply by virtue of the dominance of non-native plants, urban gardens in Britain are an extremely important nature conservation resource. This is because they are, as a land use type, spatially and temporally complex; indeed far more so than natural habitats. They are also mega-diverse in terms of plant species, many of which are cultivated aliens. Total plant diversity in Sheffield gardens was assessed as 438 species per 0.01 ha (Thompson et al. 2003). To put this into perspective the most diverse parts of the wet tropics support > 200 tree species per 0.1ha and the richest Mediterranean vegetation (Israel) has around 250 species per 0.1 ha (Crawley 1997). There are also very great differences in the plant species present between individual gardens; ongoing human agency (the independent decisions of 16 million gardeners) works to maintain and expand diversity, as this is culturally valued by many gardeners. As more than 70,000 garden plant taxa are currently commercially available in Britain (Lord 2007) and this total is probably growing, it is almost inevitable that garden plant diversity will continue to be extremely high.

Even if BUGS or Jennifer Owen had never existed it would still have been clear to the author and his co-workers that our vegetation types support a wide diversity of invertebrates, birds, amphibian, and small mammals. We see these every time we take research measurements, or harvest biomass for growth analysis. The larvae of most invertebrates (with the exception of butterflies) are not particularly host-plant specific, and many alien plant species, are in any case related to native species. Even butterflies, the cause *célèbre* of exclusive native plant-native invertebrate relationships, show signs of adaptability to other food plants in urban contexts. In Davis, California, the larvae of nearly all the native butterflies now depend on introduced alien plants (Shapiro 2002).

So there is good evidence to support the notion that hybrid native-exotic vegetation and even entirely exotic vegetation play a positive role in supporting a rich native invertebrate fauna and as a result vertebrates that feed on these species. What about the bigger picture in relation to urban ecology as a whole? In Britain we now recognize that in order to maximize biodiversity value in urban landscapes it is necessary to create vegetation types that mirror the content and structure of either i) gardens, ii) post industrial derelict land, or iii) "ancient" managed native woodlands and grasslands. All of these are complex and dynamic, although for very different reasons, because species complements change rapidly (particularly in the first two) in space and time. Our urban green space staple, the traditional 19th century park of widely spaced large trees and hectares of closely mown grass is much less good as biodiversity habitat for organisms other than those restricted to tree canopy or mown grassland.

There are many parallels between the green space of American and British cities, however, American suburban gardens are very different from British gardens. Indeed many have a similar vegetation structure to urban parks, closely mown grass and tall trees (Hefland et al. 2006). House blocks are large, and the suburbs cover huge tracts of land, as is strikingly obvious when one descends to Chicago's O'Hare airport on a clear day. In Britain, approximately 25% of cities are composed of gardens (Loram et al. 2007); it would seem likely that this figure is higher in the United States (although comparable data have proved difficult to find) and hence the significance of gardens is potentially greater still. Data discussed in Milesi et al. (2005) suggests that garden lawns in the United States account for a total area of at least 60,000 km^2, and possibly considerably more. This suggests that in addition to public green space, increasing the complexity of gardens should be one of the main targets of urban nature conservation. It seems unlikely to the author that this cultural shift can be achieved without a step-wise approach, starting with planting that is more familiar and moving to that which is potentially much wilder looking as changes in visual norms become embedded. The willingness of residents to make changes to their garden landscapes has been discussed in Helfand et al. (2006). Emphasizing highly colorful vegetation types, including non-invasive exotic species where these are culturally valued as much as the most attractive native species, is likely to assist in achieving an increase in plant diversity and spatial complexity.

2.2 OUR APPROACH TO CREATING NATURALISTIC HERBACEOUS VEGETATION IN PRACTICE

In contrast to conventional design practice, we normally create our vegetation types by sowing seed *in situ*, where it is to grow, and we have developed, and continue to refine, sophisticated techniques to ensure that what is created closely resembles what was envisaged at the design stage.

Establishing herbaceous vegetation by sowing seed *in-situ* avoids many of the carbon expenditures associated with the growing and transportation of conventional nursery grown plants. Because we need our vegetation types to meet the expectations of urban green space managers and visitors in terms of appearance and function, we have invested much time in understanding how to engineer vegetation with high forb-species richness, and develop management techniques to retain this, *albeit* in modified form, in the longer term (e.g., Hitchmough et al. 2008). An example of our research to make sowing highly predictable in terms of the number of emerged seedlings of each species sown is shown in Figure 1.

FIGURE 1: Testing field emergence of species used in our research to ensure the composition of vegetation created in practice closely resembles the design model. EU funded research with Jelitto Seeds, Germany.

After the existing vegetation on a site to be sown has been eliminated, a 50-75 mm deep mulch layer of sand, crushed building rubble, or composted urban green waste is spread over the surface of the soil. The actual material chosen on any given site depends on local availability, and the nature of the plant community being created. These materials typically contain relatively few weed seeds, in contrast to the topsoil lying beneath. Seed mixtures are then sown into the surface of this "sowing mulch" layer, which in turn suppresses most weed seed emergence from the soil below. In the absence of sufficient rainfall, the mulch layer is irrigated twice a week in April, the main germination and emergence window in the United Kingdom. The sown seedlings develop largely in the absence of competition from weedy species (see Figure 2), and weed management costs in the first year are low. In a project in the Sheffield Botanic Gardens, total maintenance costs for the first year to maintain a 800 m^2 sown area in a weed-free state was 14 hours (Hitchmough, unpublished data). Seed costs per m^2 typically vary from £1.00-£3.00 ($1.70 - $5.11 USD). The costs of planting to achieve a similar vegetation type are typically 10 to 15 times higher. A greater understanding of what types of vegetation we make and how, can be gained from our research websites (http://shef.ac.uk/landscape/staff_minisites/james/, http://www.nigeldunnett.co.uk/index.html), a textbook (Dunnett and Hitchmough 2004), plus various published papers (e.g, Hitchmough et al. 2004, Hitchmough and De La Fleur 2006).

Making examples of our vegetation types in public and institutional landscapes in Britain, often on a large scale, has been an important contributor to the evolution of our research agenda. This "road testing" is critical to our understanding of establishment phenomena, large-term management in practice, and also how people respond to the appearance of these types of vegetation. Examples of our vegetation can be seen for example, at: The Eden Project, Cornwall (Figure 3); National Botanical Garden of Wales; The Royal Horticultural Society Gardens at Wisley, Surrey (Figure 4); Harlow Carr, Yorkshire (Figure 5); The Sheffield Botanic Gardens; plus a number of urban parks, green spaces, and commercial landscapes across Britain.

We have also developed the idea of the "managed gap" as a way of addressing concerns about the escape of non-native species. When North American prairie vegetation is used in Britain, for example, most species can only persist and recruit successfully from self-sown seed when sown into an area surfaced with sand or a similar granular mineral (to check slug predation) and burnt in spring to restrict the invasion of C3 grasses. Without these simple, low intensity practices (the managed gap) this community is rapidly replaced by weedy native species (Hitchmough and de La Fleur 2006). There are aspects of the managed gap in nearly all of our designed plant communities, including of course, those composed entirely of native species, many of which also cannot persist unless specific management actions are applied to them in perpetuity.

A central idea in our research has been to create vegetation that is spatially complex in both space and time and contains a high diversity of species. To contribute to this we have explored how to create herbaceous

FIGURE 2: North American prairie vegetation emerging through jute erosion matting out of a sand mulch layer in a public park project in Sheffield, United Kingdom. Note the absence of weed growth.

FIGURE 3: Tall-grass prairie vegetation created by sowing seed *in situ* at the Eden Project, St. Austell, Cornwall in 2000.

FIGURE 4: Second generation dry steppe-prairie vegetation 6 months after sowing at RHS Wisley, Surrey, United Kingdom. At this point in time the scene is dominated by the shade intolerant lower layer. In the second and subsequent growing seasons the predominantly leafless flowering stems of medium and tall species that are present in the ground layer at low density will emerge to provide a complex vertical structure.

vegetation composed of multiple layers of species "stacked" on top of one another. Typically this entails a low growing, spring flowering shade tolerant understory layer (Figure 6), a mid-canopy late spring to summer flowering layer and a taller mid-summer to autumn flowering layer (Ahmad and Hitchmough 2007). Species selection, sowing and emergence density, are key tools in successfully achieving these goals. We have pursued these complex layered structures to maximize resource utilization within the vegetation to restrict invasion of weedy species from outside, to maximize the duration of flowering, and to maximize opportunities for wildlife, and in particular invertebrates – the bulk of the visual biodiversity.

We are now developing more sophisticated "second generation" communities in which most of the plant diversity is held within the ground

FIGURE 5: Wet meadow vegetation containing native and non-native species, but dominated by Himalayan *Primula* species. Established by sowing in Harlow Carr Garden, Harrogate, United Kingdom.

FIGURE 6: North American prairie vegetation with an understory of shade tolerant, winter-green, spring flowering European woodland forbs; an example of a simple and robust multi-layer vegetation we have developed to minimize maintenance inputs.

layer, with the plants present in the mid- and tall canopy layers present at much lower densities to prevent the elimination of shade intolerant ground layers species. These plant communities are created by ensuring most of the seed sown is of ground layer species (typically around 70% on a target seedling emergence basis) with intermediate canopy layers at 20% of target seedling emergence and tall canopy species 10% or less.

2.3 CONCLUSION

In this paper I have discussed the reasoning behind our development of naturalistic, but sometimes non-native herbaceous vegetation to explore some of the bigger issues about how ordinary urban citizens might engage with new forms of urban landscapes that are richer in biodiversity, and more sustainable and meaningful to people. Throughout this paper, I have adopted a cautious position on how this work might translate into practice in American cities. One of the reasons for this caution is that to Europeans, America seems more polarized in terms of perspectives on urban ecosystems and, in particular, the role of non-native species in naturalistic vegetation, although this may merely be an artifact of an outsider's view. As evidence of these contrasts I would cite the omnipresent manicured lawn and the willingness to use large quantities of embodied energy and biocides in order to conform to an "ideal lawn construct" seemingly independent of climate and location (Milesi et al. 2005; Robbins 2007). As a counterpoint to this, a nativist movement, with strongly contrasting values is pursued by some of its proponents with an almost religious fervor (Kingsbury 2004), fuelled by a sense of what has been lost. Between these positions there are obviously many people who wish to have a positive relationship with nature but who also wish to engage in aspects of human culture that they value. It is important to the author to develop and mainstream plural landscape dialogues in urban areas, and to be reflective and adaptive, rather than being in thrall to inflexible positioning of whatever sort. I hope some of the ideas in this paper may at least prompt reflection on such approaches for the design and management of urbanized landscapes in the U.S.

REFERENCES

1. Ahmad, H., and J.D. Hitchmough. 2007. Germination and emergence of understorey and tall canopy forbs used in naturalistic sowing mixes. A comparison of performance in vitro v. the field. Seed Science and Technology. 35(3): 624-637.
2. BUGS - Biodiversity of Urban Gardens Study, University of Sheffield. 2007. http://www.bugs.group.shef.ac.uk/index.html. (accessed October 10, 2008).
3. Brown, C.S. and R.l. Bugg. 2001. Effects of established perennial grasses on introduction of native forbs in California. Restoration Ecology. 9: 38-48.
4. Crawley, M.J. 1997. Biodiversity, pp. 595-632. In Crawley, M.J. (Ed.). Plant Ecology. Blackwell, Oxford.
5. Dunnett, N, C. Swanwick, H. Woolley. 2002. Improving Urban Parks, Play Areas and Green Spaces. Office of the Deputy Prime Minister, London. pp.214.
6. Dunnett, N. and J.D. Hitchmough. 2004. The Dynamic Landscape: Design Ecology and Management of Naturalistic Urban Planting. Taylor and Francis, London, pp. 332.
7. Dunnett, N.D. and A. Clayden. 2007. Rain Gardens. Managing Water Sustainably in the Garden and Designed Landscape. Timber Press, Portland. pp 188.
8. Dunnett, N. and N. Kingsbury. 2008. Planting Green Roofs and Living Walls. Timber Press, Portland. pp 328.
9. Dunnett, N., J.D. Hitchmough, C. Jenkins, M. Tylecote, K. Thompson, R. Matthews-Joyce, and
10. D. Rae. 2007. Growing Nature – The Role of Horticulture in Supporting Biodiversity. Commission Report 244, Scottish Natural Heritage, Clydebank. pp 63.
11. Gilbert, O.L. 1989. The Ecology of Urban Habitats. Chapman and Hall, London. pp 369.
12. Grime J.P. 2001. Plant Strategies, Vegetation Processes and Ecosystem Properties. New York, Wiley. pp 417.
13. Grime, J.P, J.G. Hodgson, and R. Hunt. 2007. Comparative Plant Ecology; A Functional Approach to Common British Species. Second Edition. Castlepoint Press, Dalbeattie. pp 748.
14. Helfand, G.E., J.S. Park, J.I. Nassauer, and S. Kosek. 2006. The economics of native plants in residential landscape designs. Landscape and Urban Planning. 78: 229-240.
15. Hitchmough, J.D., M. De La Fleur, and C. Findlay. 2004. Establishing North American prairie vegetation in urban parks in northern England: Effect of sowing season, sowing rate and soil type. Landscape and Urban Planning. 66: 75-90.
16. Hitchmough, J.D. and M. De La Fleur. 2006. Establishing North American prairie vegetation in urban parks in northern England: Effect of management and soil type on long-term community development. Landscape and Urban Planning. 78: 386-397.
17. Hitchmough, J.D., A. Paraskevopoulou, and N. Dunnett. 2008. Influence of grass suppression and sowing rate on the establishment and persistence of forb dominated urban meadows. Urban Ecosystems.11: 33-44.
18. Jager, H. 1877. Lehrbuch der Gartenkunst. Hugo Voigt, Berlin. pp 687.

19. Jones, T.A. 2003. The restoration gene pool concept: beyond the native versus non-native debate. Restoration Ecology. 11(3): 281-290.
20. Kingsbury, N. 2004. Contemporary overview of naturalistic planting design, pp 58-96. In Dunnett, N. and J.D. Hitchmough, (Eds.). The Dynamic Landscape: Design, Ecology and Management of Naturalistic Urban Planting. Taylor and Francis, London.
21. Loram, A., J. Tratalos, P.H. Warren, and P. Gaston. 2007. Urban domestic gardens. (X): the extent and structure of the resource in five major cities. Landscape Ecology. 22(4): 601-615.
22. Lord, T. 2007. RHS Plant Finder 2007-2008. Dorling Kindersley, London. pp 970
23. Luken, J.O. 1990. Directing Ecological Succession. Chapman and Hall, London. pp 251.
24. Luscombe, G. and R. Scott. 2004. Wildflowers Work; a guide to creating and managing new wildflower landscapes. Third Edition, Landlife, Liverpool. pp 48.
25. Met Office. 2005. Climate Change and the Greenhouse Effect. A briefing from the Hadley Centre. DEFRA, London. pp 71.
26. Milesi, C., S.W. Running, C.D. Elvridge, J.B. Dietz, B.T. Tuttle, and R.R. Nemani. 2005. Mapping and modeling the biochemical cycling of turfgrasses in the United States. Journal of Environmental Management. 36(3): 426-438.
27. Nassauer, J.I. 1995. Messy ecosystems, orderly frames. Landscape Journal. 14(2): 161-170.
28. National Gardening Association. 2004. Environmental Lawn and Garden Survey. South Burlington, Vermont. pp 46.
29. Oehme, W. and J. Van Sweden. 2002. Bold Romantic Gardens. Spacemaker, Washington. pp 310.
30. Oudolf, P. and N. Kingsbury. 2005. Planting Design. Gardens in Time and Space. Timber Press, Portland. pp 175.
31. Owen, J. 1991. The Ecology of a Garden: The First Fifteen Years. Cambridge University Press. Cambridge. pp 403.
32. Pollan, M. 1991. Second Nature, A Gardeners Education. Bloomsbury. London. pp 279.
33. Pywell, R.F., J.M. Bullock, D.B. Roy, L. Warman, K.J. Walker, and P. Rothery. 2003. Plant traits as predictors of performance in ecological restoration. Journal of Applied Ecology. 40(1): 65-77.
34. Preston, C., D. Pearman, and T. Dines. 2002. New Atlas of the British and Irish Flora. Centre for
35. Ecology and Hydrology and Botanical Society for the British Isles. Oxford University Press. Oxford. pp 910.
36. Rappaport, B. 1993. The John Marshall Law Review. Volume 26, Summer 1993, Number 4. http://www.epa.gov/greenacres/weedlaws/. (accessed August 25, 2008).
37. Robbins, P. 2007. Lawn People, How Grasses, Weeds and Chemicals Make Us Who We Are. Temple University Press, Philadelphia. pp 208.
38. Robinson, W. 1870. TheWild Garden. John Murray, London. pp 304.
39. Shapiro, A.M. 2002. The Californian urban butterfly population is dependent upon alien plants. Diversity and Distributions. 8: 31-40.

40. Thompson, K., K.C. Austin, R.M. Smith, P.H. Warren, P.G. Angold, and K.J. Gaston. 2003. Urban domestic gardens (I): putting small-scale plant diversity in context. Journal of Vegetation Science. 14: 71-78.
41. Widrlechner, M.P., J.R. Thompson, J.K. Iles, and P.M. Dixon. 2004. Models for predicting the risk of naturalization of non-native woody plants in Iowa. Journal of Environmental Horticulture. 22: 23-31.

CHAPTER 3

Urban Cultivation in Allotments Maintains Soil Qualities Adversely Affected by Conventional Agriculture

JILL L. EDMONDSON, ZOE G. DAVIES, KEVIN J. GASTON, AND JONATHAN R. LEAKE

3.1 INTRODUCTION

Agriculture, at all scales of production, is dependent on the natural capital of soils which yield a flow of services upon which humans depend, not only for food, fibre and biomass production, but also for other ecosystem services such as provision of fresh water, regulation of nutrient cycling, flood mitigation, water purification, carbon sequestration and climate regulation (Kibblewhite, Ritz & Swift 2008; Haygarth & Ritz 2009; Dominati, Patterson & Mackay 2010; Robinson et al. 2013). During the 20th century, the rising demand for food globally was met by conversion of natural and semi-natural habitats into agricultural land, and the intensification of farming methods, including mechanization and use of synthetic fertilizers (Robinson & Sutherland 2002; Haygarth & Ritz 2009). However, intensification of agriculture has depleted the natural capital of soil organic

---

© Edmondson, J. L., Davies, Z. G., Gaston, K. J., Leake, J. R. (2014), Urban cultivation in allotments maintains soil qualities adversely affected by conventional agriculture. Journal of Applied Ecology, 51: 880–889. doi: 10.1111/1365-2664.12254. Creative Commons Attribution license (http://creativecommons.org/licenses/by/3.0/).

carbon (SOC) and nutrients resulting in serious losses of regulating and supporting ecosystem services (Franzluebbers 2002). These include impaired water and nutrient holding capacity, reduced pollutant immobilization and water filtration, loss of soil aggregates and strength (Watts & Dexter 1997) leading to increased erosion, CO_2 release to the atmosphere and eutrophication of aquatic ecosystems (Robinson & Sutherland 2002; Loveland & Webb 2003; Dominati, Patterson & Mackay 2010; Robinson et al. 2013). Loss of organic matter (OM) content is of particular concern for food security as yields of staple cereal crops typically increase linearly with SOC concentration (Lal 2010).

One of the greatest challenges now facing humanity is to improve the sustainability of agriculture and reduce its environmental impact, whilst also meeting the food demands of the growing global population, which exceeds 7 billion (DEFRA 2010; Godfray et al. 2010). A crucial goal in agricultural sustainability is to reverse the historic losses of SOC from farmland and to increase soil C : N ratios which are important controls on nutrient cycle regulation (Robinson et al. 2013). High C : N-rich soil amendments are particularly important in reducing the risk of N leaching from soils (Dungait et al. 2012).

Concurrent with the intensification of agriculture has been rapid urbanization; over half of the world's population is now residing in cities and towns (UN 2008). Indeed, urban areas are increasing in areal extent faster than any other land use (Hansen et al. 2005), a trend set to continue as the proportion of people living in cities and towns rises to 70% by 2050 (UN 2008). This land-use change is further exacerbated by the expansion of urban areas outpacing population growth, particularly in developed regions such as Europe (EEA 2006). These dynamics bring about a number of significant challenges. Of increasing concern is the food security of urban inhabitants as they become physically more detached from primary food production (Howe & Wheeler 1999).

However, an estimated 800 million people currently practise some form of urban food production globally, with much borne out of necessity for subsistence in the developing world (Lee-Smith 2010). Urban horticulture operates over spatial scales ranging from potted plants, to vegetable plots in gardens, to allotments, community gardens and city farms (Howe & Wheeler 1999). In Europe, allotments are a common feature of urban areas and in areal extent are often the main areas of own-grown food production. In the UK, there are c. 330 000 allotment plots, and a standard plot is 250 m^2, giving a total area nationally likely to be >8000 ha (Crouch & Ward 1997). Allotments represent a unique type of greenspace, designated specifically for food production (van den Berg et al. 2010). Peak allotment provision in the UK occurred during the First and Second World Wars (Crouch & Ward 1997; Martin & Marsden 1999), and during the latter, allotments and gardens provided c. 10% of food consumed in the UK because of the 'Dig for Victory' campaign whilst comprising <1% of the area of arable cultivation (Crouch & Ward 1997; Keep 2009).

After a post-war decline in own-growing and associated decrease in plot provision, there has been a resurgence in UK allotment demand reflected in increased waiting lists over the past 17 years, with over 90 000 people now waiting for a plot (Campbell & Campbell 2011). The increase in interest in agriculture is not confined to the UK, for example own-growing in the USA has risen (Viljoen & Bohn 2012) as a result of a recognition of the importance of provision of healthy food, particularly to disadvantaged neighbourhoods in combination with the availability of 'vacant lots' within urban areas (Grewel & Grewel 2012). Amongst scientists, policymakers, the media and public, there is increasing awareness of the multiple benefits of 'own-growing' including access to nutritious fresh produce, stress relief, improved psychological well-being and physical fitness (Martin & Marsden 1999; Leake, Adam-Bradford & Rigby 2009; van den Berg et al. 2010; Kortright & Wakefield 2011). The UK government £30 million Healthy Towns Initiative launched in 2008 funded projects aimed at increasing participation in own-growing to promote healthier lifestyles and tackle the problem of sedentary behaviour, low consumption of fresh fruit and vegetables, and obesity. Other motivations for own-growing include more sustainable living in response to threats from climate change, peak oil and unsustainable food production systems (Hopkins 2008), widespread concerns about chemical residues of pesticides in conventional agriculture, genetically modified crops and 'food miles'. More recently, the increase in own-growing has been attributed to rising global food prices (DEFRA 2010).

Soils in urban greenspaces have recently been shown to make an important contribution to provision of ecosystem goods and services especially in holding large stocks of SOC (Pouyat, Yesilonis & Nowak 2006; Churkina, Brown & Keoleian 2010; Edmondson et al. 2011, 2012, 2014). However, we currently know nothing about how soil management for own-growing in allotments impacts on the main soil quality indicators. Do these soils suffer significant depletion in SOC and nitrogen stocks compared to other urban greenspaces, as might be expected on the basis of the effects of cultivation seen in conventional agriculture? Are higher SOC stocks maintained under perennial woody fruit bushes and trees, where soil may be less disturbed, compared to frequently dug ground used for annual herbaceous crops?

In this paper, we investigate topsoil properties at allotment sites across an entire mid-sized UK city, including SOC concentration, total nitrogen (TN) concentration, C : N ratio and soil bulk density (BD), and compare them to urban domestic gardens, non-domestic greenspace and regional agricultural soils. The comparisons with other urban greenspace soils were made to determine whether allotment cultivation significantly impacts urban soil quality within the same city on the same soil types, and these other greenspaces provide a 'control' for soil properties that are affected by the urban environment such as air pollutants. The soil properties were selected as they are positively associated with regulating and supporting ecosystem services (Franzluebbers 2002) and can be directly managed for ecosystem service provision (Kibblewhite, Ritz & Swift 2008; Dominati, Patterson & Mackay 2010). SOC is particularly important as it has a direct positive influence on both ecosystem function including water and nutrient holding capacity, and crop growth and C : N ratio is one of the major controls of both N and C cycling in the soil (Powlson et al. 2011; Dungait et al. 2012). BD is a direct measure of soil pore space, which provides an indication of the ability of soil store water and the rate of storm water infiltration (Lal 2007; Dominati, Patterson & Mackay 2010).

Using a questionnaire, we examine plot management practices which may influence soil quality in allotments including the prevalence of on-site composting; inputs of manure, fertilizer and commercial compost; and the burning or removal of OM for disposal off-site.

We hypothesize that (i) intensively managed urban allotments will maintain higher soil quality, as indicated by the above parameters when compared to regional agricultural soil, and (ii) cultivation on allotments will negatively affect soil properties in comparison with other types of urban greenspace, to a greater extent in beds used for annual crops than under woody fruit bushes and trees.

3.2 MATERIALS AND METHODS

3.2.1 STUDY AREA

Our study focussed on Leicester, a mid-sized UK city in the East Midlands of England (52°38′N, 1°08W), covering an area of c. 73 km^2 (defined by the unitary authority boundary), with a human population of c. 330,000 (Leicester City Council 2013; Fig. 1a). The region experiences a temperate climate, receiving 606 mm of precipitation annually and average annual daily minimum and maximum temperatures of 5·8 and 13·5 °C, respectively (Met Office 2009). More than 75% of land in the East Midlands is agricultural, of which arable farming is dominant (Rural Business Research 2012). Soils within the city are deep clays, deep loam and seasonally wet deep clays and loam, according to the National Soil Map for England and Wales produced by Cranfield University. The main soil series in the city and its agricultural hinterland are Hanslope, Whimple, Salop, Beccles 3, Ragdale and Fladbury 1.

Allotment provision in Leicester peaked in the 1930s, with one household in three renting a plot (Crouch & Ward 1997). Today, the city has 46 allotment sites (Fig. 1b), 45 of which are owned by Leicester City Council with 3200 individual plots (Leicester City Council 2012) that in total cover c. 2% of the cities greenspace. Within the city, greenspace constitutes 56% of the total area with 32% managed on a small scale privately in domestic gardens, and the remaining 68% is non-domestic greenspace generally managed on a large scale by Leicester City Council or large institutions.

3.2.2 SOIL SURVEY

Fifteen allotment sites were selected to provide representative samples from across the city (Fig. 1b), with permission obtained to sample from 27

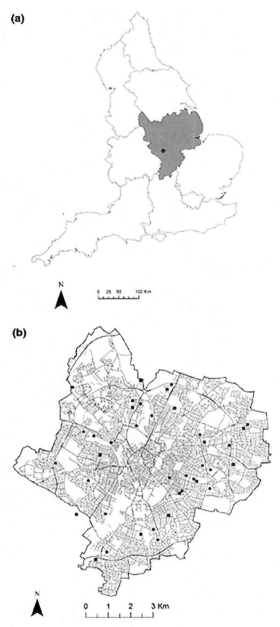

FIGURE 1: (a) The geographical location of the East Midlands within England and our study city, Leicester, and (b) the position of allotments within Leicester. Square symbols represent allotment sites sampled; circular symbols are unvisited allotment sites.

plots. Where permission was granted, the cultivation on the allotment plot was assessed, specifically the presence of annual herbaceous vegetable crops (which generally constitute the largest cultivated area) and perennial fruit bushes and trees. In all plots, duplicate soil cores were taken under annual vegetable crops and, where available, another duplicate set of samples were taken under woody fruit bushes or trees. Samples were taken from the topsoil layer in two depth increments (0–7 cm and 7–14 cm), using specialist corer that removes undisturbed soil samples for BD analysis (Edmondson et al. 2011).

Sample locations for soils in other urban greenspaces were generated in a GIS using two high spatial resolution data sets. The first, LandBase was produced by Infoterra (http://geosurveysolutions.com/landbase; accessed April 2014) and categorized land cover within the city into eight different classes (inland water, bare ground, artificial surface, buildings, herbaceous vegetation, shrubs, tall shrubs and trees; Davies et al. 2013). The LandBase data set used high-resolution LiDar data to stratify vegetation by height. This data set determined the extent of greenspace within the city and the extent of the different vegetation land-cover classes used in this study (herbaceous vegetation and a combined shrubs, tall shrubs and tree category). The second data set, MasterMap, provided by Ordnance Survey (http://www.ordnancesurvey.co.uk/business-and-government/products/mastermap-products.html), was used to split the two land-cover classes by land use into domestic gardens and non-domestic greenspace. Random sample points were generated within the GIS for the different non-domestic greenspace land-cover categories and, at each, four replicate soil samples were taken at the two depth intervals. The sampling strategy for domestic gardens used a street layer created in the GIS and 45 roads were selected at random. Each of these roads was visited and, if there were residential properties present and authorization from a householder was granted, soil cores were taken from the back garden. In domestic gardens, cores were extracted from herbaceous areas within the garden and/or within the vicinity of shrubs and trees (where gardens contained both land-cover classes cores were taken beneath both herbaceous vegetation and shrubs and trees). In total, a further 136 sites were sampled within the urban greenspace of the city. Similarly, soil samples were taken from randomly selected agricultural sites (arable n = 16; pasture n = 12), within a 7·5-km buffer zone around the unitary authority boundary of Leicester (see Table S1 in Supporting Information for sample site GPS coordinates).

3.2.3 SOIL SAMPLE PREPARATION AND ANALYSIS

Soils were dried at 105 °C for 24 h, weighed, ball-milled to homogenize and passed through a 1-mm sieve. Material >1 mm was weighed and then removed from the soil total weight (Edmondson et al. 2011). Soil BD was converted to g cm^{-3}. The homogenized samples were analysed for C and TN in an elemental analyser (VarioEL Cube; Isoprime, Hanau, Germany; Edmondson et al. 2012). SOC density (mg cm^{-3}) was calculated for each individual sample using SOC concentration (mg g^{-1}) and BD (g cm^{-3}) following the approach of Edmondson et al. (2012).

3.2.4 ALLOTMENT QUESTIONNAIRE

All allotment holders present at the time of the site visit were asked to complete a questionnaire (see Appendix S1, Supporting Information) about plot management. The questionnaire assessed the length of time the plot had been held by the present person; types of OM added; types of fertilizer used; OM burning or removal from the plot. In total, 75 plot holders, including those where soil was sampled, answered the questionnaire.

3.2.5 STATISTICAL ANALYSIS

The effects of urban allotment vs. agricultural land use (arable and pasture) on soil properties, including effects in relation to soil depth, were analysed using two-way ANOVA. The effect of urban land use (allotment, domestic garden and non-domestic greenspace), soil depth and vegetation cover (tree and shrub or herbaceous) on soil properties was analysed using three-way ANOVA. The Tukey *post hoc* test compared differences ($P < 0.05$) between means (Zar 1999). All data were checked for homogeneity of variance and normality prior to analysis and, where necessary, were transformed. Analyses were conducted in PASW Statistics 18.

3.3 RESULTS

3.3.1 ALLOTMENT MANAGEMENT

The length of time the 75 allotment holders had managed their plots ranged from <1 to 50 years, with a median duration of 5 years and with 16% of respondents having held their plots for more than 15 years. In total, 95% of the respondents composted on their plot, with 73% adding household fruit and vegetable waste to their allotment compost. Nearly half of the respondents added commercial compost to their plot soils (Table 1). Three-quarters of respondents added manure and a similar proportion bought other fertilizers (Table 1). These included general purpose mineral fertilizer, chicken manure and fish blood and bone, with 53%, 42% and 27% of respondents using these products, respectively, and a minority using tomato feed, liquid seaweed and lime.

Biomass that is slow to compost, including tree, shrub or hedge trimmings, sweetcorn stalks and brassica roots, together with diseased plants and noxious weeds, was burnt on-site by 68% of respondents (Table 1). A smaller proportion of allotment holders acknowledge removing these kinds of wastes, and autumn leaves, from their plots for disposal elsewhere (Table 1).

3.3.2 THE EFFECT OF OWN-GROWING VS. CONVENTIONAL AGRICULTURE ON SOIL PROPERTIES

Soil organic carbon density (mg cm^{-3}) was significantly higher in allotments compared to soils from surrounding agricultural land, with arable land most seriously depleted in SOC having 65% lower concentrations than allotment soils (Fig. 2a). Soil TN density (mg cm^{-3}) was also significantly reduced in arable fields, with 25% greater TN densities in both pasture and allotment soils (Fig. 2b). As with SOC density, soil C : N ratio

Table 1. Responses of allotment holders to a questionnaire focused on plot management. Number of survey respondents = 75

Questions	Yes (%)	No (%)	No answer (%)
Compost production on allotments			
Do you compost your waste allotment material?	95	5	0
Do you compost household vegetable matter on your allotment?	72	27	1
Inputs to allotments			
Do you add commercial compost to your allotment?	45	50	5
Do you add manure to your allotment?	75	20	5
Do you add any fertilizer to your allotment?	73	21	5
Removals from allotments			
Do you burn material from your allotment?	68	28	4
Do you remove any tree, shrub or hedge trimmings from you allotment?	17	63	20
Do you remove any autumn leaves from your allotment?	8	72	20

was 36% greater in allotments than in conventional agriculture but, in this case, there was no significant difference between pasture and arable fields (Fig. 2c). Soil BD was 15% lower in allotments and pasture compared to arable fields (Fig. 2d). There was no effect of soil depth on SOC density, C : N ratio or BD, or any interaction between land use and depth (Table 2). Soil TN density declined significantly with depth (Table 2), driven by the responses of pasture and arable soils only (see Fig. S1, Supporting Information).

3.3.3 THE EFFECT OF ALLOTMENTS VS. OTHER URBAN GREENSPACE LAND USES ON SOIL PROPERTIES

Soil organic carbon concentration (mg g^{-1}) was significantly higher in gardens beneath woody vegetation than in all herbaceous vegetation (at least 37%) and 25% greater than under woody vegetation in non-domestic land (Fig. 3a; Table 3). There was no difference in SOC concentration between soils beneath woody and herbaceous vegetation on allotments and beneath herbaceous vegetation throughout land-use types. Consequently, there was a significant interaction between land use and vegetation on SOC concentration (Table 3).

There was a significant land-use effect on soil C : N ratio (Table 3), with lowest values in non-domestic greenspaces and higher values in gardens between 7–14 cm depth, compared to allotments (Fig. 3b). There was also a significant effect of land-cover type on C : N ratio and there was a significant interaction between land use and soil depth (Table 3, Fig. 3b).

Greenspace land use had no effect on soil BD (Table 3). There was significantly lower soil BD beneath trees and shrubs compared to herbaceous vegetation. This effect was driven by differences arising in the non-domestic greenspaces but not in allotments resulting in a significant interaction between vegetation and land use (Fig. 3c, Table 3). Soil BD beneath woody vegetation in non-domestic greenspace was 17% lower than soils beneath herbaceous vegetation throughout the land-use categories and at least 11% lower than under woody vegetation in domestic gardens or allotments (Fig. 3c). BD significantly increased with depth across all urban greenspace land uses for both herbaceous and woody vegetation (Table 3).

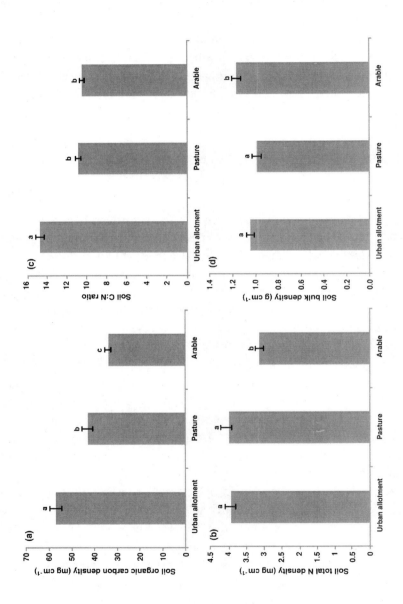

FIGURE 2: (a) Mean soil organic carbon density; (b) soil nitrogen density; (c) soil C : N ratio; (d) soil bulk density in urban allotment and agricultural soils. Error bars are ±1 standard error; letters show significant differences between land uses (Tukey's test $P < 0.05$).

Table 2. Two-way ANOVA testing the effects of land use (urban allotments vs. intensive agriculture) and depth (0–7 cm, 7–14 cm) on soil organic carbon density, C : N ratio and soil bulk density. Numbers in bold indicate a significant effect

Transformation	Factor	d.f.	F	P value
Soil organic carbon density (mg cm^{-3})				
Log$_{10}$	Land use	2,90	**32·294**	**<0·001**
	Soil depth	1,90	2·297	0·112
	Land use × soil depth	2,90	1·073	0·378
Soil nitrogen density (mg cm^{-3})				
Log$_{10}$	Land use	2,89	**7·721**	**0·001**
	Soil depth	1,89	4·060	0·047
	Land use × soil depth	2,89	1·792	0·173
Soil C : N ratio				
Log$_{10}$	Land use	2,91	**66·202**	**<0·001**
	Soil depth	1,91	0·123	0·727
	Land use × soil depth	2,91	0·172	0·842
Soil fine earth bulk density (g cm−3)				
	Land use	2,91	**6·479**	**0·002**
	Soil depth	1,91	0·004	0·947
	Land use × soil depth	2,91	1·031	0·361

3.4 DISCUSSION

3.4.1 THE PROPERTIES OF ALLOTMENT, DOMESTIC GARDEN AND NON-DOMESTIC GREENSPACE SOILS

Until recently, in the absence of city-scale sampling, soils in urban areas have often been represented as functionally degraded, low in OM and compacted. This follows from research on urban soils mainly focussed on

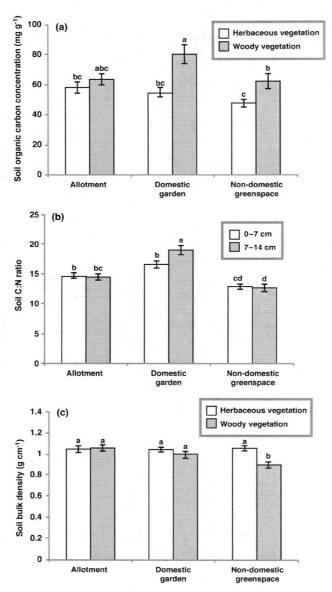

FIGURE 3: (a) Mean soil organic carbon concentration beneath woody and herbaceous vegetation; (b) C : N ratio at 7 and 14 cm soil depth; (c) soil bulk density beneath woody and herbaceous vegetation in three urban greenspace land-use types. Error bars are ±1 standard error; letters show significant differences between land uses (Tukey's test $P < 0.05$).

Table 3. Three-way ANOVA testing effects of urban land use (allotment, domestic garden and non-domestic), vegetation type (herbaceous or tree and shrub) and depth (0–7 cm, 7–14 cm) on soil organic carbon concentration, C : N ratio and soil bulk density. Numbers in bold indicate a significant effect.

Transformation	Factor	d.f.	F	P value
Soil organic carbon concentration (mg g^{-1})	Land use	2,283	4·579	**0·011**
	Vegetation type	1,283	10·271	**0·002**
	Soil depth	1,283	8·916	**0·003**
	Land use × vegetation	2,283	3·193	**0·043**
	Land use × depth	2,283	0·483	0·618
	Vegetation × depth	1,283	0·173	0·678
	Land use × vegetation × soil depth	2,283	0·656	0·520
Soil C : N ratio				
Log$_{10}$	Land use	2,282	76·216	**<0·001**
	Vegetation type	1,282	8·237	**0·004**
	Soil depth	1,282	0·699	0·404
	Land use × vegetation	2,282	2·911	0·056
	Land use × depth	2,282	3·540	**0·030**
	Vegetation × depth	1,282	0·736	0·392
	Land use × vegetation × soil depth	2,282	1·485	0·228
Soil bulk density (g cm^{-3})				
	Land use	2,268	2·361	0·096
	Vegetation type	1,268	11·304	**<0·001**
	Soil depth	1,268	12·408	**<0·001**
	Land use × vegetation	2,268	3·945	**0·020**
	Land use × depth	2,268	0·241	0·786
	Vegetation × depth	1,268	0·251	0·617
	Land use × vegetation × soil depth	2,268	0·195	0·823

highly altered and disturbed areas, often associated with land redevelopment generating 'technosols' whose formation and functioning are the result of anthropogenic activities (Lehmann & Stahr 2007), but are not representative of typical urban soils. Furthermore, it has often been assumed that urban centres are devoid of functional soil, for example in the UK national SOC inventory (Bradley et al. 2005) it has been assumed that city centres contain no SOC, and soils in suburban areas hold half of the SOC concentration of regional pasture soils. Until recently, these assumptions remained untested. Empirical evidence has now challenged these assumptions on two fronts. First, high spatial resolution GIS has revealed the extent of urban greenspace, even in built-up city centres, is greater than previously recognized, for example Leicester contains 56% greenspace, including a very large number of small patches undetected by lower spatial resolution data sets (Davies et al. 2013). Secondly, measurements of urban SOC stocks (Pouyat, Yesilonis & Nowak 2006; Churkina, Brown & Keoleian 2010), which include some studies at the citywide scale, have revealed SOC concentrations and soil BD values comparable to those in semi-natural ecosystems (Edmondson et al. 2011, 2012). In the present paper, we extend these findings to show that across the suite of soil properties measured within allotments, soil quality was consistently high, compared to soils from the surrounding agricultural region, and against English national data (Carey et al. 2008). Whilst arable agriculture is the dominant land use in the Leicester region, allotment soil properties compare favourably to those found in semi-natural habitats. For example, when compared to English lowland woodland soils and grasslands of neutral pH, SOC storage was c. 1 kg m^{-2} greater and TN storage was similar (0·55, 0·61 and 0·53 kg m−2 for allotments, neutral grasslands and lowland woodlands, respectively; Carey et al. 2008). Soil BD was slightly higher in allotments when compared to these two semi-natural habitats ranging from 1·1 g cm^{-3} in allotments, 0·9 g cm^{-3} in neutral grasslands, down to 0·8 g cm^{-3} in lowland woodland soils (Carey et al. 2008). Soil C : N ratio was considerably higher in lowland woodlands (17·7) than in allotment (14·7) and neutral grassland soils (14·1; Carey et al. 2008).

The modest differences between soil properties in allotments compared to other urban greenspaces, and the indicators of high soil quality in all these greenspaces, affirm the new paradigm of typical soils in urban areas being of high ecological and ecosystem service value (Edmondson et al. 2011; Edmondson et al. 2012); however, research must be conducted in cities world-wide to further support these findings. This parallels the recent paradigm shift in recognition of the importance of urban areas for biodiversity. The 'urban desert' myth (Braat & ten Brink 2008) was overturned by systematic data collection across multiple UK cities, revealing that native and alien species richness and habitat diversity exceeded that in the wider countryside on a unit area basis (Loram, Warren & Gaston 2008; Loram et al. 2008).

It is clear that urban soils not only play very important roles in the delivery of supporting and regulating ecosystem services such as carbon, water and nutrient storage, but also in the provisioning service of food production. Most supporting ecosystem services depend on SOC (Powlson et al. 2011), so the finding that allotment soils contain more SOC than the soils in non-domestic greenspaces is important. Although garden soils had slightly higher SOC than in allotments, this was strongly driven by values beneath trees. Extra accumulation of SOC under trees and shrubs in gardens is likely to occur due to reduced disturbance and increased leaf litter, composts and mulch inputs (Osmond & Hardy 2004), compared to other greenspace soils. In addition, as the city of Leicester expanded over agricultural land, albeit before the advent of modern agriculture that intensified SOC loss, it is more likely that SOC storage has increased in gardens under trees and shrubs, than allotment soils have significantly lost SOC compared to the pre-urbanization concentrations in agricultural land. Furthermore, the lower SOC concentrations in non-domestic greenspaces compared to allotment soils suggest that the additional carbon inputs to allotments, especially manure and compost, are important in maintaining or increasing SOC storage.

The absence of beneficial effects of woody vegetation on SOC in allotment soils, in contrast to the effects seen in domestic and non-domestic greenspaces, is probably explained by the woody plants on allotments being of low stature and biomass. They comprise woody-stemmed fruit bushes, and small fruit trees, often grafted onto dwarfing rooting stocks and will not be very long established as the median duration of plot holding was 5 years. Many local authorities discourage or forbid cultivation of fruit trees and bushes on allotments and require removal of such plants before plots are allocated to new tenants, so old established fruit trees are rare on allotments compared to gardens.

3.4.2 COMPARISON OF ALLOTMENT AND AGRICULTURAL SOILS

The remarkable contrast in soil quality indicators (higher SOC, C : N, TN and lower BD) between allotments and arable fields reveals the effectiveness of management achieved by own-growers. Furthermore, it demonstrates the extent to which modern agricultural practices have degraded soil natural capital – which has profound implications for the loss of ecosystem service provision (Loveland & Webb 2003; Lal 2004), including reduced structural stability, water and nutrient holding capacity and impaired regulation of N mineralization and supply to plants (Quinton et al. 2010; Dungait et al. 2012). In terms of provisioning ecosystem services by own-growing in allotments, both the historical records of production during the world wars and more recent UK trials conducted by the Royal Horticultural Society and 'Which?' Magazine showed fruit and vegetable yields of 31–40 t ha^{-1} year^{-1} (Tomkins 2006), 4–11 times the productivity of the major agricultural crops in the Leicestershire region (DEFRA 2013). Importantly, depletion of SOC in conventional agricultural fields is now thought to be an important factor constraining productivity as many arable soils have suboptimal concentrations (Lal 2010).

However, our data revealing the maintenance of soil quality in allotments indicate that benefits obtained from ecosystem services do not necessarily have to be traded off against each other in the manner currently seen in conventional agriculture. Indeed, allotments not only provide yields rarely matched by commercial horticulture (Tomkins 2006), but simultaneously provide exceptionally high delivery of a wide portfolio of other ecosystem services. These include cultural services such as aesthetic value, together with physical and psychological benefits (Leake, Adam-Bradford & Rigby 2009; Kortright & Wakefield 2011). Most importantly, we show that the soil quality indicators underpinning the delivery of supporting ecosystem services are not compromised by the delivery of provisioning and cultural ecosystem services for which allotments are most valued. Urban agriculture is already a well-established management practice in urban greenspaces globally, and interest in own-growing is increasing. Consequently, policy and planning at local, national and international scales should seek to capitalize on this resurgence in interest and further encourage urban agriculture as a means to improve food security within cities and towns, as this can deliver additional food without compromising soil quality. This is in contrast to conventional agriculture in which intensification of production generally leads to the loss of soil OM and quality (Lal 2010).

The maintenance of this multifunctionality of allotments rests on substantial inputs of OM and nutrients to these soils including manures, and own-produced composts, all of which have been shown to increase SOC and TN concentrations (Lal 2004, 2008). However, it is important to recognize that many of these inputs involve a 'subsidy' from agriculture and fisheries such as cow and chicken manure, commercial composts and purchased vegetable and fruit waste composted on allotments. This subsidy from agriculture may be justified by higher yields obtained by own-growing, but tempers any claim that allotment cultivation is completely sustainable. In addition, 55% of respondents used a synthetic fertilizer, many of which are derived from, or produced using, petrochemicals. The increasing use of large-scale composting of putrescible household wastes by local councils instead of landfilling opens the possibility for reduced dependence on agricultural products and greater sustainability if these composts can be substituted on allotments for other organic carbon and nutrient sources.

We found evidence of both environmentally favourable and unfavourable management practices on allotments. For example, compost heaps are recognized as an indicator of urban biodiversity and are of particular importance as habitats for invertebrate communities (DEFRA 2003). However, other practices may be less favourable, and 68% of respondents reported burning material, a frequency far greater than in a recent survey reporting 15% of gardeners use bonfires to manage waste (Loram et al. 2011). Whilst application of ash and char from these fires onto allotment soils could further improve soil quality, as the biochars produced are a highly stable form of OC (Lehmann 2007), bonfires are detrimental to air quality and a risk to human health in highly populated urban areas.

3.5 CONCLUSIONS

This research demonstrates that own-growing in urban allotments, in contrast to arable crop production, does not trade off the soil quality measures that are positively associated with regulating and supporting ecosystem services, in order to deliver provisioning ecosystem services. Typical urban soils are shown to be comparable to semi-natural ecosystems and of considerably better quality than agricultural soils, and this is maintained under cultivation in allotments, which receive regular organic inputs from manures and composts. Allotment cultivation may provide a model for understanding management systems for sustainably delivering multiple ecosystem services without the provision of one type of service compromising the delivery of another. Further work is now required to quantify the ecosystem services provided by allotments, the potential and actual yield of crops in urban environments, and the area currently under cultivation. For urban allotment cultivation to be more sustainable, efforts should be made to replace OM and nutrient inputs derived directly from agriculture with those derived from composting putrescible wastes in cities. Our findings lend additional support to the view that own-growing provides multiple human and environmental benefits and has a role to play in more sustainable living in urban areas.

REFERENCES

1. van den Berg, A.E., van Winsum-Westra, M., de Vries, S. & van Dillen, S.M.E. (2010) Allotment gardening and health: a comparative survey among allotment gardeners and their neighbours without an allotment. Environmental Health, 9, 74–86.
2. Braat, L. & ten Brink, P. (eds) (2008) The cost of policy inaction. The case of not meeting the 2010 biodiversity target. Study/Report for the European Commission, DG Environment under contract ENV.G.1/ETU/2007/0044.
3. Bradley, R.I., Milne, R., Bell, J., Lilly, A., Jordan, C. & Higgins, A. (2005) A soil carbon and land-use database for the United Kingdom. Soil Use and Management, 21, 363–369.
4. Campbell, M. & Campbell, I. (2011) Allotment waiting lists in England. Transition Town West Kirkby in conjunction with the National Society of Allotment and Leisure Gardens. www.transitiontownwestkirkby.org.uk (accessed May 2012).

5. Carey, P.D., Wallis, S., Chamberlain, P.M., Cooper, A., Emmett, B.A., Maskell, L.C. et al. (2008) Countryside Survey: UK Results from 2007. NERC/Centre for Ecology & Hydrology (CEH Project Number:C03259).
6. Churkina, G., Brown, D.G. & Keoleian, G. (2010) Carbon stored in human settlements: the conterminous United States. Global Change Biology, 16, 135–143.
7. Crouch, D. & Ward, C. (1997) The Allotment Its Landscape and Culture. Five Leaves Publications, Nottingham, UK.
8. Davies, Z.G., Dallimer, M., Edmondson, J.L., Leake, J.R. & Gaston, K.J. (2013) Identifying potential sources of variability between vegetation carbon storage estimates for urban areas. Environmental Pollution, 183, 133–142.
9. DEFRA (2003) Measuring Progress: Baseline Assessment. DEFRA, London, UK.
10. DEFRA (2010) Food 2030 Strategy Report. DEFRA, London, UK.
11. DEFRA (2013) Agriculture in the English Regions 2012, 2nd Estimate DEFRA, London, UK.
12. Dominati, E., Patterson, M. & Mackay, A. (2010) A framework for classifying and quantifying the natural capital and ecosystem services of soils. Ecological Economics, 69, 1858–1868.
13. Dungait, J.A.J., Cardenas, L.M., Blackwell, M.S.A., Wu, L., Withers, P.J.A., Chadwick, D.R. et al. (2012) Advances in the understanding of nutrient dynamics and management in UK agriculture. Science of the Total Environment, 434, 39–50.
14. Edmondson, J.L., Davies, Z.G., McCormack, S.A., Gaston, K.J. & Leake, J.R. (2011) Are soils in urban ecosystems compacted? A citywide analysis. Biology Letters, 23, 771–774.
15. Edmondson, J.L., Davies, Z.G., McHugh, N., Gaston, K.J. & Leake, J.R. (2012) Organic carbon hidden in urban ecosystems. Scientific Reports, 2, 963.
16. Edmondson, J.L., Davies, Z.G., McCormack, S.A., Gaston, K.J. & Leake, J.R. (2014) Land-cover effects on soil organic carbon stocks in a European city. Science of the Total Environment, 472, 444–452.
17. EEA. (2006) Urban sprawl in Europe. The ignored challenge. Report No. 10. European Environment Agency, Copenhagen.
18. Franzluebbers, A.J. (2002) Soil organic matter stratification ratio as an indicator of soil quality. Soil and Tillage Research, 66, 95–106.
19. Godfray, H.J.C., Beddington, J.R., Crute, I.R., Haddad, L., Lawrence, D., Muir, J.F. et al. (2010) Food security: the challenge of feeding 9 billion people. Science, 327, 812–818.
20. Grewel, S.S. & Grewel, P.S. (2012) Can cities become self-reliant in food? Cities, 29, 1–11.
21. Hansen, A.J., Knight, R.L., Marzluff, J.M., Power, S., Brown, K., Gude, P.H. & Jones, K. (2005) Effects of exurban development on biodiversity: patterns, mechanisms and research needs. Ecological Applications, 15, 1893–1905.
22. Haygarth, P.M. & Ritz, K. (2009) The future of soils and land use in the UK: soil systems for the provision of land-based ecosystem services. Land Use Policy, 26S, S187–S197.
23. Hopkins, R. (2008) The Transition Handbook: From Oil Dependency to Local Resilience. Green Books, London.

24. Howe, J. & Wheeler, P. (1999) Urban food growing: the experience of two UK cities. Sustainable Development, 7, 13–24.
25. Keep, M. (2009) Agriculture: historical statistics. Standard note SN/SG/3339. House of Commons Library, London.
26. Kibblewhite, M.G., Ritz, K. & Swift, M.J. (2008) Soil health in agricultural systems. Philosophical Transactions of the Royal Society B: Biological Sciences, 363, 685–701.
27. Kortright, R. & Wakefield, S. (2011) Edible backyards: a qualitative study of household food growing and its contributions to food security. Agriculture and Human Values, 28, 39–53.
28. Lal, R. (2004) Soil carbon sequestration impacts on global climate change and food security. Science, 304, 1623–1627.
29. Lal, R. (2007) Soil science and the carbon civilisation. Soil Science Society of America Journal, 71, 1425–1437.
30. Lal, R. (2008) Carbon sequestration. Philosophical Transactions of the Royal Society B: Biological Sciences, 363, 815–830.
31. Lal, R. (2010) Beyond Copenhagen: mitigating climate change and achieving food security through soil carbon sequestration. Food Security, 2, 169–177.
32. Leake, J.R., Adam-Bradford, A. & Rigby, J.E. (2009) Health benefits of 'grow your own' food in urban areas: implications for contaminated land risk assessment and management. Environmental Health, 8, 56–61.
33. Lee-Smith, D. (2010) Cities feeding people: an update on urban agriculture in equatorial Africa. Environment and Urbanisation, 22, 483–499.
34. Lehmann, J. (2007) A handful of carbon. Nature, 447, 143–144.
35. Lehmann, A. & Stahr, K. (2007) Nature and significance of anthropogenic urban soils. Journal of Soils and Sediments, 7, 247–260.
36. Leicester City Council. (2012) http://www.leicester.gov.uk/your-council-services/lc/parks-green-spaces/allotments-4-all/ (accessed August 2012).
37. Leicester City Council. (2013) http://www.leicester.gov.U.K./your-council-services/council-and-democracy/city-statistics/ (accessed April 2013).
38. Loram, A., Warren, P.H. & Gaston, K.J. (2008) Urban domestic gardens (XIV): the characteristics of gardens in five cities. Environmental Management, 42, 361–376.
39. Loram, A., Thompson, K., Warren, P.H. & Gaston, K.J. (2008) Urban domestic gardens (XII): the richness and composition of the flora in five cities. Journal of Vegetation Science, 19, 321–330.
40. Loram, A., Warren, P.H., Thompson, K. & Gaston, K.J. (2011) Urban domestic gardens: the effects of human interventions on garden composition. Environmental Management, 48, 808–824.
41. Loveland, P. & Webb, J. (2003) Is there a critical level of organic matter in the agricultural soils of temperate regions: a review. Soil and Tillage Research, 70, 1–18.
42. Martin, R. & Marsden, T. (1999) Food for urban spaces: the development of urban food production in England and Wales. International Planning Studies, 4, 389–412.
43. Met Office. (2009). http://www.metoffice.gov.U.K./climate/U.K./averages/ (accessed December 2009).
44. Osmond, D.L. & Hardy, D.H. (2004) Characterization of turf practices in five North Carolina communities. Journal of Environmental Quality, 33, 565–575.

45. Pouyat, R.V., Yesilonis, I.D. & Nowak, D.J. (2006) Carbon storage by urban soils in the United States. Journal of Environmental Quality, 35, 1566–1575.
46. Powlson, D.S., Gregory, P.J., Whalley, W.R., Quinton, J.N., Hopkins, D.W., Whitmore, A.P., Hirsch, P.R. & Goulding, K.W.T. (2011) Soil management in relation to sustainable agriculture and ecosystem services. Food Policy, 36, 72–87.
47. Quinton, J.N., Govers, G., Van Oost, K. & Bardgett, R.D. (2010) The impact of agricultural soil erosion on biogeochemical cycling. Nature Geosciences, 3, 311–314.
48. Robinson, D.A. & Sutherland, W.J. (2002) Post-war changes in arable farming and biodiversity in Great Britain. Journal of Applied Ecology, 39, 157–176.
49. Robinson, D.A., Hockley, N., Cooper, D.M., Emmett, B.A., Keith, A.M., Lebron, I. et al. (2013) Natural capital and ecosystem services, developing an appropriate soils framework as a basis for valuation. Soil Biology and Biochemistry, 57, 1023–1033.
50. Rural Business Research (2012) Farm Business Survey - East Midlands region commentary. Rural Business Research, DEFRA, London.
51. Tomkins, M. (2006) The Edible Urban Landscape: an assessment method for retro-fitting urban agriculture into an inner London test site. MSc Thesis, University of East London, London, UK.
52. UN. (2008) World Urbanization Prospects: The 2007 Revision. United Nations, New York.
53. Viljoen, A. & Bohn, K. (2012) Scarcity and abundance: urban agriculture in Cuba and the US. Architectural Design, 82, 16–21.
54. Watts, C.W. & Dexter, A.R. (1997) The influence of organic matter in reducing the destabilization of soil by simulated tillage. Soil and Tillage Research, 42, 253–275.
55. Zar, J.H. (1999) Biostatistical Analysis, 4th edn. Prentice Hall, New Jersey.

Additional supplementary information tables available online at http://onlinelibrary.wiley.com/doi/10.1111/1365-2664.12254/suppinfo.

CHAPTER 4

Lead Levels in Urban Gardens

ANNIE KING, PETER GREEN, GUADALUPE PENA, WENDY CHEN, AND LOUIS SCHUETTER

4.1 INTRODUCTION

According to Lawson [1], Mayor Pingree (Detroit, IL) proposed and promoted production of Pingree Potato Patches on donated vacant lots during the depression of 1893. Following the success of these gardens, others were created in Boston, Chicago, New York and Philadelphia. As noted in Figure 1, the popularity of urban gardens subsided and rose again during various times in US history. By the 1970's the American Community Gardening Association was formed by activists across the country.

Today, nonprofit organizations like the Center for Land-Based Learning (Winters, CA) promote urban farming in West Sacramento, CA and other locales through its California Farm Academy (Figures 2a,2b,3a and 3b) [2]. Also, urban farming was promoted in an exhibit at the 2014 California State Fair (Figure 3c).

© King A, Green P, Pena G, Chen W, Schuetter L (2015) Lead Levels in Urban Gardens. Journal of Horticulture 2:133. doi: 10.4172/2376-0354.1000133. Creative Commons Attribution license (http://creativecommons.org/licenses/by/3.0/).

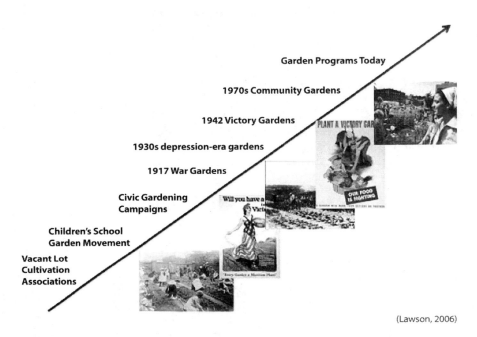

(Lawson, 2006)

FIGURE 1: Community Garden Development in the US.

FIGURE 2A: Amending the soil for urban farming in West Sacramento, CA.

FIGURE 2B: Early stages of garden. Center for Land-Based Learning West Sacramento Urban Farm Program, 2014. Center for LandBased Learning West Sacramento Urban Farm Program, 2014.

As in many urban centers, Sacramento, CA also supports development of community gardens. Presently, two gardens for the homeless are under development in the Alkali Flats area of Sacramento, characterized by beautiful old homes and revitalized small to medium size businesses. A typical vacant lot donated for garden development is shown in Figure 4. The project is affiliated with a UC Davis student organization (Multiculturalism in Agriculture, Natural Resources and Related Sciences, MANRRS). Under the supervision of their advisor, members of the organization decided to assess content of specific metals in surface and subsurface levels of soil at the 3 initial sites (Figure 5). This paper reports results of the research.

FIGURE 3A: Ready for harvest, urban farming in West Sacramento, CA.

FIGURE 3B: Innovative planter boxes. Center for Land-Based Learning West Sacramento Urban Gardening Program, 2014.

FIGURE 4: Early 1900's home site adjacent to an industrial area slated for development of a community garden. MANRRS, 2013.

FIGURE 5: MANRRS members -from right, 1st (Gaby Pedroza) and 3rd (Matthew Warren) - at a potential garden site.

4.2 METALS AND OTHER ELEMENTAL CONTAMINANTS

Several elements—occurring where unwanted or in forms/ concentrations that are detrimental to humans and the environment—can be considered contaminants [3,4]. Some contaminating elements are metals such as mercury, lead, cadmium, thallium and beryllium; some are non-metals (fluorine) while others fall into an intermediate class called semi-metals (for instance, arsenic and selenium). Hawkes [5] noted that several of the toxic metals are dense and are sometimes called 'heavy metals' that are >0.18 ounce, oz/0.39 inches^3, in^3 (>5 grams/centimeter^3, >5 g/cm^3) while Duffus [6] disagreed with use of the terminology because toxicity is not always associated with density or heaviness. Indeed, many dense elements have little toxicity (rare earths elements such as cerium, lanthanum and yttrium) or are so uncommon that they are 'precious' metals–gold and platinum [7]. More complicated are the transition metals (for instance, iron, chromium, manganese and nickel) that are indeed relatively dense and required by humans and other organisms in appropriate concentration ranges for proper health [4,8].

There are 5 elements that have no known beneficial role in human, other animal health or in plants [4]. Cadmium, produced from melting copper ores, iron or zinc, is used to make batteries, plastics and as a possibly restricted pigment in paints [4,9]. The use of thallium in rat poison has been banned in the US; it is mainly used in chemical and medicinal (nuclear imaging) research [10]. Presently, beryllium is primarily used in highly specialized industrial operations, for instance, as metal alloys for aerospace operations, in nuclear reactors or as an alloy and an oxide in microwave ovens and electrical equipment [11]. Uranium is extensively used in military munitions and nuclear reactors [12]. Lead is the most widespread insoluble heavy metal due to long-term use in paint and gasoline [4,13] (Figure 6). Small amounts occur naturally; therefore, it can be detected anywhere. Some plants are highly tolerant and may accumulate large concentrations while others absorb iron very slowly [14].

For the purpose of urban gardening, there are two major questions relative to elemental contaminants. Which toxic elements might occur in the soil? What are their plausible pathways for human exposure? Some elements can be found in water soluble forms, and can be taken up by plant roots, leading to ill effects in the plants or in those who consume them. Elements which are not water soluble may still be taken up on fine particles swept along in the water or may cause exposure as dust that is inhaled, licked off children's fingers or consumed from the surface of produce [4].

4.3 LEAD POISONING

As the most widespread heavy metal, lead has been used by societies in ancient and modern history. It was found in the 6,400 B. C. Neolithic settlement of Çatalhöyük in central modern day Turkey [15]. Ancient Roman society was the first group in recorded history that incorporated lead into

FIGURE 6: A malleable piece of lead found in a garden site. MANRRS, 2014.

daily products such as face powders, mascaras and rouges as well as a pigment in many paints [15]. Also, lead was used as an additive to heighten the sweet taste of wine and in lead pipes for water transport systems [15].

As a dense, soft and malleable metal, lead has useful physical and chemical properties; as such, before it was considered a health hazard, lead was added to many US products to enhance performance. In the early 1900's, lead was found in US gasoline, paints and pipes (Figure 7).

Since the 1990's, numerous studies have confirmed the dangerous side-effects of lead for adults and its neurotoxicity in growing children [16]. It is well known that lead poisoning has greater effects on fetuses and young children than on adults due to the rapidly developing nervous systems of the young. The adverse effects for children include permanent

FIGURE 7: A malleable piece of lead found in a garden site. MANRRS, 2014.

damage to the brain and nervous system, lower IQ, behavioral problems and slow growth [16].

Magyar et al. [17] elucidated the etiology of neurotoxicity by revealing the effect of lead binding in proteins needed for human metabolic function. Due to its cationic property, lead has the ability to compete with zinc (Figure 8). Zn (II) binds in a 4-coordinate mode with sulfur in

FIGURE 8: Lead (Pb) binds with three sulfur groups of proteins to replace zinc (Zn) that binds with four sulfur groups. The geometry of the proteins is altered due to Pb binding, thereby changing their functionality and ultimately leading to symptoms of lead poisoning, especially in children [17].

proteins while lead (II) binds in a 3-coordinate lead (II)– sulfur mode. Altered geometry due to the binding of lead causes improper function/dysfunction of proteins, leading to developmental toxicity related to childhood lead poisoning.

Figure 9 shows a painter with the characteristic wrist drop (peripheral neuropathy) caused by licking the tip of his brushes to produce fine points, thereby constantly exposing himself to lead [18]. In adults, consuming a dangerous amount of lead increases infertility in women, promotes cardiovascular disease, decreases mental activity and reduces red blood cells causing anemia [19].

As noted above, before lead was confirmed as a neurotoxin, it was widely used in gasoline and paints. In the US, the Lead-Based Paint Poisoning Prevention Act was signed into law in 1971; it was followed by the 1990 Clean Air Act, prohibiting use of lead in many products [20,21]. Use of lead in gasoline and paint in the past explains the reason why urban soil, especially in industrial areas, tends to contain higher levels of lead than that in rural areas. For homes built before 1940, building age in the strongest statistical predictors of lead in soil [22].

Paint from older homes is deposited in soil due to exterior deterioration, remodeling, renovation (blasting, sanding and/or scraping) and/or

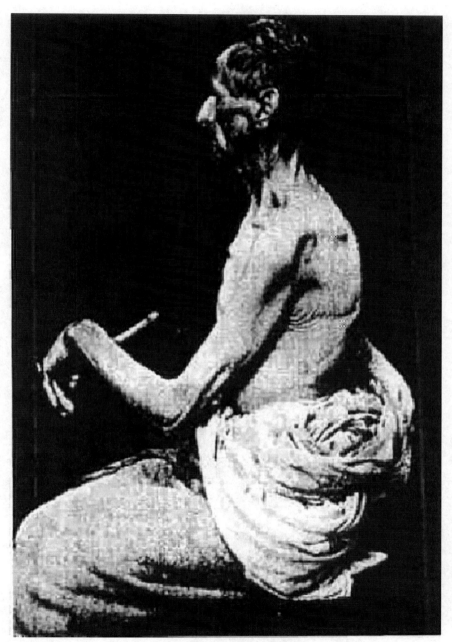

FIGURE 9: American painter with characteristic wrist drop caused by neurological damage from high lead exposure in paint [18].

weather [22]. Thus, it is particularly important to assess lead content in older home sites slated for development as urban gardens.

4.4 SPECIFIC METALS AND LEAD IN 3 SITES

4.4.1 COLLECTING SOIL SAMPLES

Initially, 3 project sites (Lots 1, 2 and 3) were sampled for content of specific metals and subsequently, lead, during the winter of 2013. Lots were divided into 3 regions of approximately equal size and further subdivided into right and left areas creating 6 sub sections per lot. Triplicate samples of surface soil at 0 to 4 in (0 to 10.16 cm) and subsurface soil at 12 to 16 in (30.48 to 40.64 cm) were collected from each sub region. Precautions were taken to avoid inclusion of organic matter in samples. Depending on the size of the lot, samples were taken at 10 to 20 feet (3.05 to 6.10 meters) apart. Samples from the right and left side of each lot were pooled and analyzed in duplicate for metal content. Triplicate samples of each subsections were collected and combined for analysis in duplicate for lead content.

4.4.2 ANALYSIS FOR METALS AND LEAD

Soil samples (0.035 oz, 1 g) were mixed with concentrated nitric acid in a 1:1 ratiofor 12 to 16 hours to dissolve organic material and present metals in their elemental forms. Mixtures were placed in a sonicator (for vibration) with heating in a fume hood for 1 hour, then diluted in deionized distilled water at 1:10. Samples of the solutions were analyzed in an Inductively Coupled Plasma Mass Spectrometer (Department of Civil and Environmental Engineering, University of California, Davis, CA).

4.4.3 SPECIFIC METALS AND LEAD IN SOIL OF 3 LOTS

Except for lead, analysis showed no abnormally high concentrations of specific metals in the soil of each lot. The screening level for lead is set at <400 parts per million (ppm, milligram/kilogram) and is meant to note a safe level for children playing in residential soil [23,24]. Soil was analyzed to determine levels that exceeded this standard (<400 ppm) and new recommendations proposed by the Technical Review Workgroup of the Environmental Protection Agency [24].

The initial analyses for determination of overall lead content for each lot. This information along with established and proposed recommendations was used to decide if further analyses were warranted for any particular lot. Except for quantity of lead (641.5 ppm) in the left side subsurface of Lot 3, all levels for lots were <400 ppm. This value for lead (641.5 ppm) indicated that more analyses should be conducted in Lot 3 (dubbed the Long Lot because of it shape).

4.5 DETERMINATION OF LEAD IN THE LONG LOT

4.5.1 COLLECTING SOIL SAMPLES

During spring of 2013 and winter of 2014, the Long Lot was divided into approximately 3 equal regions from left to right and regions were further subdivided into 3 sections from front to rear to produce 9 sub sections (Figure 10,11a and 11b). Triplicate samples were collected from each sub section.

4.5.2 ANALYSIS FOR LEAD

Samples from subsections were combined and analyzed in duplicate as delineated above for subsurface soil.

4.6 SUBSURFACE LEAD IN LONG LOT SOIL

Results from analysis of subsurface lead content in the Long Lot during spring of 2013 and winter of 2014. The first observation is that in 2013,

FIGURE 10: Sub sections of Lot 3, the long lot in alkali flats (Sacramento, CA). MANRRS, 2013.

Lead Levels in Urban Gardens

FIGURE 11A: MANNRS members, Lupe Pena, removes organic matter to sample soil and b. Wendy Chen, samples the subsurface. MANRRS, 2014.

there were some extremely high levels of lead in the soil of the Long Lot. These high values (>2,000 ppm) may have been caused by rusted lead pipes, pieces of lead (Figure 6), old paint cans and other industrial waste illegally dumped on the lot. These items, when exposed, were removed along with debris in 2014. The second observation is that lead content for 2014 was lower than that for 2013. By winter of 2014, various groups were prematurely removing small trees and roots and tilling the soil for planting. As well, some small garden plots within the Long Lot had been planted and partially harvested (Figure 12).

FIGURE 11B: MANRRS, 2014.

Undoubtedly, mixing the soils at varying levels affected the results for 2014. However, results for both years indicated that for most sub regions (9), lead levels exceeded 400 ppm, because lead content in the Long Lot exceeded limits for planting in the soil, planter boxes with permanent barriers (Figure 13a and 13b) are being used and precautions will be taken to cover paths and picnic areas.

4.7 NEW RECOMMENDATIONS FOR LEAD IN GARDENS

In December, 2013, the TRW, composed of representatives from all regions of the US (the U.S. EPA Office of Solid Waste and Emergency Response/Office of Superfund Remediation and Technology Innovation) met to discuss new recommendations for lead content in gardens. As stated above, the present CADPH (2014) recommended screening level for lead in bare soil is <400 ppm. The TRW recommended new levels and practices as delineated [24]. A much lower safe level for lead content (<100 ppm)

Lead Levels in Urban Gardens

FIGURE 12: Premature tilling and planting of vegetables causing mixing of soil in the Long Lot during winter of 2014. MANRRS, 2014.

in gardens was proposed because not all gardening exposure pathways for lead are included in the development of the soil screening levels (<400 ppm) set for the safety of children playing in soil. The TRW recommendations account for (a) consumption of home-grown produce, (b) lengthy duration of soil contact, (c) possible ingestion of soil during gardening activities and (d) exposure to soil tracked into homes [24].

Using these new recommendations from TRW for safe levels of lead in gardens, only Lot 1 would be safe for gardening while gardeners in Lot 2 with 100–400 ppm of lead should follow precautions provided [24]. Additionally, gardeners should use plants that absorb lead slowly (Figure 14). These plants include apples, melons, okra, oranges, peppers, beans, corn and peas (Craigmill and Harivandi 2010). Gardeners using the Long Lot would continue to use planter boxes with barriers and/or all other precautions set forth.

FIGURE 13A: Planter boxes with barriers in the long lot.

FIGURE 13B: Planter box with soil in the long lot.

FIGURE 14: Corn, grown in Lot 2 (containing 100 to 400 ppm lead) due to its lower lead uptake. MANRRS, 2014.

We concluded that development of fast, accurate kits that analyze lead in various ranges from 0 to 2000 ppm would be of value to several community groups or individuals with plans to use urban sites for gardens (Figure 15). This is particularly applicable for sites where houses were built prior to 1970.

FIGURE 15: (a) Director of community garden project, Janet Little, reveals plans (b) for use of planter boxes in the Long Lot due to analysis of high lead content.

REFERENCES

1. Lawson LJ (2005) PowerPoint. City bountiful: A century of community gardening in America, Berkeley, University of California Press.
2. CLBL (Center for Land-Based Learning), Personal correspondence, Winters, CA.
3. Singh R, Gautam N, Mishra A, Gupta R (2011) Heavy metals and living systems: An overview. Indian J Pharmacol 43: 246-253
4. Green PG (2014) Personal correspondence. Department of Civil & Environmental Engineering, University of California, Davis, CA.
5. Hawkes SJ (1997) What is a "heavy metal"? J ChemEduc 74: 1374.
6. Duffus JH (2002)"Heavy metals"–a meaningless term. ChemInternat'l 74: 793-807.
7. Ames Laboratory - Rare-earth Center of the Nation (2013)
8. Golub M, GoyerR (2004) Issue paper on the human health effects of metals.
9. EPA (Environmental Protection Agency) (2014) Cadmium Fact Sheet - Environmental Protection Agency.
10. CPCS (California Poison Control System) (2007) Thallium Poisoning. The Official Newsletter of the California Poison Control System. School of Pharmacy, University of California, San Francisco, CA.
11. EPA (Environmental Protection Agency) (2013a) Basic information about beryllium in drinking water | basic water.
12. NEI, Nuclear Energy Institute - Nuclear Fuel Supply (2014)
13. Ruby MV, Schoof R, Bratlin W,Goldade M, Post G,et al.(1999) Advances in evaluating the oral availability of inorganics in soil for use in human health. EnvirSci and Tech 33: 3697-3705.
14. Craigmill A,HarivandiaA (2010)Home gardens and lead - What you should know about growing plants in lead-contaminated soil. University of California Agriculture and Natural Resources.
15. Acharya S (2013) Lead between the lines. Nat Chem 5: 894.
16. Needleman H (2004) Lead poisoning. Annu Rev Med 55: 209-222.
17. Magyar JS, Weng TC, Stern CM, Dye DF, Rous BW, et al. (2005) Reexamination of lead(II) coordination preferences in sulfur-rich sites: implications for a critical mechanism of lead poisoning. J Am ChemSoc 127: 9495-9505.
18. Moyer M (2014) Peripheral neuropathy - metals in medicine and the environment faculty.
19. Oregon Health Authority (2014) Public Health.
20. PUBLIC LAW 91-695-JAN. 13. 1971.Public law 91-695 Be ...
21. EPA (Environmental Protection Agency) (2013b) Overview - The Clean Air Act Amendments of 1990.
22. EPA (Environmental Protection Agency) (2012) Chapter 3. Lead in soil: Why is it a problem?
23. CADPH (California Department of Public Health) (2014) Testing your home for lead in paint and soil.
24. TRW-EPA(Technical Review Workgroup of the Environmental Protection Agency) (2013). Gardening and reducing exposure to lead-contaminated n soils.

PART II

THE BENEFITS OF GREEN INFRASTRUCTURE

CHAPTER 5

Urban Community Gardeners' Knowledge and Perceptions of Soil Contaminant Risks

BRENT F. KIM, MELISSA N. POULSEN, JARED D. MARGULIES, KATIE L. DIX, ANNE M. PALMER, AND KEEVE E. NACHMAN

5.1 BACKGROUND

Urban community gardens—gardens tended by multiple households in an urban neighborhood—may offer a range of benefits. Studies have observed associations between community gardening and health [1]–[8], social [6], [9], and economic benefits [6], [7], [10], and gardening in general has been associated with cardiovascular [11], [12] and mental [13]–[15] health benefits. Historically, backyard and community gardens have made substantial contributions to the food supply; World War II "Victory Gardens" have been credited with providing an estimated 40% of the U.S. vegetable supply [16]. In urban settings, community gardens—and urban green spaces in general—may confer an additional set of social benefits [17]–[20] and ecosystem services [21], [22]. Urban green spaces also provide educational opportunities for urban residents, for whom parks and

---

© Kim BF, Poulsen MN, Margulies JD, Dix KL, Palmer AM, Nachman KE (2014) Urban Community Gardeners' Knowledge and Perceptions of Soil Contaminant Risks. PLoS ONE 9(2): e87913. doi:10.1371/journal.pone.0087913. Creative Commons Attribution License (http://creativecommons.org/licenses/by/4.0/).

gardens may be their primary source of experience, knowledge, and valuation of nature.

Gardening in urban settings may also present health risks, including those stemming from exposure to contaminants such as heavy metals, organic chemicals, and asbestos that may be present in urban soils. Urban soils are often close to pollution sources, such as industrial areas and heavily trafficked roads. As a result, many soil contaminants have been found at higher concentrations with increasing proximity to urban centers [23]. In Baltimore, Maryland, prior soil analyses (Table S1 in File S1) have revealed high concentrations of lead at some sites [24]–[28], reflecting the city's long history of industrial activity, incinerators, and vehicular traffic, and raising concerns about lead exposure [24]. Table S2 in File S1 summarizes some of the more common urban soil contaminants, their sources, and health effects associated with exposure.

Gardeners can be exposed to contaminants by inadvertently ingesting soil, inhaling soil particles, or via dermal contact. Soil ingestion is of particular concern among children, who may ingest larger quantities of soil than adults (e.g., by putting their hands in their mouths), absorb higher levels of certain contaminants into their bloodstream [29], and are generally more sensitive to their effects. People who consume produce grown in contaminated environments also risk ingesting soil particles on the surfaces of plants [30]. Contaminants in soils including lead [31], cadmium [32], and arsenic [33] may accumulate in the tissues of vegetables grown in contaminated soils, posing another potential route of ingestion.

Urban gardeners may be unaware of how to manage these risks. Harms et al. [34], [35] surveyed 121 urban farmers and gardeners from Kansas, Indiana, and Washington, most of whom indicated they do not have sufficient knowledge of how to minimize health risks associated with gardening in contaminated environments and want more information on soil testing and best management practices. Gardeners may also benefit from information on soil remediation, i.e. removing, destroying, detoxifying, immobilizing or containing soil contaminants [36].

The purpose of our study is to characterize urban community gardeners' knowledge of risks associated with contaminated garden soils, their perceptions of these risks, their knowledge of how to assess and reduce these risks, the sources they draw upon for information on soil contamination, and the information and training needs they have related to soil contamination.

5.2 METHODS

To characterize urban community gardeners' knowledge and perceptions of soil contamination risks, we conducted surveys among urban community gardeners and semi-structured interviews with key informants in the gardening community.

5.2.1 GARDENER SURVEYS

We conducted brief verbal surveys in-person or by phone with Baltimore community gardeners. The survey included questions regarding demographics, garden site history, and knowledge, perceptions, and practices related to soil contamination. To be eligible to participate, gardeners had to be at least 18 years of age and have been gardening at their current site for at least 6 months.

We partnered with the Community Greening Resource Network (CGRN) to identify gardens from which to recruit survey participants. CGRN is Baltimore's gardening support network and maintains a registry of community gardens in the Baltimore metropolitan area. We randomly selected 30 gardens from the CGRN registry of 70 food-producing community gardens, contacting leaders at the selected gardens to identify opportunities to survey gardeners. After experiencing difficulty reaching some garden leaders, we included additional gardens – recommended to us by representatives in the gardening community or identified through personal contacts – whose leaders were willing to help us arrange surveys.

As an incentive for participating gardeners, we collected soil samples from represented community gardens, sent the samples for analysis at the U.S. Department of Agriculture (USDA) soils lab, shared the results with garden leaders, and offered guidance in interpreting the results.

5.2.2 KEY INFORMANT INTERVIEWS

We conducted semi-structured interviews with 18 purposively selected informants knowledgeable about community gardening and soil contamination in Baltimore City: representatives from City government urban agriculture-related programs (4), federal agency employees (2), a representative of a Baltimore community gardening organization (1), agricultural extension employees (2), Master Gardeners - trained volunteers who advise and educate the public on gardening (2), community garden leaders (4), and urban farmers (3). We distinguish farming from gardening by the intent to produce goods for sale.

Interviews focused on informants' perceptions of community gardeners' concerns about soil contamination, barriers to soil testing, and information needs related to soil contamination. When applicable, informants were also asked relevant questions about their roles and perspectives related to their employment in city, state, or federal agencies.

To identify major themes in the qualitative data, three members of the research team first developed a codebook that was organized by axial codes and sub-codes. Two researchers coded each transcript using Atlas/ti (v7); when discrepancies arose, we included all quotes assigned to a particular code by either researcher. We then generated reports of the text assigned to each code, writing reflective memos and pulling out illustrative quotes for each theme.

5.2.3 ETHICAL CONSIDERATIONS

The Johns Hopkins School of Public Health Institutional Review Board (IRB) approved this study. Study participants provided verbal informed consent prior to participating in surveys and interviews. Oral consent was deemed adequate by the IRB, eliminating the need to record identifying information in study documents. An IRB-approved oral consent script was read by trained investigators to study participants. A dated questionnaire served as a record that the oral consent process had been completed.

5.3 RESULTS

5.3.1 GARDENER DEMOGRAPHICS

Seventy gardeners, representing 15 community gardens from a range of socioeconomic census tracts, responded to our survey. Most were female (66%), lived within a quarter-mile of their garden plots (76%), and had been at their current gardens for less than four years (76%). The median age of surveyed gardeners was 45. See Figure 1 for additional gardener demographic information.

5.3.2 GARDENING PRACTICES AND HARVEST USE

Most (73%) surveyed gardeners indicated they avoid using commercial pesticides and fertilizers, relying instead on practices such as composting and mulching to promote soil fertility and suppress pests. Others (19%) reported using one or more commercial fertilizers and/or insecticides, several of which are allowed for use under USDA organic standards. Interview informants indicated that Baltimore's community gardeners generally garden without chemical inputs.

Among surveyed gardeners, 86% grew produce for home consumption, while the other 14% grew produce primarily for soup kitchens and other charitable uses. Among gardeners who grew produce for home consumption, almost half (45%) supplied over 60% of their family's produce intake from their community garden during the growing season.

5.3.3 GENERAL KNOWLEDGE AND CONCERNS ABOUT CONTAMINANTS

To assess their knowledge about chemical contaminants, surveyed gardeners were asked to list the soil contaminants they are aware of (Table 1).

Most (66%) gardeners mentioned lead, and to a lesser extent, other trace elements (19%) and some types of organic chemicals (36%).

Gardeners were also asked to list any health concerns they have as community gardeners (Table 2); half (51%) cited soil contaminants as among their concerns. When asked to express their overall levels of concern about contaminants in their gardens, the average response was 2.3 on a scale of one to five, with five being the most concerned. There was no apparent association between levels of concern and whether gardeners thought their soil had been tested, or what they thought the test results indicated (Table 3).

When asked to list the ways in which one might come into contact with contaminants, most (70%) surveyed gardeners mentioned ingestion (e.g., "eating crops"). They did not specifically mention incidental ingestion, e.g., accidentally swallowing small amounts of soil while gardening. Other responses included dermal contact with (63%), and inhalation of (39%) contaminants.

Through interviews it became clear that lead is the contaminant of greatest concern among informants and, based on informants' perceptions, also the most common contaminant concern among gardeners. Informants expressed particular concerns about the vulnerability of children to contaminants—and specifically to lead—as compared to adults; among gardens where children may be present, some informants emphasized the heightened importance of testing their soil and making sure children do not ingest it. Informants were also concerned about other contaminants such as trash, drug paraphernalia, and animal feces, as well as potential contaminants in fill dirt, compost, and water. Informants also expressed concerns about chemical inputs, such as pesticides, and indicated that gardeners may view their use as more harmful to health than contaminants directly in soil. Table S3 in File S1 illustrates the range of concerns noted in these discussions.

Most informants did not express a high level of concern about soil contaminants. Frequently, informants indicated that their concerns about soil contamination were alleviated by the use of raised beds or after seeing safe results come back from soil tests. Informants also made repeated comments about soil quality, suggesting issues of soil fertility may be more salient than contaminant concerns.

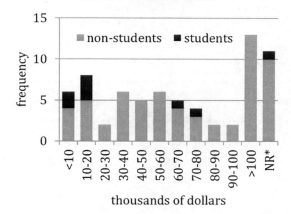
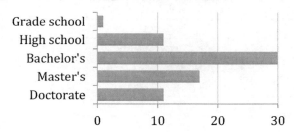
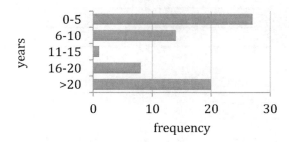

FIGURE 1: Additional gardener demographic information. * NR = No response.

Table 1. Open-ended responses to questions about soil contaminant knowledge: "What soil contaminants are you aware of that urban gardeners should be concerned about in general?" and "As a community gardener, do you have any concerns about hazards to your health?"

Response	%
Heavy metals and other trace elements	71
Non-specific	20
Lead	66
Arsenic	11
Mercury	4
Chromium	4
Cadmium	3
Copper	1
Organic chemicals	36
Petrochemicals (e.g., fuel, oil)	19
Pesticides	13
Persistent organic pollutants	7
Automotive fluids	6
Chemicals (non-specific)	16
Biological hazards	11
Human excreta	7
Animal excreta	6
Building materials (e.g., asbestos, asphalt, roofing tar)	11
Foreign objects (e.g., trash, needles)	21
Other	9
No response	10

> For me, the most important thing is that we have good soil structure here. ... So, really my energies have been not around contaminations, but just building healthy soil so that we get the best vegetable production out of here. (Community garden leader)

Table 2. Open-ended responses to "As a community gardener, do you have any concerns about hazards to your health?"

Response	%
Soil contaminants	51
Non-specific	20
Organic chemicals (e.g., pesticides)	16
Heavy metals and other trace elements	11
Trash	11
Discarded needles	9
Human or animal excreta	4
Crime	6
Animal pests	4
Injury	3
Air quality	3
No concerns	44

In discussing gardeners' levels of awareness or concern about soil contamination, informants' views varied widely. Several had little confidence that gardeners think about soil contamination as an issue or are aware that soil testing can and should be conducted. Informants working with municipal programs related to community gardening noted that few people ask about soil contamination when starting a garden. At the other end of the spectrum, some informants noted broad concern about soil contamination among community gardeners.

> We talk about air. We talk about water. ... Nobody talks about soil, and, essentially, it became very obvious that soil's probably the most contaminated thing that we have in our environment, particularly in urban areas. (Master Gardener)

> I think each year, the new gardeners ask do we have to be concerned about soil, and I say we tested it and everything was okay. (Community garden leader)

Table 3. Gardeners' levels of concern about contaminants in their garden, by perceived soil test status.

"Has your soil been tested for contaminants?"	"Did the results reveal a problem with contamination?"	Number of respondents	Average level of concern (1–5)* among respondents
No	NA	14	2.5
Unsure	NA	16	1.7
Yes	No	20	2.6
Yes	Unsure	9	2.0
Yes	Yes**	11	2.4

NA: Not applicable.
*On a scale of one to five, with five being the most concerned.
**8 of these 11 respondents indicated they discontinued growing food crops in contaminated areas; two indicated the soil was remediated; one was unsure whether corrective action was taken.

> And I've noticed that most gardens want raised beds, because they think there is a lead issue. (City government representative)

Informants noted that knowledge and concerns about contaminants vary with different populations. Younger and more educated individuals, for example, were thought to have greater awareness of soil contaminant issues. A few informants noted that soil contamination was of less concern for gardeners and volunteers at urban farms, because they trusted that the appropriate steps had been taken to ensure the safety of the soil. One urban farmer noted that community members were concerned about soil contamination when the farm was first getting started, but once it became "established", these concerns disappeared.

5.3.4 SITE HISTORY

One of the first steps in determining soil safety is learning how a particular site was used. This was a top concern of one City government representative, who worried that by testing soil without the knowledge of a site's history, gardeners may be unaware of potential contaminants:

> If you do a test for lead and other heavy metals and you pat yourself on the back and you go on, are you missing the fact that there used to be a gas station on that site and there could be types of contaminants that you don't even know how to test for that could pose a risk?

Most (73%) surveyed gardeners said they knew the site history of their gardens. Likewise, the community garden leaders and urban farmers we interviewed indicated they knew the past use of their garden and farm sites.

When asked how they learned about their site's history, most community garden leaders and urban farmers we interviewed indicated they spoke to residents in the surrounding area. One urban farmer said they would start by referencing Sanborn Maps, which are available through local libraries and depict historical land uses from 1867 to 1970. Surveyed gardeners reported obtaining information on site histories primarily from other gardeners (42%), from neighbors (26%) or based on their own observations (23%). A small proportion (7%) had obtained information from a government office, such as the Department of Planning.

When asked if site history is important information in determining if a site is suitable for gardening, nearly all (99%) surveyed gardeners agreed. In contrast, one City government representative suggested that most gardeners would not be interested in trying to uncover information on site history, noting, "I think, based on the people I've met and talked to, they just wanna grow something."

Informants also suggested that gardeners may lack the expertise necessary to conduct a site history. One City government representative noted that in an ideal world, assistance would be provided to new gardens to test the soil and "sit down with somebody and go over the site history in a way that's simple and doesn't take too long and is very clear." One federal agency employee indicated that expert guidance is the "crucial part" of a Phase 1 Environmental Site Assessment, in which an auditor reviews historical and other records, visits the site, and interviews previous landowners and other informants:

> [T]he site history will get you ... maybe 85% there.... [T]here's nothing about [a Phase 1 assessment], less judgment, that a person can't do at the library. But that is still missing that crucial part of the equation—the expertise piece.... Because you'll see maybe it was a paint factory. Well, will everybody think about, "Okay, well, how was a paint made at that time"? Well, it was linseed oil and the white lead was actually mixed in, and it was about at 40% lead.

Another federal agency employee described additional limitations of site histories, noting that "the use and dumping on backyards and gardens is so idiosyncratic that it's impossible to learn what happened even ten years before," and that conducting sporadic site histories on a per-garden basis may not reveal evidence of contaminants from other parts of the city (e.g., from nearby industries that have since shut down). For these reasons, this informant recommended a more comprehensive approach of conducting site histories and soil testing at a city-wide level.

5.3.5 SOIL TESTING

One theme that emerged during informant interviews was the barriers that deter gardeners from testing their soil for contaminants.

Cost was perceived to be prohibitive, particularly in situations in which a gardener wanted to test for a contaminant outside the scope of the usual metals panel, such as asbestos. According to informants, these situations also required additional knowledge about what to test for and how to find a service that offered those tests.

Informants also suggested that gardeners might perceive the steps involved in taking and sending away soil samples to be cumbersome or too complicated. Some informants suggested the need for a local testing service or a government-funded public service for soil testing, although not all agreed that a local testing service would be worth the cost.

There should be an immediate way to get testing ... because some people will not go through the process of sending something away. (Community garden leader)

I don't really see a huge a demand out there for this kind of information ... it takes a whole lot to get the right people together to have a soil-testing lab here, in the city. And then, again, it might not even be used. (City government representative)

Other barriers mentioned by informants included fear of discovering contamination after having already made investments in the land, and the need to document the exact locations from where soil samples are taken within a garden (since contaminant levels may vary spatially across a garden).

A few informants also noted that once soil tests are conducted, gardeners might have difficulty interpreting the results. Our survey results also hinted at this – in responding to questions about tests for contaminants, several gardeners referenced nutrient levels and soil tilth, suggesting that some gardeners may conflate tests of soil fertility with tests for contaminant levels.

Several informants also perceived a lack of scientific consensus about what levels of contamination are considered safe.

[H]ow much lead is too much lead? I have read different numbers. In Canada, the safe level is different than in the United States, and I think that in Europe it's different. (City government representative)

[T]here's a lot of conflicting information from EPA and different universities about what an action level would be for total lead... (Agricultural extension employee)

Both federal agency employees – experts in contamination – also noted imperfections in the science in determining risk standards.

5.3.6 REDUCING EXPOSURE TO CONTAMINANTS

Another aim of this study was to explore knowledge and practices related to reducing exposure when working in potentially contaminated gardens.

We asked surveyed gardeners how they thought one should approach working in contaminated environments, and what they would do if their soil was found to be contaminated; these results are summarized in Table 4.

Among interviewed informants, most cited building raised beds and filling them with clean, imported soil as the safest and easiest way to manage potential soil contamination. Among surveyed gardeners, using raised beds was a common practice. The majority (74%) reported growing at least some crops in raised beds, and 50% said they use raised beds exclusively. Some informants, however, alluded to concerns regarding limitations of raised beds. One federal agency employee noted the possibility that the soil used to fill raised beds may be contaminated, particularly if it was taken from a questionable source, and that plant roots may extend down into contaminated soils below the raised bed, potentially allowing contaminants to enter plant tissues. One urban farmer also suggested that people may be exposed to contaminants from soil not covered by the raised bed (e.g., if native soil is kicked up), and that gardeners who use raised beds might underestimate these risks and not test the underlying soil.

We also asked informants and surveyed gardeners about soil remediation. One City government representative suggested that gardeners may not necessarily know how to remediate the soil and that guidance is needed to provide direction. When surveyed gardeners were asked, for example, whether they thought planting sunflowers in contaminated soil would effectively remediate it, 9% incorrectly said yes and 51% were unsure.

5.3.7 INFORMATION SOURCES

Another aim of this study was to understand where gardeners obtain information about soil contamination. Surveyed gardeners (see Table 5) and interviewed informants most commonly mentioned gardening support institutions, particularly the agricultural extension office and its Master Gardener program.

Gardeners' Knowledge and Perceptions of Soil Contaminant Risks 117

Table 4. Open-ended responses to questions about reducing exposure in contaminated environments.

Response	%
Stop growing produce in contaminated areas, and/or stop eating produce grown in contaminated areas	50
Remove surface contaminants	26
Wash produce	26
Peel root crops	3
Remediate soil	26
Install a barrier over contaminated soil	9
Add soil amendments (e.g., compost or minerals)	9
Bioremediate, phytoremediate, and/or mycoremediate	9
Remove contaminated soil	9
Remediate (non-specific)	4
Grow in raised beds or containers	17
Only grow certain crops (e.g., not root vegetables)	13
Wear gloves	9
Wash hands	6
Apply mulch (e.g., to reduce splashing on crops)	3
Continue using the same methods	3
Seek out more information	29
Don't know	24

Table 5. Open-ended responses to "Where do you get information on gardening practices?"

Response	%
Gardening support organizations	84
Extension office/Master Gardeners	37
CGRN	19
Other	4
Online	53
Other gardeners	44
Books/magazines	29
Friends/family	16

One theme that emerged from informant interviews was the need for a central repository where gardeners could access information about soil contamination. Most informants thought this should be offered through an organization that gardeners already associate with gardening information. Compared to the more formal services of the agricultural extension, the community-based CGRN was cited as having "the biggest direct communication with community gardeners in the city" and being "more accessible" than more "bureaucratic" organizations. One informant noted, however, that while it provides a valuable network for gardeners, within CGRN "a lot of misinformation gets shared." The agricultural extension was thought to be the traditional place where gardeners and farmers would think to access soil contamination information, but informants noted it had "not historically had a real urban presence" and was not prepared to deal with issues common in cities, such as urban soil contamination. One City government representative saw the municipal government as best positioned to gather, hold, and disseminate information on soil contamination:

> [G]overnment can play a really important role in doing the due diligence and gathering all of that stuff and then making it publicly available. ... I think we have the institutional longevity to hold on to that [information]. ... And we need to have this historical data so if that [soil] test has already been done you don't need to go do it again.

5.3.8 INFORMATION NEEDS

Through informant interviews, we aimed to identify urban community gardeners' information needs related to soil contamination. Responses fell under four main topics: site history, soil testing, remediation, and minimizing exposure (see Table 6).

Regarding how best to present this information to gardeners, the overriding theme was that it must be concise, clearly organized, and use simple, straightforward language that speaks to people of varying educational levels. One City government representative noted that the information that

Table 4. Open-ended responses to questions about reducing exposure in contaminated environments.

Site history	How to find information about past uses of a plot of land
	Which contaminants to test for, given specific past land uses
	Geographic areas of the city where there are likely to be high levels of contamination
Soil testing	Importance of obtaining a soil test prior to gardening
	Which contaminants to test for
	Why to test for certain contaminants and not others
	Where to get soil testing done
	How much soil testing costs
	How to correctly take a soil sample for a soil test
Remediation	Best practices for remediating contaminated urban soils
Minimizing exposure	How to reduce exposure risks when gardening
	Contamination risks associated with imported materials such as compost or mulch

is needed already exists, but should be combined "in a document with clear instructions that a layperson would feel comfortable using."

One community gardening organization representative also placed value in communicating the "fluid" nature of determining what levels of contaminants are considered safe, and that the "best way ... [to approaching contaminant issues is] not black and white." Furthermore, informants emphasized the need to balance risk reduction messages related to soil contamination with the health, social, and environmental benefits of gardening, as well as "the values in gardening that are beyond measure."

> [W]e don't want to create barriers. We want more people to be growing food. (City government representative)

5.3.9 DISSEMINATING INFORMATION

Another consideration is how best to disseminate information about soil contamination to community gardeners. Informants had a broad range of suggestions, and several noted that a combination of dissemination strategies – including print, online, and face-to-face information – is needed in order to reach all types of gardeners.

Most informants expressed a need for more interactive, face-to-face methods of dissemination, such as individual consultations, workshops, or a citywide gardening conference. The important role of Master Gardeners was noted, for, as stated by one City government representative, they are "already tapped into the lives of the gardeners out there in the world."

> [N]o matter how hard we try we may never reach half the people who want to garden. Because they're not going to ask, they're not going to look, they're not going to read, they're not going to do a Web search. ... So only by person-to-person communication pushed out from the community master gardeners. (Federal agency employee)

5.3.10 TRAINING NEEDS

While we did not ask informants about their level of knowledge related to soil contamination, many spontaneously acknowledged confusion and a lack of understanding about the issue. One federal agency employee recommended that to help urban community gardeners make decisions about the safety of garden sites, training is needed to provide plant and soil experts with expertise on soil contamination.

> [T]he only really education I've had about soil is what we had in our Master Gardener class. And to be honest, that was very cursory, tip of the iceberg, basic soil composition. And I don't really remember ... there being a lot of information shared about contamination. (Community garden leader)

5.4 DISCUSSION

Through surveys with urban community gardeners and key informant interviews, we characterized urban community gardeners' knowledge and perceptions of soil contaminant risks, including their knowledge of how to assess and reduce these risks, sources of information on soil contamination, and information needs related to soil contamination.

5.4.1 KNOWLEDGE AND CONCERNS

Our results suggest that concern about soil contaminants among community gardeners in Baltimore is generally low, particularly among established gardens. Informants indicated this is likely because gardeners assume soil contamination has already been addressed through safe soil test results, remediation, or the use of raised beds. Concern may be warranted, however, since prior studies of Baltimore soils suggest that soil contaminant levels vary widely [24]–[26]—even within the same garden plot [25]—and at some sites lead levels greatly exceed EPA screening levels (Table S1 in File S1). Soil lead levels have also been shown to increase over time due to atmospheric deposition [37]. Informants called for extra precautions where children may be present in gardens, echoing evidence of children's vulnerability to soil contaminants [24], [29].

Surveyed gardeners' knowledge and concerns related to soil contaminants largely focused around lead. Their awareness may have been informed by recent state and city interventions in Baltimore aimed at raising awareness of child lead poisoning [38], [39]. Gardeners' concerns were in accordance with tests of Baltimore soils (Table S1 in File S1), which identified high levels of lead more often than other trace elements included in analyses. Gardeners demonstrated inconsistent awareness about other potential contaminants.

Among key informants, issues that affect gardeners' ability to cultivate plants often appeared to be more salient than contamination concerns. Additionally, our results suggest that Baltimore's gardeners are more concerned about chemicals added to the gardening environment than what contaminants may already be present in soil. Gardeners' concerns about pesticides reflect the results of prior surveys that found the primary reason consumers purchase organic produce is to reduce exposure to pesticides and other chemicals [40].

Our results identified areas where gardeners' knowledge and concerns may not be concomitant with the potential health risks associated with urban soil contaminants. Efforts to address discrepancies in gardeners' knowledge, however, must be carefully crafted so as to not elevate levels of concern beyond those at which they would discontinue gardening altogether. Informants also made the important point that risk reduction messages must be balanced with the health, social, and environmental benefits of gardening.

5.4.2 SITE HISTORY

Our results suggest gardeners recognize the importance of knowing a garden site's prior uses. Several informants indicated, however, that gardeners may lack the motivation, information and expertise to determine accurately the prior use of their garden site, or to anticipate the contaminants that may be present as a result. City-wide documentation of site histories may be an effective means to alleviate these responsibilities from gardeners.

5.4.3 SOIL TESTING

Our findings also revealed potential barriers to soil testing, including not knowing how to properly sample soil from a garden, where to send soil samples for testing, and which contaminants to test for under various circumstances, as well as the perception that testing is too expensive, complicated, or cumbersome. Even when soil tests are conducted, gardeners may have difficulty interpreting the results. Given surveyed gardeners' knowledge and concerns were largely centered around lead, they may interpret a negative test result for lead as a "clean bill of health" and neglect to consider the presence of other contaminants. These and other concerns speak to the potential value of providing gardeners with cost-assistance and guidance on testing soil and interpreting results. Such services could, for example, be included as part of a lease to adopt city-owned vacant lots.

5.4.4 REDUCING EXPOSURE TO CONTAMINANTS

When surveyed gardeners were asked to list practices to reduce exposure in contaminated environments (Table 4), several best management practices [25], [41], [42] were notably absent from responses, including reducing soil ingestion among children (e.g., by washing their hands, and reducing hand-to-mouth contact), growing produce away from busy streets, railways, and older buildings, and removing shoes to avoid tracking contaminants into the home. Few respondents alluded to the use of mulch (3%) to reduce splashing on crops; or the removal of surface contaminants, e.g., by washing produce (26%) and peeling root crops (3%). Other gaps in practices included the application of soil amendments (9%) to dilute contaminants and/or reduce their mobility or bioavailability (e.g., applying phosphorus to reduce the bioavailability of lead [29]), though such amendments may also increase the mobility or bioavailability of certain contaminants [43]. Some gardeners were quick to acknowledge their limited knowledge on how to approach contaminated environments, and indicated they would seek out more information (29%) or take the conservative approach of not growing produce in and/or eating produce from contaminated areas (50%).

Contaminant concerns among gardeners and informants were often alleviated by the use of raised beds, which were viewed as an easy and effective solution to managing soil contamination. As some informants noted, raised beds do not remedy the presence of contaminated soil surrounding the bed, which may be kicked up during gardening activities. Clark and colleagues [37] raise particular concerns regarding children: based on a model specific to lead-contaminated gardens that considered incidental soil ingestion, inhalation of ambient air, and consumption of tap water and garden-grown produce, an estimated 72–91% of children's lead exposure is via incidental soil ingestion. Because raised beds only cover a small percentage of land, they offer limited protection against incidental ingestion via hand-to-mouth behavior among children playing in areas with contaminated soils. Raised bed soils may also become contaminated over time; lead levels measured in urban raised beds in Dorchester, Massachusetts were found to increase by roughly 185 parts per million over a four year period due to wind-transported fine grain soil [37]. Another study explored concerns related to the use of timbers in the construction of raised beds, detecting elevated levels of arsenic in garden plots framed by chromated copper arsenate treated lumber and elevated levels of polycyclic aromatic hydrocarbons in plots framed by railroad ties [44]. In addition to these concerns, as one informants noted, soil used to fill raised beds may be contaminated, and plant roots may extend into contaminated soils below the bed. While raised beds provide some protection against contaminant exposure, they are not a panacea, and recommendations for their use should be tempered with information about their limitations.

5.4.5 INFORMATION AND TRAINING NEEDS

Informants voiced a need for specific information related to the management of soil contamination and indicated that gardeners need a central place where they can access such information. They noted several potential organizations that could serve such a role. Informants suggested collaboration between such organizations and City government to develop and disseminate a single set of information could yield the greatest reach.

Informant interviews suggest the major challenges in providing such information are the complexity and uncertainty surrounding the issue. Thus, there may be a role for two levels of guidance: additional training for gardening experts, to help them better understand the issues around soil contamination and how to effectively communicate risks to community gardeners; and concise, straightforward messaging for gardeners.

5.4.6 STUDY LIMITATIONS

Our sample population was small, and the median income bracket among surveyed gardeners ($50,000 – 60,000) and percentage with a bachelor's degree (83%) were high relative to the population of Baltimore City in 2007–2011 [45]. For these reasons, our study population may not be representative of the average Baltimore gardener. Our qualitative findings may also be unique to the Baltimore context; however, given the lack of research on this topic, we believe the results of this study can be used as a starting point to inform educational interventions for reducing soil contamination risks among gardeners in a variety of urban contexts.

5.5 CONCLUSIONS

Through this study, we identified a range of factors, challenges, and needs related to Baltimore community gardeners' perceptions of risk related to soil contamination, including low levels of concern and inconsistent levels of knowledge about heavy metal and organic chemical contaminants, barriers to investigating a garden site's history and conducting soil tests, limited knowledge of best practices for reducing exposure, and a need for clear and concise information on how best to prevent and manage soil contamination. Key informants discussed various strategies for developing and disseminating educational material to gardeners. For some challenges, such as barriers to conducting site history and soil tests, some informants recommended city-wide interventions that bypass the need for gardener knowledge altogether. In cases where public health messages about the risks from soil contaminants are implemented, informants stressed the importance of crafting messages in ways that do not dissuade gardeners from continuing to garden in urban environments. Given the health, social, environmental, and economic benefits associated with participating in and supporting urban green spaces, it is critical to protect the viability of urban community gardens while also ensuring a safe gardening environment.

REFERENCES

1. Alaimo K, Packnett E, Miles RA, Kruger DJ (2008) Fruit and vegetable intake among urban community gardeners. J Nutr Educ Behav 40: 94–101 doi:10.1016/j.jneb.2006.12.003.

2. Blair D, Giesecke CC, Sherman S (1991) A dietary, social and economic evaluation of the Philadelphia urban gardening project. J Nutr Educ 23: 161–167. doi: 10.1016/s0022-3182(12)81191-5
3. McCormack LA, Laska MN, Larson NI, Story M (2010) Review of the nutritional implications of farmers' markets and community gardens: a call for evaluation and research efforts. J Am Diet Assoc 110: 399–408 doi:10.1016/j.jada.2009.11.023.
4. Litt JS, Soobader MJ, Turbin MS, Hale JW, Buchenau M, et al. (2011) The influence of social involvement, neighborhood aesthetics, and community garden participation on fruit and vegetable consumption. Am J Public Health 101: 1466–1473 doi:10.2105/AJPH.2010.300111.
5. Armstrong D (2000) A survey of community gardens in upstate New York: implications for health promotion and community development. Health Place 6: 319–327. doi: 10.1016/s1353-8292(00)00013-7
6. Patel IC (1991) Gardening's socioeconomic impacts. J Ext 29.
7. Wakefield S, Yeudall F, Taron C, Reynolds J, Skinner A (2007) Growing urban health: community gardening in South-East Toronto. Health Promot Int 22: 92–101 doi:10.1093/heapro/dam001.
8. Twiss J, Dickinson J, Duma S, Kleinman T, Paulsen H, et al. (2003) Community gardens: lessons learned from California Healthy Cities and Communities. Am J Public Health 93: 1435–1438. doi: 10.2105/ajph.93.9.1435
9. Kuo FE, Sullivan WC, Coley RL (1998) Fertile ground for community: inner-city neighborhood common spaces. Am J Community Psychol 26: 823–851.
10. Voicu I, Been V (2006) The effect of community gardens on neighboring property values. Real Estate Econ 36: 241–283. doi: 10.1111/j.1540-6229.2008.00213.x
11. Caspersen CJ, Bloemberg M, Saris WHM, Merritt RK, Kromhout D (1991) The prevalence of selected physical activities and their relation with coronary heart disease risk factors in elderly men: The Zutphen Study, 1985. Am J Epidemiol 133: 1078–1092.
12. Magnus K, Matroos A, Strackee J (1979) Walking, cycling, or gardening, with or without seasonal interruption, in relation to acute coronary events. Am J Epidemiol 110: 724–733.
13. Kaplan R (1973) Some psychological benefits of gardening. Environ Behav 5: 145–162 doi:10.1177/001391657300500202.
14. Fabrigoule C, Letenneur L, Dartigues JF, Zarrouk M, Commenges D, et al. (1995) Social and leisure activities and risk of dementia: a prospective longitudinal study. J Am Geriatr Soc 43: 485–490.
15. Simons LA, Simons J, McCallum J, Friedlander Y (2006) Lifestyle factors and risk of dementia: Dubbo Study of the elderly. Med J Aust 184: 68–70. doi: 10.1161/01.str.29.7.1341
16. Brown KH, Jameton AL (2000) Public health implications of urban agriculture. J Public Health Policy 21: 20–39. doi: 10.2307/3343472
17. Kuo FE (2001) Coping with poverty: impacts of environment and attention in the inner city. Environ Behav 33: 5–34 doi:10.1177/00139160121972846.
18. Kuo FE, Taylor AF (2004) A potential natural treatment for attention-deficit/hyperactivity disorder: evidence from a national study. Am J Public Health 94: 1580–1587. doi: 10.2105/ajph.94.9.1580

19. Wells NM (2000) At home with nature: effects of "greenness" on children's cognitive functioning. Environ Behav 32: 775–795. doi: 10.1177/00139160021972793
20. Kuo FE, Sullivan WC (2001) Environment and crime in the inner city: does vegetation reduce crime? Environ Behav 33: 343–367 doi:10.1177/0013916501333002.
21. Bolund P, Hunhammar S (1999) Ecosystem services in urban areas. Ecol Econ 29: 293–301 doi:10.1016/S0921-8009(99)00013-0.
22. Andersson E, Barthel S, Ahrné K (2007) Measuring social-ecological dynamics behind the generation of ecosystem services. Ecol Appl A Publ Ecol Soc Am 17: 1267–1278. doi: 10.1890/06-1116.1
23. Meuser H (2010) Causes of soil contamination in the urban environment. In: Alloway BJ, Trevors JT, editors. Contaminated urban soils. Springer. pp. 29–94.
24. Mielke HW, Anderson JC, Berry KJ, Mielke PW, Chaney RL, et al. (1983) Lead concentrations in inner-city soils as a factor in the child lead problem. Am J Public Health 73: 1366–1369. doi: 10.2105/ajph.73.12.1366
25. Chaney R, Sterrett SB, Mielke HW (1984) The potential for heavy metal exposure from urban gardens and soils. In: Preer JR, editor. Proc. symp. heavy metals in urban gardens. USDA ARS. pp. 37–84.
26. Pouyat R V, Yesilonis ID, Russell-Anelli J, Neerchal NK (2007) Soil chemical and physical properties that differentiate urban land-use and cover types. Soil Sci Soc Am J 71: 1010 doi:10.2136/sssaj2006.0164.
27. Schwarz K, Pickett STA, Lathrop RG, Weathers KC, Pouyat R V, et al. (2012) The effects of the urban built environment on the spatial distribution of lead in residential soils. Environ Pollut 163: 32–39 doi:10.1016/j.envpol.2011.12.003.
28. Yesilonis ID, Pouyat RV, Neerchal NK (2008) Spatial distribution of metals in soils in Baltimore, Maryland: role of native parent material, proximity to major roads, housing age and screening guidelines. Environ Pollut 156: 723–731 doi:10.1016/j.envpol.2008.06.010.
29. Hettiarachchi GM, Pierzynski GM (2004) Soil lead bioavailability and in situ remediation of lead-contaminated soils: a review. Environ Prog 23: 78–93 doi:10.1002/ep.10004.
30. Morgan R (2013) Soil, heavy metals, and human health. In: Brevik EC, Burgess LC, editors. Soils and human health. CRC Press. pp. 59–82.
31. Finster ME, Gray KA, Binns HJ (2004) Lead levels of edibles grown in contaminated residential soils: a field survey. Sci Total Environ 320: 245–257 doi:10.1016/j.scitotenv.2003.08.009.
32. Smolders E (2001) Cadmium uptake by plants. Int J Occup Med Environ Health 14: 177–183.
33. Ramirez-Andreotta MD, Brusseau ML, Artiola JF, Maier RM (2013) A greenhouse and field-based study to determine the accumulation of arsenic in common home-grown vegetables grown in mining-affected soils. Sci Total Environ 443: 299–306 doi:10.1016/j.scitotenv.2012.10.095.
34. Harms AMR (2011) Determining and meeting the educational needs of students and urban gardeners and farmers on urban soil quality and contamination topics. Master's Thesis, Kansas State University.

35. Harms AMR, Presley DR, Hettiarachchi GM, Thien SJ (2013) Assessing the educational needs of urban gardeners and farmers on the subject of soil contamination. J Ext 51.
36. Meuser H (2012) Soil remediation and rehabilitation: treatment of contaminated and disturbed land. Alloway BJ, Trevors JT, editors. Spinger. p. 128.
37. Clark HF, Hausladen DM, Brabander DJ (2008) Urban gardens: lead exposure, recontamination mechanisms, and implications for remediation design. Environ Res 107: 312–319 doi:10.1016/j.envres.2008.03.003.
38. Maryland Department of the Environment (2000) State, city unveil new lead awareness campaign. MD Environ 4.
39. City of Baltimore Health Department (2010) Data watch: Maryland Department of the Environment releases 2009 lead poisoning data. Available: http://baltimorehealth.org/press/2010-08-27-lead-report-pr.pdf. Accessed 01 January 2014.
40. Hughner S, McDonagh P, Prothero A, Shultz CJ, Stanton J (2007) Who are organic food consumers? A compilation and review of why people purchase organic food. J Consum Behav 6: 94–110 doi:10.1002/cb.
41. U.S. Environmental Protection Agency (2011) Brownfields and urban agriculture: interim guidelines for safe gardening practices. Available: http://www.epa.gov/brownfields/urbanag/pdf/bf_urban_ag.pdf. Accessed 2014 Jan 1.
42. Kessler R (2013) Urban gardening: managing the risks of contaminated soil. Environ Health Perspect 121: A327–A333. doi: 10.1289/ehp.121-a326
43. Scheckel KG, Diamond GL, Burgess MF, Klotzbach JM, Maddaloni M, et al. (2013) Amending soils with phosphate as a means to mitigate soil lead hazard: a critical review of the state of the science. J Toxicol Env Heal B Crit Rev 16: 337–380 doi:10.1080/10937404.2013.825216.
44. Heiger-Bernays W, Fraser A, Burns V, Diskin K, Pierotti D, et al. (2009) Characterization and low-cost remediation of soils contaminated by timbers in community gardens. Int J Soil, Sediment Water 2: 1–19.
45. U.S. Census Bureau (2013) Baltimore City, Maryland. state & county quickfacts. Available: http://quickfacts.census.gov/qfd/states/24/24510.html. Accessed 2013 June 28.

Additional supplementary information tables available online at http://journals.plos.org/plosone/article?id=10.1371/journal.pone.0087913.

CHAPTER 6

Sustainable Water Management for Urban Agriculture, Gardens and Public Open Space Irrigation: A Case Study in Perth

RAJU SHARMA DHAKAL, GEOFF SYME, EDWARD ANDRE, AND CHARLES SABATO

6.1 INTRODUCTION

Urban agriculture has become increasingly popular across the world that includes a variety of activities: community gardens and fruit orchard, home gardens and veggie patches, urban forest, public open spaces, reserves, urban forest and recreational landscaping [1]-[5]. Urban agriculture differs from traditional agriculture as it is integrated into densely populated areas with limited land for food production and recreation space [4]. Urban agriculture can bring diverse vegetative structures back into urban system, support local bio-diversity, and provide ecosystem services across fragmented habitats and spatial levels [6] that in turn can reduce the impact of climatic variability [7]. In addition to food production, urban agriculture can cater for a wide range of urban community needs, including cultivation of vegetables, medicinal plants, spices, mushroom, fruit trees, ornamental plants, and other productive plants [5] [8]. The production of

---

© Dhakal, R. , Syme, G. , Andre, E. and Sabato, C. (2015) Sustainable Water Management for Urban Agriculture, Gardens and Public Open Space Irrigation: A Case Study in Perth. Agricultural Sciences, 6, 676-685. doi: 10.4236/as.2015.67065. Creative Commons Attribution International License (CC BY) (http://creativecommons.org/licenses/by/4.0/).

crop and agricultural goods, within and around cities, with a motivation of personal consumption or income generation [9] [10] thus integrates the local, urban and suburban economic and ecological system [1].

Urban agriculture has a vital role in enhancing food production and bio-diversity, but that comes with significant costs and constraints [11] [12]. Albeit not required, urban agriculture utilizes significant amount of scheme water for growing foods and crops, which is usually expensive than agricultural water supplies [4] [7]. On the other hand, reducing outdoor use of scheme water for agriculture activities is a major component of many strategies to reduce urban water use and ensure reliable indoor water supply [4]. For instance, almost 40% of the scheme water is consumed for agricultural irrigation activities in urban and regional councils of Perth metropolitan. In drought period, the agricultural irrigation is normally restricted with a variety of bans (daytime and winter sprinkler ban), and demand management practices [13]-[16]. As a result, urban agricultural activities are not always supplied with sufficient irrigation, especially when they require most, hence affecting the continuity of food production and other agricultural activities. This condition is expected to be continued in WA, since a gap between water demand and supply is predicted to be 120 GL by 2030 [15]. In this context, an alternative irrigation system utilizing locally available fit-for-purpose water sources (e.g. groundwater) could have multiple benefits from helping water authorities in augmenting water supply and ensuring cheap and reliable irrigation for urban agricultural activities.

Previous studies in Australia and other countries have shown that alternative irrigation systems using groundwater and recycled wastewater are widely accepted for urban and regional agriculture, forestry and recreational landscaping [7] [17]-[22]. Wong [19] suggests that agriculture, garden and park irrigation are important avenues to utilize recycled water and nutrients within the build environment. This supports the integrated land and water management practices at respective levels by reducing water import into and net discharge out of the environment. Further, well-established urban agriculture activities would have potential to mitigate and adapt the climate change by reducing the urban heat island effects, managing micro-climate, and enhancing biodiversity and ecology [7].

Similar studies have shown a growing acceptance among Australian communities towards alternative irrigation systems [17] [18] [22]-[24]. Hurlimann [17] observed that the majority of Mawson Lake community in South Australia accepted the irrigation use of recycled water as a better option compared to drinking water for their home gardens, veggie patches and other urban agriculture activities. Similarly, Australia-wide case studies conducted by Davis and Farrelly [22]-[24] have shown that a number of alternative water systems can be best utilized for efficient irrigation system. In context of WA, a number of studies consider groundwater as a reliable and sustainable source for outdoor irrigation activities [16] [18] [25]-[27]. These studies indicate that using groundwater as an alternative source for urban agriculture is technically feasible and receiving growing community acceptance all over Australia.

In this context, a suburban area in Perth ("The Green") was selected for this study that has alternative irrigation system via third pipe network. The system utilized local groundwater from shallow aquifer (20 - 60 m below the ground surface). 5 communal bores abstract the groundwater and supply to the irrigation ring without any treatment for irrigating the private gardens and the public open space in every alternate day [28]. This innovative irrigation system was investigated in terms of irrigation efficiency and its utility for urban agriculture. For that, total household drinking water and irrigation consumption, and total public open spaces usage in "The Green" were analyzed and compared with that of the surrounding suburban areas and Perth metropolitan. Further, public acceptance towards the groundwater as an alternative irrigation source was analyzed.

6.2 DESCRIPTION OF THE STUDIED SYSTEM

This study was carried out in "The Green" suburban community at Butler, Western Australia (Figure 1), where urban agricultural practices and recreational landscaping were being irrigated with an efficient irrigation system. Butler is a Greenfield suburban area of City of Wanneroo, which is 35 KM north of Perth CBD. The development of "The Green" began in 2005 and still to finish. "The Green" was compared as an experimental area with its neighbouring suburban development, mainly Ridgewood as

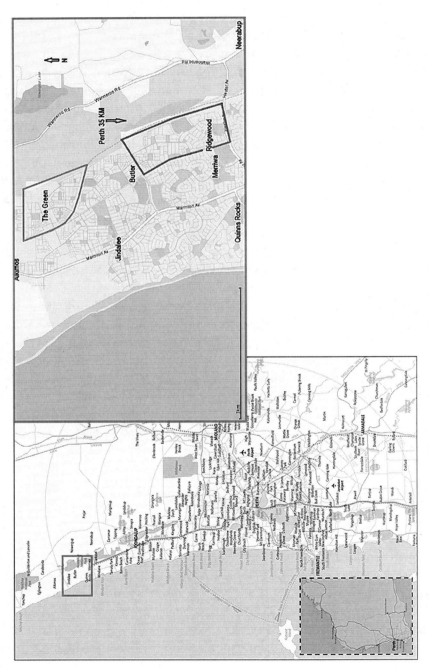

FIGURE 1: Location of the research area (Source: Contrywide Publication, Google Maps).

control and Perth metropolitan city. Ridgewood is an established metropolitan suburban area having similar geography, climate, and socio-demography; but lacking the groundwater irrigation system and having a separate activity locus.

The irrigation system utilised the local groundwater without treatment, hence only used for irrigating home gardens, veggie patches, fruit orchards, community gardens, verges, public parks and ovals, urban forest, plantations, reserves, and bushlands [22] [29]. The irrigation system incorporated water smart technologies and water sensitive land management practices for the efficient consumption and optimisation of the groundwater supplied for outdoor agricultural activities, which include:

1) Auto-operated irrigation system
   a) Weather station;
   b) Soil moisture sensors.
2) Irrigation techniques for achieving efficiency and reducing human contacts
   a) Night time irrigation;
   b) Drips and sprinklers irrigation.
3) Soil conditioning and mulching
4) Water efficient agricultural activities at home
5) Water efficient agriculture, forestry, and recreational landscaping at community

6.2.1 AUTOMATIC IRRIGATION SYSTEM

All agricultural and outdoor activities in "The Green" were automatically supplied with the local groundwater on the basis of local weather condition. Real time weather information was obtained from a local meteorological station (Figure 2(a)); such as temperature, rainfall, relative humidity, wind velocity, etc. This information was coupled with soil moisture information received from in-situ soil moisture sensors (Figure 2(b)) across "The Green" in controlling and operating the irrigation system. Thus established automated irrigation system not only provided irrigation virtually always when required, but also optimized the irrigation supply by avoiding overwatering, and irrigation after rain.

6.2.2 EFFICIENT IRRIGATION TECHNIQUES

The gardens, parks, and urban agricultural activities in "The Green" were provided night time irrigation (10 p.m.-6 a.m.) that avoided evaporation loss, and also reduced possible health hazards to humans a direct contact with the groundwater. A number of efficient irrigation techniques were utilised, such as: unique pop-up sprinklers, and subsurface drip reticulation. The sprinklers were designed for spraying bigger droplets that would avoid wind-drifting and supplying enough water even in shorter operation windows. Similarly, subsurface drip-pipes (Figure 3(a)) supplied irrigation near the root zone of crops that not only improved irrigation efficiency but also reduce evaporation loss.

6.2.3 SOIL CONDITIONING AND MULCHING

When preparing the garden beds and lands for other agricultural activities, the soil condition was improved with sufficient soil mixture, soil conditioner, and mulch as shown in Figure 3(a) and Figure 3(b). This would not only enhance the soil quality, fertility, as well as the water holding capacity but also reduce the evaporation loss from the surface.

6.2.4 WATER EFFICIENT AGRICULTURAL ACTIVITIES AT HOME

Water efficient food production and gardening activities were encouraged at each household to reduce irrigation use. As shown in Figures 4(a)-(c), vegetable gardens and front gardens were established with less water demanding crops, vegetable, hardy turf, and bush. Mostly native plants were used, lawn areas were reduced to improve irrigation efficiency.

Sustainable Water Management for Urban Agriculture 135

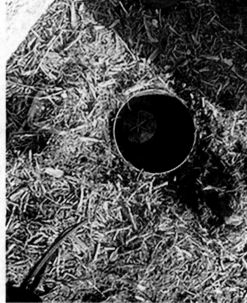

FIGURE 2: A local meteorological station (a) and soil moisture sensor (b) associated with the third-pipe irrigation system in "The Green".

FIGURE 3: Photographs of garden bed preparation (a) and mulching (b) in "The Green".

6.2.5 WATER EFFICIENT AGRICULTURE, FORESTRY, AND RECREATIONAL LANDSCAPING AT COMMUNITY

In "The Green", community gardens, public parks, and recreational landscaping were designed in water efficient way. Usual sprinklers were replaced with subsurface drip irrigation practices (Figure 3(a) and Figure 5(c)) and the lawn areas were dropped and replaced with less water demanding natives and bushes (Figure 5(a)). Trees and bushland (Figure 5(b)) were retained in the parks, so that these parks could be utilized for multiple purposes, such as: playground and recreational activities, community gardening, improving bio-diversity, urban cooling, and community appearance.

Furthermore, a higher density development was adopted in "The Green" that reduced residential garden areas and eventually the residential irrigation demand. The reduced residential gardens were, however, compensated with increased community gardens, public open spaces and reserves [28] [30]. In addition, wide range of water sensitive land management practices were adopted, namely: porous pavement, bio-retention trenches and basins, grassed swales, terraced gardens, and artificial water bodies [22]. These practices would help reducing irrigation demand, improving irrigation efficiency, facilitating aquifer recharge, and recycling urban water and nutrients within the build environment. These innovative designs facilitated integrated and sustainable water management at local and urban level. The innovative irrigation and water sensitive land management practices were expected to be an important avenue for ensuring efficient and integrated land and water management [14], and improving neighbourhood appearance and liveability [31] at various spatial level.

6.3 RESEARCH METHOD

A case study with mixed methodology was adopted to evaluate the agricultural irrigation efficiency and water conservation as a result of the fit-for-purpose irrigation system and water efficient urban development. This paper utilizes the secondary data on drinking water consumption, irrigation usage in gardens and parks and land use pattern to analyze the scheme

FIGURE 4: Photographs of veggie patches (a) and (b), and home garden (c) in "The Green".

water saving and irrigation efficiency at "The Green". The drinking water consumption and irrigation usage data were obtained from the Western Australian Water Corporation and land use data were obtained from the City of Wanneroo. At the same time, the qualitative information from survey and stakeholders interviews were analyzed to understand community acceptance and socio-economic challenges associated with the alternative irrigation system. The data were sorted, managed and analyzed using computer software: Microsoft Excel 2007, IBM SPSS 22, IBM SPSS Amos 22 and NVivo 9.

The drinking water supply was metered and measured in KL/year/household, whereas the groundwater irrigation supply was not metered. Hence a bulk amount of residential groundwater consumption was divided by the number of households connected to the irrigation system to get the average groundwater usage (in KL) per household per year. Similarly, the annual public open space irrigation usage was measured with the meter installed in each public parks and verges and given in ML/year.

The total household water usage was calculated as a sum of average drinking water consumption and irrigation usage. The comparative analysis of drinking water consumption data across the studied areas explained the drinking water conservation, whereas the analysis of total domestic water (Drinking and groundwater) usage data provided the net water efficiency situation at "The Green". The analysis of drinking water conservation was not restricted only for the survey participants. It utilized the data for the whole studied suburban areas to explore a complete picture of water conservation and irrigation efficiency scenarios.

6.4 RESULTS AND DISCUSSIONS

6.4.1 WATER CONSERVATION SCENARIO

In "The Green", both drinking water and groundwater irrigation were supplied; whereas in Ridgewood and Perth metro region, only drinking water was supplied. "The Green" was started since 2007 but the number of households connected to the groundwater irrigation system was very low until 2010, hence only the data from 2011 were used for the analysis. In

FIGURE 5: Public parks with (a) native plants, (b) trees and bushland, and (c) recreational landscaping in "The Green".

Table 1, the total household water consumption in "The Green" (drinking water and groundwater irrigation) is compared with that of Ridgewood and Perth metropolitan (only drinking water).

The average drinking water consumption in "The Green" was significantly lower compared to Ridgewood and Perth metropolitan for all times. A typical household in "The Green" consumed only half of the drinking water used by an average Perth Metropolitan household. Such a significant water savings in "The Green" was mainly because of groundwater irrigation system that replaced the drinking water usage in garden irrigation and other outdoor agricultural activities.

As shown in Table 1, the total household water consumption in "The Green" in 2012 appeared to be significantly higher than neighbouring suburban areas and metropolitan average. It could be attributed to increased usage of groundwater (188 KL) for new garden establishment, and other once-off usage such as construction works. It became further evident from continuous reduction in total water consumption in next two consecutive years (Table 1).

It should be noted that a newly established garden or lawn in Perth metropolitan could get irrigation exemption for up to 42 days in summer and 35 days in winter. During exemption period, a significant amount of water (10 mm/day in summer, and 7.5 mm/day in winter) would be consumed [34]. This was supposed to be the main reason for the higher amount of groundwater consumption in "The Green" given the number of newly established garden and lawns. This figure could get higher, but the water efficient irrigation system and land management practices help to restrain it.

As shown in Figure 6, the household irrigation consumption in "The Green" appeared to be significantly higher than allocated, whereas the public parks irrigation consumption figures were far below than the allocation limit. This could be linked again to the large number of irrigation exemptions for newly established gardens across "The Green" suburb in 2013, which was supported with the reduced consumption in successive years (Table 1). Whereas the groundwater consumption for public open space irrigation in "The Green" was significantly lower than the allocation limit as well as the average public open space irrigation in surrounding suburban areas and metropolitan figures. This indicates that the water

Table 1. Water consumption (KL/household) in "The Green", Ridgewood, Butler, and Perth metropolitan region [32] [33].

Areas\Years	2005	2006	2007	2008	2009	2010	2011	2012	2013	2014
Perth Metro*	375.0	387.5	362.5	362.5	352.5	347.5	344.3	331.5	336.6	347.5
Ridgewood	265.9	178.7	165.0	253.8	300.7	302.6	285.2	285.5	292.6	282.9
Butler (except "The Green")	258.7	282.6	371.1	391.0	364.2	346.2	333.6	290.9	269.5	278.3
The Green-Drinking Water				6.7	37.9	91.3	116.9	154.4	167.6	172.3
-Groundwater							54.1	188.8	167.5	115ᵠ
-Total				6.7	37.9	91.3	171.0	343.3	335.1	287.3ᵠ

*Household water consumption for Perth Metropolitan is calculated as a multiplication of average household size (2.6) with the average per-capita water consumption for each year. ᵠThe allocated groundwater for residential irrigation in "The Green" is approximately 115 KL/household for 2013/14.

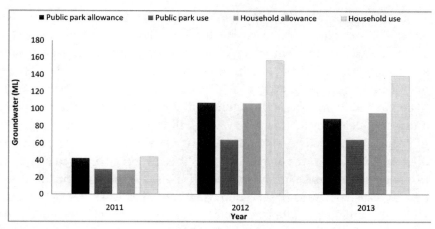

FIGURE 6: Total groundwater allocation and consumption in "The Green".

efficient irrigation technology and the water sensitive land management practices could significantly reduce the irrigation demand of public parks, verges, and other green infrastructures at the urban setting. The findings supports the empirical ideas on irrigation efficiency and urban water conservation put forth by Wong [19], Water Corporation [15], and Barron, Wendling, Tucker, Green, Devkota and Donn [18].

It is equally important to note that the irrigation in "The Green" is sourced from superficial aquifer, which is directly recharged by rainfall. The water sensitive land management practices implemented in "The Green" were reported to increase the aquifer recharge by 383 ML per year than that of pre-development conditions. It was also noticed that after abstracting 209 ML/year for groundwater irrigation network, still there would be an increase in net aquifer recharge by 174 ML/year [35]. Such an increase in aquifer recharge indicates that the groundwater would be a sustainable source for irrigating urban agriculture, vegetation, and recreational landscaping as shown by previous studies of Western Australian Planning Commission [14], and Nolasco [4].

The irrigation trial has been operated for seven years but still approximately 20% of blocks are to be developed. Though new blocks are yet to be connected, the trend in water saving and irrigation efficiency is quite promising. Almost 50% less drinking water demand at residential settings and significant reduction in irrigation for agricultural activities in "The Green" than surrounding suburban areas and metropolitan average clearly indicate that the trialled system will achieve its target even at the full residential development of the suburb. However, an overconsumption of groundwater that was evident in "The Green" could be linked mainly to irrigation exemptions and other once-off usage. These transitional irrigation inconsistencies, as observed in Mawson Lakes Australia [17], would gradually settle down after the suburban areas completely developed and irrigation system fully connected. Having said that, the complete analysis for the factors and parameters associated with the success of the irrigation trial requires completion of the residential development and longitudinal data on usage and behaviour towards water and irrigation systems. Joint effort of Urban Agriculturist, water providers and urban planners.

6.4.2 INHERENT SOCIO-ECONOMIC CHALLENGES

The community perceptions were found to be positive towards the efficient irrigation system and a majority of the consumers were reported to be satisfied with the system in "The Green". The higher level of satisfaction was mainly associated with the automatic irrigation operation, water savings, environmental benefits, and the trust on irrigation service providers. However, there were some social and economic challenges, mainly lack of clarity in institutional roles, and management of consumer expectations that need to be addressed for better management of potential alternative irrigation systems. This study shows that the fit-for-purpose irrigation with integrated land and water management brings the community members, government authorities, and service providers together to plan, implement and develop sustainable urban agricultural practices, and share mutual benefits.

6.4.3 CHALLENGES IN SYSTEM REPLICATION

The qualitative data analysis clearly shows that the majority of residents participated positively towards the efficient irrigation system for food production and agricultural activities at their home and community. Further, it shows an increasing awareness towards the efficient gardens and irrigation system in "The green" community. This is an important finding for the future development of urban agricultural activities with reliable efficient irrigation systems in similar location and climate across Australia.

Based on the findings of this study, alternative irrigation system sourced from rainwater has been successfully implemented in a neighbouring suburban area (Evermore Height, Alkimos). Successive new alternative irrigation projects in the Perth metropolitan and regional areas have also being formulated and developed taking Butler trial as a successful urban agriculture irrigation model [30]. These findings and successful replications clearly demonstrate that the fit-for-purpose irrigation system is instrumental in sustainable development of urban agriculture across Australia.

6.5 CONCLUSION

An alternative fit-for-purpose irrigation system was trialled in "The Green" community at Butler, Perth to understand sustainable water management for urban agriculture. The quantitative and qualitative data were collected and analyzed. The study suggested that a fit-for-purpose irrigation was a sustainable alternative for urban agriculture. Additionally, it offers significant irrigation efficiency in urban agriculture, and consequent reduction in water demand at urban residential settings. The water quality issues associated with fit-for-purpose irrigation appear to be nominal and do not affect the community acceptance. This indicates that the fit-for-purpose irrigation system with water efficient land management practices is highly encouraging for the sustainable development of urban agriculture and recreational landscaping across spatial levels.

REFERENCES

1. Alaimo K, Packnett E, Miles RA, Kruger DJ (2008) Fruit and vegetable intake among urban community gardeners. J Nutr Educ Behav 40: 94–101 doi:10.1016/j.jneb.2006.12.003.
2. Blair D, Giesecke CC, Sherman S (1991) A dietary, social and economic evaluation of the Philadelphia urban gardening project. J Nutr Educ 23: 161–167. doi: 10.1016/s0022-3182(12)81191-5
3. McCormack LA, Laska MN, Larson NI, Story M (2010) Review of the nutritional implications of farmers' markets and community gardens: a call for evaluation and research efforts. J Am Diet Assoc 110: 399–408 doi:10.1016/j.jada.2009.11.023.
4. Litt JS, Soobader MJ, Turbin MS, Hale JW, Buchenau M, et al. (2011) The influence of social involvement, neighborhood aesthetics, and community garden participation on fruit and vegetable consumption. Am J Public Health 101: 1466–1473 doi:10.2105/AJPH.2010.300111.
5. Armstrong D (2000) A survey of community gardens in upstate New York: implications for health promotion and community development. Health Place 6: 319–327. doi: 10.1016/s1353-8292(00)00013-7
6. Patel IC (1991) Gardening's socioeconomic impacts. J Ext 29.
7. Wakefield S, Yeudall F, Taron C, Reynolds J, Skinner A (2007) Growing urban health: community gardening in South-East Toronto. Health Promot Int 22: 92–101 doi:10.1093/heapro/dam001.
8. Twiss J, Dickinson J, Duma S, Kleinman T, Paulsen H, et al. (2003) Community gardens: lessons learned from California Healthy Cities and Communities. Am J Public Health 93: 1435–1438. doi: 10.2105/ajph.93.9.1435
9. Kuo FE, Sullivan WC, Coley RL (1998) Fertile ground for community: inner-city neighborhood common spaces. Am J Community Psychol 26: 823–851.
10. Voicu I, Been V (2006) The effect of community gardens on neighboring property values. Real Estate Econ 36: 241–283. doi: 10.1111/j.1540-6229.2008.00213.x
11. Caspersen CJ, Bloemberg M, Saris WHM, Merritt RK, Kromhout D (1991) The prevalence of selected physical activities and their relation with coronary heart disease risk factors in elderly men: The Zutphen Study, 1985. Am J Epidemiol 133: 1078–1092.
12. Magnus K, Matroos A, Strackee J (1979) Walking, cycling, or gardening, with or without seasonal interruption, in relation to acute coronary events. Am J Epidemiol 110: 724–733.
13. Kaplan R (1973) Some psychological benefits of gardening. Environ Behav 5: 145–162 doi:10.1177/001391657300500202.
14. Fabrigoule C, Letenneur L, Dartigues JF, Zarrouk M, Commenges D, et al. (1995) Social and leisure activities and risk of dementia: a prospective longitudinal study. J Am Geriatr Soc 43: 485–490.
15. Simons LA, Simons J, McCallum J, Friedlander Y (2006) Lifestyle factors and risk of dementia: Dubbo Study of the elderly. Med J Aust 184: 68–70. doi: 10.1161/01.str.29.7.1341

16. Brown KH, Jameton AL (2000) Public health implications of urban agriculture. J Public Health Policy 21: 20–39. doi: 10.2307/3343472
17. Kuo FE (2001) Coping with poverty: impacts of environment and attention in the inner city. Environ Behav 33: 5–34 doi:10.1177/00139160121972846.
18. Kuo FE, Taylor AF (2004) A potential natural treatment for attention-deficit/hyperactivity disorder: evidence from a national study. Am J Public Health 94: 1580–1587. doi: 10.2105/ajph.94.9.1580
19. Wells NM (2000) At home with nature: effects of "greenness" on children's cognitive functioning. Environ Behav 32: 775–795. doi: 10.1177/00139160021972793
20. Kuo FE, Sullivan WC (2001) Environment and crime in the inner city: does vegetation reduce crime? Environ Behav 33: 343–367 doi:10.1177/0013916501333002.
21. Bolund P, Hunhammar S (1999) Ecosystem services in urban areas. Ecol Econ 29: 293–301 doi:10.1016/S0921-8009(99)00013-0.
22. Andersson E, Barthel S, Ahrné K (2007) Measuring social-ecological dynamics behind the generation of ecosystem services. Ecol Appl A Publ Ecol Soc Am 17: 1267–1278. doi: 10.1890/06-1116.1
23. Meuser H (2010) Causes of soil contamination in the urban environment. In: Alloway BJ, Trevors JT, editors. Contaminated urban soils. Springer. pp. 29–94.
24. Mielke HW, Anderson JC, Berry KJ, Mielke PW, Chaney RL, et al. (1983) Lead concentrations in inner-city soils as a factor in the child lead problem. Am J Public Health 73: 1366–1369. doi: 10.2105/ajph.73.12.1366
25. Chaney R, Sterrett SB, Mielke HW (1984) The potential for heavy metal exposure from urban gardens and soils. In: Preer JR, editor. Proc. symp. heavy metals in urban gardens. USDA ARS. pp. 37–84.
26. Pouyat R V, Yesilonis ID, Russell-Anelli J, Neerchal NK (2007) Soil chemical and physical properties that differentiate urban land-use and cover types. Soil Sci Soc Am J 71: 1010 doi:10.2136/sssaj2006.0164.
27. Schwarz K, Pickett STA, Lathrop RG, Weathers KC, Pouyat R V, et al. (2012) The effects of the urban built environment on the spatial distribution of lead in residential soils. Environ Pollut 163: 32–39 doi:10.1016/j.envpol.2011.12.003.
28. Yesilonis ID, Pouyat RV, Neerchal NK (2008) Spatial distribution of metals in soils in Baltimore, Maryland: role of native parent material, proximity to major roads, housing age and screening guidelines. Environ Pollut 156: 723–731 doi:10.1016/j.envpol.2008.06.010.
29. Hettiarachchi GM, Pierzynski GM (2004) Soil lead bioavailability and in situ remediation of lead-contaminated soils: a review. Environ Prog 23: 78–93 doi:10.1002/ep.10004.
30. Morgan R (2013) Soil, heavy metals, and human health. In: Brevik EC, Burgess LC, editors. Soils and human health. CRC Press. pp. 59–82.
31. Finster ME, Gray KA, Binns HJ (2004) Lead levels of edibles grown in contaminated residential soils: a field survey. Sci Total Environ 320: 245–257 doi:10.1016/j.scitotenv.2003.08.009.
32. Smolders E (2001) Cadmium uptake by plants. Int J Occup Med Environ Health 14: 177–183.

33. Ramirez-Andreotta MD, Brusseau ML, Artiola JF, Maier RM (2013) A greenhouse and field-based study to determine the accumulation of arsenic in common homegrown vegetables grown in mining-affected soils. Sci Total Environ 443: 299–306 doi:10.1016/j.scitotenv.2012.10.095.
34. Harms AMR (2011) Determining and meeting the educational needs of students and urban gardeners and farmers on urban soil quality and contamination topics. Master's Thesis, Kansas State University.
35. Harms AMR, Presley DR, Hettiarachchi GM, Thien SJ (2013) Assessing the educational needs of urban gardeners and farmers on the subject of soil contamination. J Ext 51.
36. Meuser H (2012) Soil remediation and rehabilitation: treatment of contaminated and disturbed land. Alloway BJ, Trevors JT, editors. Spinger. p. 128.
37. Clark HF, Hausladen DM, Brabander DJ (2008) Urban gardens: lead exposure, recontamination mechanisms, and implications for remediation design. Environ Res 107: 312–319 doi:10.1016/j.envres.2008.03.003.
38. Maryland Department of the Environment (2000) State, city unveil new lead awareness campaign. MD Environ 4.
39. City of Baltimore Health Department (2010) Data watch: Maryland Department of the Environment releases 2009 lead poisoning data. Available: http://baltimorehealth.org/press/2010-08-27-lead-report-pr.pdf. Accessed 01 January 2014.
40. Hughner S, McDonagh P, Prothero A, Shultz CJ, Stanton J (2007) Who are organic food consumers? A compilation and review of why people purchase organic food. J Consum Behav 6: 94–110 doi:10.1002/cb.
41. U.S. Environmental Protection Agency (2011) Brownfields and urban agriculture: interim guidelines for safe gardening practices. Available: http://www.epa.gov/brownfields/urbanag/pdf/bf_urban_ag.pdf. Accessed 2014 Jan 1.
42. Kessler R (2013) Urban gardening: managing the risks of contaminated soil. Environ Health Perspect 121: A327–A333. doi: 10.1289/ehp.121-a326
43. Scheckel KG, Diamond GL, Burgess MF, Klotzbach JM, Maddaloni M, et al. (2013) Amending soils with phosphate as a means to mitigate soil lead hazard: a critical review of the state of the science. J Toxicol Env Heal B Crit Rev 16: 337–380 doi:10.1080/10937404.2013.825216.
44. Heiger-Bernays W, Fraser A, Burns V, Diskin K, Pierotti D, et al. (2009) Characterization and low-cost remediation of soils contaminated by timbers in community gardens. Int J Soil, Sediment Water 2: 1–19.
45. U.S. Census Bureau (2013) Baltimore City, Maryland. state & county quickfacts. Available: http://quickfacts.census.gov/qfd/states/24/24510.html. Accessed 2013 June 28.

CHAPTER 7

Where is the UK's Pollinator Biodiversity? The Importance of Urban Areas for Flower-Visiting Insects

KATHERINE C. R. BALDOCK, MARK A. GODDARD,
DAMIEN M. HICKS, WILLIAM E. KUNIN, NADINE MITSCHUNAS,
LYNNE M. OSGATHORPE, SIMON G. POTTS,
KIRSTY M. ROBERTSON, ANNA V. SCOTT,
GRAHAM N. STONE, IAN P. VAUGHAN, AND JANE MEMMOTT

7.1 INTRODUCTION

Animal pollination is essential for reproduction in many plant species [1,2] and has been valued globally at €153 billion p.a. (2005) [3] and at more than £510 million p.a. for UK crop production (2009) [4]. However, declines have been reported for all key insect pollinator groups, including honeybees, bumblebees, solitary bees and hoverflies [5–8]. Habitat loss and fragmentation (including urbanization), pesticides, pathogens and their interactions are all proposed drivers of pollinator decline [9,10].

© Baldock KCR et al. 2015 Where is the UK's pollinator biodiversity? The importance of urban areas for flower-visiting insects. Proceedings of the Royal Society. B 282: 20142849. http://dx.doi.org/10.1098/rspb.2014.2849. Creative Commons Attribution license (http://creativecommons.org/licenses/by/4.0/). Used with the permission of the authors.

Pollinators have been widely studied in agricultural systems and natural habitats, but urban areas remain under-studied and their suitability for pollinators is unclear. Urbanization represents a major proposed cause of insect decline [11], particularly through alteration of ecological features important to pollinators, such as food and nesting sites [12,13]; many previous studies have found a decrease in the species richness of pollinating insects with increased urbanization (e.g. [14,15]), a trend mirrored in many other animal groups [16,17]. However, urban habitats can contain remarkably high pollinator species richness; for example, 35% of UK hoverfly species were recorded in a single garden [18], half of the German bee fauna has been recorded in Berlin [19], and some studies show a positive effect of urbanization on certain bee taxa, including bumblebees [20] and cavity-nesting bees [21,22]. Urbanization can also change community composition through novel combinations of available species [23], and communities may shift from more specialized to more generalist species [24,25].

Urban land is expanding in the UK [26] and Europe [27], and in 2008 the global proportion of people living in urban areas crossed the 50% threshold [28]. Here, we undertake the first systematic survey of pollinators across the three main land use types in the UK, comparing plant-pollinator communities in thirty-six 1 km2 sites in urban areas, farmed landscapes and nature reserves (defined here as land with protected status). We used quantified flower-visitation networks to address three objectives. (i) To compare the abundance, species richness and diversity of insect flower-visitors among the three landscapes. We predict that all measures will be highest in nature reserves and lowest in the urban areas, as previous studies have shown negative impacts of urbanization on insect species richness and abundance [13,29], and intensive agriculture can negatively affect pollinating insects [30,31]. (ii) To compare the composition of insect flower-visitor communities among landscapes. We predict that urbanization will filter out habitat specialists and rare species (e.g. [24]). (iii) To compare insect flower-visitation patterns in urban habitats with those in farmland and in nature reserves. Given that cities often support higher plant species richness [16], we predict that urban pollinators will visit more plant species than their counterparts in other habitats and thus be more generalized in diet.

7.2 MATERIAL AND METHODS

7.2.1 FIELD SITE SELECTION

The 36 sites were located in and around 12 large UK urban centres (10 cities and two large towns, all termed cities hereafter) with populations over 150 000. Cities were blocked into four regional groups of three (for city list and map, and selection details, see electronic supplementary material, appendix S1). In each city, we selected a site triplet comprising one urban, one farmland and one nature reserve site. Urban sites were located within the respective city boundary, with matched farmland and nature reserve sites within 10 km of the city boundary. Nature reserve sites were located in National Nature Reserves, Local Nature Reserves or Sites of Special Scientific Interest. Sites were selected using GIS, such that the proportion of habitat types in each site matched those found in the surrounding city, farmland or nature reserve (for full details of methods see electronic supplementary material, appendix S1). All except three of the 36 sites were 100 ha in size; the exceptions were the Edinburgh triplet, in which restrictions on the size of available nature reserves resulted in the selection of 75 ha sites.

7.2.2 SAMPLING FLOWERS, FLOWER-VISITORS AND FLOWER-VISITOR INTERACTIONS

Each of the 36 sites was sampled four times between 30 May and 19 September 2011 at approximately monthly intervals. Plants and pollinators were sampled along a 2 m × 1 km transect in each site, with sections allocated proportionately to all habitat types comprising more than 1% of the selected site (e.g. pasture, crops, hedgerow and woodland on the farm sites; see electronic supplementary material, appendix S1 for a full list of habitat types). Transects in residential areas were positioned along the boundary between pavements and residential gardens, so that 1 m of the transect width was located in gardens and the other 1 m of the transect width on pavements and road verges. See electronic supplementary material, appendix S1 for further details of site and transect selection.

Flowers were sampled at 10 m intervals along each transect. All flowering plant species in a 0.5 × 0.5 m quadrat were identified and the number of floral units (defined as an individual flower or collection of flowers that an insect of 0.5 cm body length could walk within or fly between) counted for each species. A floral unit comprised a single capitulum for Asteraceae, a secondary umbel for Apiaceae and a single flower for most other taxa (see electronic supplementary material, appendix S2 for full details). Grasses, sedges and wind-pollinated forbs were not sampled.

Flower-visitor interactions were quantified by walking along each transect and collecting all insects (except thrips, order Thysanoptera) on flowers up to 1 m either side of the transect line to a height of 2 m. Each transect was walked twice with a 10-min gap between the two samples to allow disturbed flower-visitors to return. All insects were identified by taxonomists (see Acknowledgements), 95% to species and the remainder to morphologically distinct genera or families. The plant species from which each insect was sampled was identified, 88% to species and the remainder to genus. Sampling for flower-visitors and their interactions took place between 09.00 and 17.00 h on dry, warm, non-windy days spanning the activity periods of diurnally active UK pollinators [32].

7.2.3 DATA ANALYSIS

All analyses were performed using R v. 3.1.1 [33]. Generalized linear mixed models (GLMM) were fitted using the R package lme4 [34], with a Gaussian error distribution unless otherwise stated. Post hoc Tukey tests were conducted using the multcomp package [35]. The effect of landscape type on the response variable was tested using a log-likelihood ratio test [36] comparing models with and without landscape type included. The effect of region (Scotland, north England, southwest England/Wales, southeast England) was tested but there was no significant effect for any of the models so the term was not included.

7.2.3.1 OBJECTIVE 1: COMPARING THE ABUNDANCE, SPECIES RICHNESS AND DIVERSITY OF INSECT FLOWER-VISITORS IN URBAN AREAS WITH THOSE IN FARMLAND AND NATURE RESERVES

We tested for the effect of landscape type on species richness and visitor abundance using GLMMs fitted using a Poisson error distribution and a negative binomial distribution respectively. Model residuals were checked for overdispersion and heteroscedasticity. Fixed effects included landscape type (urban, farmland, nature reserve), sampling month (June, July, August, September), floral abundance and proportion of woodland habitat at the site. A nested random effect term of sampling site nested within city was included to reflect the repeated measures of three sites per city. Woodland cover varied greatly among sites, particularly nature reserves, in which it covered 0–96% of site area. Woodland cover was significantly correlated with visitor abundance and therefore included in the model to account for woodland variation across sites. Flower-visitor abundance was included as a covariate in models comparing species richness to control for sample size effects. Analyses were carried out for (i) the whole dataset; (ii) separately for the two dominant insect orders, Diptera and Hymenoptera; (iii) for the key pollinator taxa of hoverflies (Diptera: Syrphidae) and bees (Apoidea: comprising bumblebees, honeybees and solitary bees); and (iv) separately for bumblebees, honeybees and solitary bees. Pollen beetles (Nitidulidae: *Brassicogethes*, *Kateretes* or *Brachypterus*) were excluded from analyses as they were not observed to move between flowers. Ants (Hymenoptera: Formicidae) and true bugs (Hemiptera) were also excluded as both are considered unimportant as pollinators in the UK [37].

Visitor diversity was calculated for each site using the inverse Simpson's index and Fisher's alpha index [38] as both are relatively robust to differences in sample size. Since Fisher's alpha index could not be calculated for some months at some sites owing to low visitor diversity both indices were calculated for data pooled across months at each site. GLMMs were used to test for differences in diversity between the three landscape types. Models contained landscape type, floral abundance and proportion of woodland as fixed effects, and city as a random effect term to reflect the nested structure of the dataset.

7.2.3.2 OBJECTIVE 2: COMPARING FLOWER-VISITOR COMMUNITY COMPOSITION ACROSS LANDSCAPE TYPES

To test if urbanization filters out rare species, we first pooled all of the data from the 36 sites and classified the visitor taxa into four categories based on their overall abundance: (i) more than 100 individuals, (ii) 21–99 individuals, (iii) 2–20 individuals and (iv) 1 individual. While these ranges are arbitrary, they encapsulate the range in abundance from common to rare. We counted the number of recorded taxa per category in each landscape to examine whether rarer species were more frequently found in particular landscape types across our whole dataset. We then recalibrated the categories to grade abundance for each triplet of sites per city so that categories reflected locally common or rare taxa: (i) more than 50 individuals, (ii) 11–49 individuals, (iii) 2–10 individuals and (iv) 1 individual recorded across all sites. We tested whether rare species (those in categories (iii) and (iv)) were found more often in farmland and nature reserve sites than in urban sites using GLMMs fitting a Poisson error distribution. Fixed effects included landscape type, floral abundance and proportion of woodland. Flower-visitor abundance was included as a covariate to control for sample size effects. The random effect term of city was included to reflect the nested structure of the dataset.

Three measures were used to assess similarity in flower-visitor community composition among the 12 sites for each landscape type: (i) Sørensen similarity index to compare species presence/absence between sites; (ii) proportional similarity; and (iii) Horn–Morisita dissimilarity index (see electronic supplementary material, appendix S3 for calculations). The latter two measures incorporate species' relative abundances and both were used as the Horn–Morisita index is independent of sample size but at the cost of being insensitive to turnover in rare species. For the Sørensen index and proportional similarity, a higher value indicates greater similarity whereas a higher Horn–Morisita index indicates lower similarity.

For each site and index, we calculated a mean value over all 11 pairwise comparisons with other sites of the same landscape type, and compared across landscape types using GLMMs, applying the logit transformation for proportions to index values to meet model assumptions. Models included landscape type, floral abundance and proportion of woodland as fixed effects, and city as a random effect term to reflect the nested structure of the dataset. Finally, we visualized variation in community composition across the 36 sites using non-metric multi-dimensional scaling (NMDS) in the R package vegan [38], in which more similar communities group more closely together.

7.2.3.3 OBJECTIVE 3: COMPARING VISITOR AND PLANT GENERALIZATION IN FLOWER-VISITOR NETWORKS ACROSS LANDSCAPE TYPES

The flower-visitor interaction data were used to construct a flower-visitor network for each of the 36 sites; data were pooled across sampling months for analyses. The R package bipartite [39] was used to calculate the following metrics to enable examination of variation in plant and visitor specialization/generalization across landscape types: 'generality', 'vulnerability', d' (species-level specialization) and $H2'$ (network-level specialization). 'Generality' and 'vulnerability' were defined by Tylianakis et al. [40] in the context of antagonistic plant–parasitoid networks, and here we refer to them as 'visitor generality' and 'plant generality', respectively. Both are measures of the number of interacting partner species weighted by relative abundance. The d' metric of specialization measures how specialized a species is with respect to available resources and $H2'$ represents the overall level of specialization of all species in a network [41]. All metrics were calculated using marginal totals (number of visits per plant species) rather than floral abundance data as the latter were not available for all plant species visited per network (as floral abundance was sampled at 10 m intervals along each transect). Abundances and marginal totals were significantly correlated for plant species with floral abundance data, thus using marginal totals was deemed appropriate. Mean d' was calculated for (i) plants and (ii) visitors in each network. These five measures (plant generality, visitor generality, mean plant specialization, mean visitor specialization and network-level specialization) were compared across landscape types using GLMMs including the fixed effects landscape type, floral abundance and proportion of woodland, and city as a random effect. Plant and visitor generality were log-transformed and the other response variables logit-transformed to meet model assumptions. d' and H2' could not be calculated for the Sheffield nature reserve site as only one plant species (*Calluna vulgaris*) was visited, so the Sheffield site triplet was excluded from these three analyses.

Finally, we compared flowering plant species richness (overall, native and non-native) and numbers of visits to native and non-native plant species between the three landscape types using GLMMs fitted with a Poisson error distribution. Plants were categorized as native or non-native to the British Isles following Hill et al. [42]. Models included landscape type, floral abundance and proportion of woodland as fixed effects, and the random effect term of site nested within city.

7.3 RESULTS

Excluding pollen beetles, ants and Hemiptera, a total of 7412 insect flower-visitors were sampled from the 36 sites, of which 67% were Diptera, 26% Hymenoptera, 5% Coleoptera and 2% Lepidoptera. This comprised 412 visitor taxa (262 Diptera, 67 Hymenoptera, 53 Coleoptera and 30 Lepidoptera) visiting 250 plant taxa, and there were 2025 unique interactions between the two groups. Of the 412 visitor taxa, 94% were distinct species or morpho-species and the remainder genus- or family-level identifications.

7.3.1 OBJECTIVE 1: COMPARING THE ABUNDANCE AND SPECIES RICHNESS OF INSECT FLOWER-VISITORS IN URBAN AREAS WITH THOSE IN FARMLAND AND NATURE RESERVES

Summed across all sites, flower-visitors were more abundant in nature reserves (3123) than farmland (2671) and urban sites (1618). Although mean numbers of flower-visitors per site at nature reserve and farmland sites were almost double those at urban sites, there was no significant difference in flower-visitor numbers between the three landscape types (figure 1a and table 1). Similarly, overall species richness for the 12 urban sites combined (147) was much lower than for all nature reserves combined (266), or all farmland sites combined (262), but there was no significant difference in the mean visitor species richness or visitor diversity between landscape types (figure 1d and table 1).

Hymenopteran abundance and species richness were not significantly different between landscape types (table 1). Bees contributed most hymenopteran visits (90%), with solitary bees, bumblebees and honeybees contributing 9%, 62% and 29% of bee visits, respectively. For bees alone, while overall abundance did not differ significantly among landscape types, bee species richness in urban landscapes was significantly higher than in farmland, and approaching significance for nature reserves ($p = 0.053$; figure 1b,e and table 1). Separate analyses for honeybees, bumblebees and solitary bees showed no significant differences in richness or abundance among landscape types (table 1).

Dipteran abundance was significantly higher in farmland and nature reserves than in urban sites, although there were no differences in richness (table 1). More specifically, hoverflies (Syrphidae) contributed a greater proportion of dipteran flower visits in urban sites (69%) than in farmland (36%) and nature reserves (49%). There were significantly more hoverflies in farmland and nature reserve sites than in urban areas (table 1 and figure 1c), although hoverfly species richness did not differ among the three landscapes (figure 1f and table 1). The net effect is that while urban sites have fewer flies, their dipteran assemblage is enriched in hoverflies relative to farms and nature reserves.

7.3.2 OBJECTIVE 2: COMPARING FLOWER-VISITOR COMMUNITY COMPOSITION ACROSS LANDSCAPE TYPES

When sites of each landscape type were combined and rarity categories assigned at a national scale, rare taxa were more often found in nature reserve and farmland than in urban sites (figure 2a; electronic supplementary

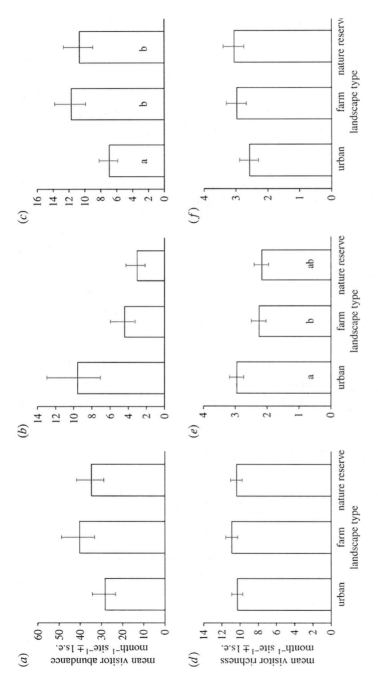

FIGURE 1: Mean (a–c) flower-visitor abundance and (d–f) visitor species richness per month per site ± 1 s.e. across the 12 cities for the three landscape types (urban, farmland and nature reserves). Landscape types significantly different from one another are indicated by different letters. Marginal (adjusted) means from the GLMMs, back-transformed to the original scale, are plotted, with standard errors based on the posterior distributions of the regression coefficients using a simulation approach implemented with the R package arm [43]. Results are shown for (a,d) all visitors combined, (b,e) bees and (c,f) hoverflies. Full GLMM results for all taxa are given in table 1.

material, appendix S4). When rarity categories were assigned at a local scale (i.e. within a triplet), there was no significant difference between landscape types in the number of rare taxa recorded and they made up a similar proportion of visitor taxa for all three landscape types (figure 2b; electronic supplementary material, appendix S4). Eleven flower-visitor species classified as nationally rare or scarce [44,45] were found, four of them in urban sites (electronic supplementary material, appendix S5).

Overall, flower-visitor communities in urban areas were more homogeneous across sites than were those from nature reserve or farmland sites (electronic supplementary material, appendix S6). Both mean Sørensen and mean proportional similarity indices were significantly higher for urban sites than for farmland and nature reserves (table 2). Mean Horn–Morisita indices (a dissimilarity index) were significantly lower in urban than farmland sites, although not lower than in nature reserves ($p = 0.09$ for the latter comparison; table 2), consistent with greater visitor community similarity among urban sites than among farmland sites.

7.3.3 OBJECTIVE 3: COMPARING VISITOR AND PLANT GENERALIZATION IN FLOWER-VISITOR NETWORKS ACROSS LANDSCAPE TYPES

Visitor generality (in terms of numbers of plant species visited) was significantly higher in urban compared with farmland and nature reserve sites (figure 3a; electronic supplementary material, appendix S7), with visitor taxa in urban sites visiting more plant species on average than those in other sites. Conversely, plant generality (in terms of numbers of visitor taxa) was significantly lower at urban sites than in farmland and nature reserves (figure 3b); thus plant species in farmland and nature reserve sites received visits from a greater variety of visitor taxa than those in urban areas. Mean visitor species-level specialization was significantly higher in urban sites compared with farmland and nature reserve sites (figure 3c), which indicates that visitors in urban areas made use of a smaller fraction of the available floral resources. There was no significant difference in plant species-level specialization between landscape types (figure 3d). Network-level specialization, which combines plants and visitors, and thus examines interaction-level specialization, was significantly higher in farmland than urban sites (figure 3e).

Plant species richness was significantly higher in urban areas than farmland (figure 3f), an effect driven by higher richness of non-native plants: while native plant species richness was not different between the three landscapes, there were significantly more non-native plant species in urban areas (figures 3g,h). Similar numbers of visits were recorded to native and non-native plant species in urban sites; by contrast, almost all flower-visitors were recorded on native plant species in farmland and nature reserve sites (figure 3j,k).

7.4 DISCUSSION

This is the first study to systematically compare pollinator communities in replicate urban and non-urban landscapes; moreover, it is based on highly resolved flower–visitor interaction networks. Our results show that while there was no difference in pollinator abundance and richness between urban, farmland and nature reserve sites, patterns varied between taxa. Bee species richness was higher and flies were less abundant in urban areas, as were hoverflies when considered separately. Urban areas had more homogeneous visitor communities than farmland or nature reserves, although they contained similar numbers of rare flower-visitor taxa. In what follows, we first address limitations of our study and then discuss our results, first in the context of our objectives, and then in the wider context of urban ecology and conservation management.

7.4.1 LIMITATIONS

There are two main limitations to our work. First, because sampling started in late May some early spring solitary bees are likely to have been missed, especially at southern sites. However, our sampling was not designed to survey each site exhaustively; rather, we aimed to sample multiple sites regularly through the year using a standardized approach to make broad cross-landscape comparisons. Second, using transect sampling rather than

Where is the UK's Pollinator Biodiversity?

Table 1. Results of GLMMs testing for differences in flower-visitor abundance, species richness and diversity between the three landscape types. Significant results are indicated in bold and there were 2 d.f. for all analyses. Means and standard errors presented are calculated from the raw data and are calculated across the pooled data (i.e. all months combined) for each site, allowing direct comparisons between abundance and richness, where monthly variation was modelled in the GLMMs, and diversity, where GLMMs pooled data across months. Significant *post hoc* Tukey tests used to test for differences between landscape pairs are shown, near-significant p-values are given in brackets and all other pairwise comparisons were not significant. UR, urban; FM, farmland; NR, nature reserve sites.

taxon or index	mean abundance, richness or diversity ± 1 s.e. across sites for all months combined			effect of landscape type		Tukey *post hoc* tests	
	urban	farmland	nature reserve	χ^2	p-value	direction	p-value
visitor abundance							
all taxa	134.83 ± 17.31	222.58 ± 43.80	260.25 ± 65.74	5.405	(0.067)	NR > UR	(0.057)
Hymenoptera	64.58 ± 12.65	51.08 ± 12.89	45.83 ± 15.31	1.575	0.455	—	—
bees	54.83 ± 11.53	45.08 ± 13.31	41.25 ± 15.00	1.315	0.518	—	—
bumblebees	34.42 ± 4.96	25.58 ± 7.57	28.75 ± 13.51	3.052	0.217	—	—
honeybees	14.50 ± 6.39	16.83 ± 5.80	10.50 ± 4.24	0.396	0.820	—	—
solitary bees	5.92 ± 2.19	4.75 ± 1.96	2.00 ± 1.02	0.863	0.650	—	—
Diptera	62.67 ± 12.03	157.83 ± 40.61	192.75 ± 50.72	12.138	**0.002**	**FM > UR** **NR > UR**	**0.003** **0.002**
hoverflies	43.42 ± 9.36	57.42 ± 12.77	94.08 ± 35.18	8.228	**0.016**	**FM > UR** **NR > UR**	**0.025** **0.021**
visitor richness							
all taxa	31.67 ± 3.58	48.25 ± 7.00	46.25 ± 8.73	0.638	0.727	—	—
Hymenoptera	11.33 ± 1.45	9.92 ± 1.28	9.00 ± 1.31	2.453	0.293	—	—
bees	9.33 ± 1.20	7.25 ± 1.09	6.25 ± 0.83	6.459	**0.040**	**FM < UR** NR < UR	**0.049** (0.053)
bumblebees	5.00 ± 0.49	4.00 ± 0.52	4.58 ± 0.62	4.177	0.124	—	—

Table 1. Continued.

solitary bees	3.42 ± 0.99	2.50 ± 0.83	1.00 ± 0.35	1.268	0.531	—	—
Diptera	17.75 ± 2.16	32.42 ± 5.75	30.33 ± 6.46	1.809	0.405	—	—
hoverflies	8.67 ± 0.83	12.17 ± 1.93	12.42 ± 2.19	1.956	0.376	—	—
visitor diversity							
inverse Simpson's	8.21 ± 1.14	10.63 ± 1.07	10.79 ± 2.03	2.439	0.295	—	—
Fisher's α	14.87 ± 2.14	20.08 ± 2.05	17.90 ± 2.90	5.762	0.056	FM > UR	(0.063)

targeted observations of each flowering plant species probably missed some rare pollinator taxa [46]. Transects, nevertheless, allow efficient sampling of many sites under time constraints [46]. Furthermore, the high plant species richness at urban sites would have resulted in a much higher sampling effort at urban sites if data had been gathered using timed observations per plant species. All insect sampling methods suffer from a variety of biases [47], and overall transect samples were deemed the most appropriate approach for this study.

7.4.2 OBJECTIVE 1: COMPARING THE ABUNDANCE AND SPECIES RICHNESS OF INSECT FLOWER-VISITORS IN URBAN AREAS WITH THOSE IN FARMLAND AND NATURE RESERVES

Other studies comparing potential pollinators between urban and non-urban habitats have found a negative effect of urbanization on the abundance and species richness of flower-visiting insects [12,13,15]. Although our study found no significant differences in overall abundance or richness among urban, farmland and nature reserve habitats for all visitor taxa combined, our

Where is the UK's Pollinator Biodiversity?

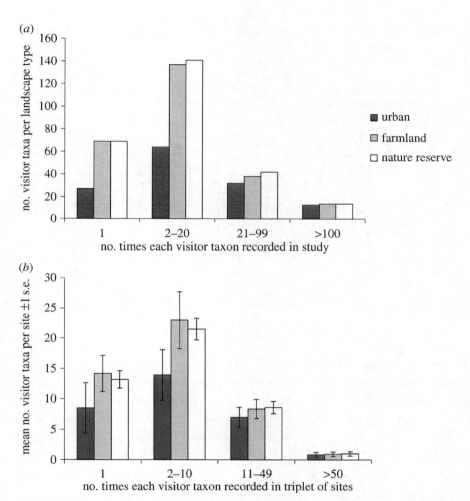

FIGURE 2: Numbers of rare, intermediate and common visitor taxa found in (a) the whole dataset and (b) individual sites. Urban sites are shown in dark grey, farmland sites in light grey and nature reserves in white.

results suggest that numbers of fly and hoverfly visitors were higher in non-urban compared with urban habitats. Deguines et al. [13] found urbanization to have a lesser effect on bees than on other insects, a result mirrored in our data with higher bee species richness in urban compared with farmland sites. Bees require two main resources: food (generally in the forms of pollen and

Table 2. Results of GLMMs testing for differences in flower-visitor community composition between the three landscape types. Significant results are indicated in bold and there were 2 d.f. for all analyses. Means and standard errors are calculated from the raw data. Significant *post hoc* Tukey tests used to test for differences between landscape pairs are shown, near-significant p-values are given in brackets and all other pairwise comparisons were not significant. UR, urban; FM, farmland; NR, nature reserve sites.

index	mean index value ± 1 s.e.			effect of landscape type		Tukey *post hoc* tests	
	urban	farmland	nature reserve	χ^2	p-value	direction	p-value
Sørensen similarity index	0.370 ± 0.018	0.272 ± 0.016	0.246 ± 0.010	20.741	<0.0001	FM < UR NR < UR	<0.0001 <0.0001
proportional similarity	0.356 ± 0.024	0.247 ± 0.013	0.234 ± 0.016	24.747	<0.0001	FM < UR NR < UR	<0.0001 <0.0001
Horn–Morisita dissimilarity index	0.531 ± 0.038	0.644 ± 0.027	0.664 ± 0.033	7.529	0.023	FM > UR NR > UR	0.030 (0.0901)

nectar) and a suitable nesting site. Food in urban areas is provided by a combination of native and introduced plant species. Although some horticultural plant varieties may not provide as much pollen or nectar as non-modified varieties (e.g. single versus double flowers [48]), many non-native plants can provide large quantities of both rewards [49]. Bees nest in a variety of locations, including soil, pre-existing cavities in walls and other structures, pithy plant stems and trees, and heterogeneous urban habitats can provide suitable nesting sites for a wide range of bee taxa [50].

Our results show that abundance and richness were no different for farmland compared with nature reserves for any of the visitor taxa. One explanation for our findings could be high habitat heterogeneity between the different nature reserves sampled, which ranged from woodland to meadow to heathland. These sites showed large differences in floral communities and flowering phenologies, and while some nature reserve sites were very good for pollinators, others, particularly woodland-dominated sites in southern England, had very few flower-visitors during our sampling period. Although all reserve sites had protected status, they were not designated on the basis of their suitability for pollinators.

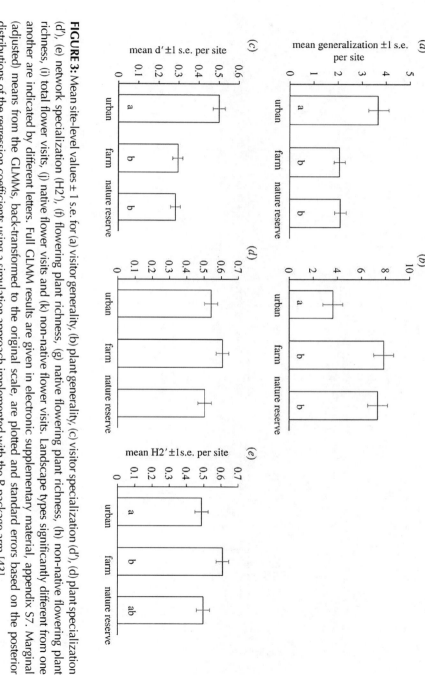

FIGURE 3: Mean site-level values ± 1 s.e. for (a) visitor generality, (b) plant generality, (c) visitor specialization (d'), (d) plant specialization (d'), (e) network specialization (H2'), (f) flowering plant richness, (g) native flowering plant richness, (h) non-native flowering plant richness, (i) total flower visits, (j) native flower visits and (k) non-native flower visits. Landscape types significantly different from one another are indicated by different letters. Full GLMM results are given in electronic supplementary material, appendix S7. Marginal (adjusted) means from the GLMMs, back-transformed to the original scale, are plotted and standard errors based on the posterior distributions of the regression coefficients using a simulation approach implemented with the R package arm [43].

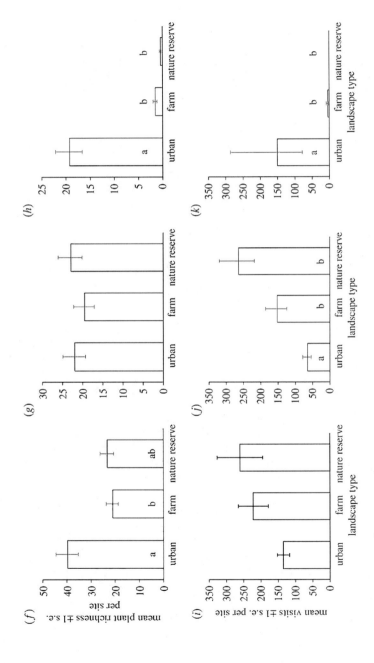

FIGURE 3: Continued.

7.4.3 OBJECTIVE 2: COMPARING THE COMPOSITION OF URBAN FLOWER-VISITOR COMMUNITIES WITH FARMLAND AND NATURE RESERVES

There was no difference in the number of rarer taxa in our dataset among urban, farmland and nature reserve sites. However, we recognize that visitor taxa classified as 'rare' in our dataset may not reflect their overall status. We recorded three species designated as priority species according to the UK Biodiversity Action Plan. *Bombus humilis* was recorded in the Cardiff urban, farmland and nature reserve sites, and two rare butterflies (*Boloria selene* and *Coenonympha pamphilus*) at nature reserve sites (electronic supplementary material, appendix S5). Hoverfly species noted as nationally scarce [45] and bee taxa noted as scarce or threatened [44] were also recorded in all three landscapes (electronic supplementary material, appendix S5). Our findings suggest that urban areas contain lower overall species richness across the wider landscape (although bee richness is comparatively high) and contain somewhat homogeneous visitor assemblages. While previous studies suggest urban areas contain fewer habitat specialists and rare species (e.g. [14]), our findings suggest that the differences between urban and non-urban habitats may not be large with respect to rare species.

7.4.4 OBJECTIVE 3: COMPARING VISITOR AND PLANT GENERALIZATION IN URBAN FLOWER-VISITOR NETWORKS WITH FARMLAND AND NATURE RESERVES

While visitors were recorded on more plant species in urban areas, they also visited a lower proportion of the plant species available compared with non-urban sites. This generates the apparently contrasting patterns in visitor generality (number of plants visited) and specialization (proportion of available plant species visited). These findings probably reflect the much higher richness of flowering plant species, driven by higher non-native richness, in urban areas. The greater generalization of urban visitors could potentially render them less effective pollinators as they are likely to be carrying more pollen species [51]. Conversely, plant generality was higher in non-urban habitats; plants were on average visited by more visitor taxa in farmland and nature reserve habitats. This can be explained by the lower plant species richness in non-urban habitats, meaning that visitor taxa had fewer plant species to visit. Overall, interactions at farmland sites were more specialized than those in urban areas, a result probably also driven by lower plant richness.

7.4.5 CONCLUSION AND FUTURE DIRECTIONS

This is the first study to compare pollinator communities in urban and non-urban habitats with replication across multiple geographically separate urban locations. Our findings suggest that urban areas can contain high bee species richness, although hoverfly abundance was lower in urban areas than elsewhere. While the effects of urbanization are likely to differ between regions and climates depending on the composition of the local pollinator fauna, urban areas are expanding globally, and natural and semi-natural habitats that support pollinator populations are likely to decrease. If high-quality urban areas are able to support good populations of insect pollinators, they could act as important source areas, refuges and corridors of favourable habitat in a hostile matrix habitat such as intensive agricultural landscapes. While there has been increasing interest in enhancing agricultural areas for pollinators, far less attention has been paid to how urban areas can be made more pollinator-friendly. Given the fact that urban areas are widespread and that there are likely to be increasing pressures on more natural areas for food and biofuel production, identifying good urban habitats for pollinators and improving their value for pollinators should be part of any strategy to conserve and restore pollinators.

REFERENCES

1. Klein AM, Vassiere BE, Cane JH, Steffan-Dewenter I, Cunningham SA, Kremen C, Tscharntke T. 2007 Importance of pollinators in changing landscapes for world crops. Proc. R. Soc. B 274, 301–313. (doi:10.1098/rspb.2006.3721)
2. Ollerton J, Winfree R, Tarrant S. 2011 How many flowering plants are pollinated by animals? Oikos 120, 321–326. (doi:10.1111/j.1600-0706.2010.18644.x)

3. Gallai N, Salles J, Settele J, Vassiere BE. 2009 Economic valuation of the vulnerability of world agriculture confronted with pollinator decline. Ecol. Econ. 68, 810–821. (doi:10.1016/j.ecolecon.2008.06.014)
4. Breeze T, Roberts SPM, Potts SG. 2012 Decline of England's bees: policy review and recommendations. Friends of the Earth report. Reading, UK: University of Reading.
5. Goulson D, Lye GC, Darvill B. 2008 Decline and conservation of bumble bees. Annu. Rev. Entomol. 53, 191–208. (doi:10.1146/annurev.ento.53.103106.093454)
6. Potts SG, Roberts SPM, Dean R, Marris G, Brown M, Jones R, Settele J. 2010 Declines of managed honeybees and beekeepers in Europe. J. Apicult. Res. 49, 15–22. (doi:10.3896/IBRA.1.49.1.02)
7. Bartomeus I, Ascher JS, Gibbs J, Danforth BN, Wagner DL, Hedtke SM, Winfree R. 2013 Historical changes in northeastern US bee pollinators related to shared ecological traits. Proc. Natl Acad. Sci. USA 110, 4656–4660. (doi:10.1073/pnas.1218503110)
8. Carvalheiro LG, et al. 2013 Species richness declines and biotic homogenisation have slowed down for NW-European pollinators and plants. Ecol. Lett. 16, 870–878. (doi:10.1111/ele.12121
9. González-Varo JP, et al. 2013 Combined effects of global change pressures on animal-mediated pollination. Trends Ecol. Evol. 28, 524–530. (doi:10.1016/j.tree.2013.05.008)
10. Vanbergen AJ and the Insect Pollinators Initiative. 2013 Threats to an ecosystem service: pressures on pollinators. Front. Ecol. Environ. 11, 251–259. (doi:10.1890/120126)
11. Jones EL, Leather SR. 2012 Invertebrates in urban areas: a review. Eur. J. Entomol. 109, 463–478. (doi:10.14411/eje.2012.060)CrossRefWeb of Science
12. Banaszak-Cibicka Z. 2012 Wild bees along an urban gradient: winners and losers. J. Insect Conserv. 16, 16 331–16 343. (doi:10.1007/s10841-011-9419-2)
13. Deguines N, Julliard R, de Flores M, Fontaine C. 2012 The whereabouts of flower visitors: contrasting land-use preferences revealed by a country-wide survey based on citizen science. PLoS ONE 7, e45822. (doi:10.1371/journal.pone.0045822)
14. Hernandez JL, Frankie GW, Thorp RW. 2009 Ecology of urban bees: a review of current knowledge and directions for future study. Cities and the Environment 2, article 3.
15. Bates AJ, Sadler JP, Fairbrass AJ, Falk SJ, Hale JD, Matthews TJ. 2011 Changing bee and hoverfly pollinator assemblages along an urban-rural gradient. PLoS ONE 6, e23459. (doi:10.1371/journal.pone.0023459)
16. Grimm NB, Faeth SH, Golubiewski NE, Redman CL, Wu J, Bai X, Briggs JM. 2008 Global change and the ecology of cities. Science 319, 756–760. (doi:10.1126/science.1150195)
17. Luck GW, Smallbone LT. 2010 Species diversity and urbanisation: patterns, drivers and implications. In Urban ecology (ed. Gaston KJ), pp. 88–119. Cambridge, UK: Cambridge University Press.
18. Owen J. 2010 Wildlife of a garden: a thirty-year study. London, UK: Royal Horticultural Society.

19. Saure C. 1996 Urban habitats for bees: the example of the city of Berlin. In The conservation of bees (eds Matheson A, Buchmann SL, Toole CO, Westrich P, Williams IH), pp. 47–53. Linnean Society Symposium Series No. 18. New York, NY: Academic Press.
20. Carré G, et al. 2009 Landscape context and habitat type as drivers of bee diversity in European annual crops. Agric. Ecosyst. Environ. 133 40–47. (doi:10.1016/j.agee.2009.05.001)
21. Cane JH, Minckley RL, Kervin LJ, Roulston TH, Williams N. 2006 Complex responses within a desert bee guild (Hymenoptera: Apiformes) to urban habitat fragmentation. Ecol. Appl. 16, 632–644. (doi:10.1890/1051-0761(2006)016[0632:CRWADB]2.0.CO;2)
22. Matteson KC, Ascher JS, Langellotto GA. 2008 Bee richness and abundance in New York City urban gardens. Ann. Entomol. Soc. Am. 101, 140–150. (doi:10.1603/0013-8746(2008)101[140:BRAAIN]2.0.CO;2)
23. Angold PG, et al. 2006 Biodiversity in urban habitat patches. Sci. Total Environ. 360, 196–204. (doi:10.1016/j.scitotenv.2005.08.035)
24. McIntyre NE, Rango J, Fagan WF, Faeth SH. 2001 Ground arthropod community structure in a heterogeneous urban environment. Landscape Urban Plan. 52, 257–274. (doi:10.1016/S0169-2046(00)00122-5)
25. Geslin B, Gauzens B, Thébault E, Dajoz I. 2013 Plant-pollinator networks along a gradient of urbanisation. PLoS ONE 8, e63421. (doi:10.1371/journal.pone.0063421)
26. UK National Ecosystem Assessment. 2011 The UK National Ecosystem Assessment: synthesis of the key findings. Cambridge, UK: UNEP-WCMC.
27. Gerard F, et al. 2010 Land cover change in Europe between 1950 and 2000 determined employing aerial photography. Prog. Phys. Geogr. 34, 183–194. (doi:10.1177/0309133309360141)
28. UNFPA. 2007 State of the World Population 2007: Unleashing the Potential of Urban Growth. New York, NY: United Nations Population Fund.
29. McKinney ML. 2008 Effects of urbanization on species richness: a review of plants and animals. Urban Ecosyst. 11, 161–176. (doi:10.1007/s11252-007-0045-4)
30. Kremen C, Williams NM, Thorp RW. 2002 Crop pollination from native bees at risk from agricultural intensification. Proc. Natl Acad. Sci. USA 99, 16 812–16 816. (doi:10.1073/pnas.262413599)
31. Ricketts TH, et al. 2008 Landscape effects on crop pollination services: are there general patterns? Ecol. Lett. 11, 499–515. (doi:10.1111/j.1461-0248.2008.01157.x)
32. Willmer PG, Stone GN. 2004 Behavioral, ecological, and physiological determinants of the activity patterns of bees. Adv. Stud. Behav. 34, 347–466. (doi:10.1016/S0065-3454(04)34009-X)
33. R Core Team. 2014 R: a language and environment for statistical computing. Vienna, Austria: R Foundation for Statistical Computing. See http://www.R-project.org/.
34. Bates D, Maechler M, Bolker B. 2013 lme4: Linear mixed-effects models using S4 classes. R package version 0.999999-2. See http://CRAN.R-project.org/package=lme4.

35. Hothorn T, Bretz F, Westfall P. 2008 Simultaneous inference in general parametric models. Biometrical J. 50, 346–363. (doi:10.1002/bimj.200810425)CrossRefWeb of Science
36. Zuur AF, Ieno EN, Walker NJ, Saveliev AA, Smith G. 2009 Mixed effects models and extensions in ecology with R. New York, NY: Springer.
37. Willmer PG. 2011 Pollination and floral ecology. Princeton, NJ: Princeton University Press.
38. Oksanen JF, et al. 2013 vegan: community ecology package. R package version 2.0–10. See http://cran.r-project.org/web/packages/vegan/index.html.
39. Dormann CF, Frund J, Bluthgen N, Gruber B. 2009 Indices, graphs and null models: analyzing bipartite ecological networks. Open Ecol. J. 2, 7–24. (doi:10.2174/1874213000902010007)
40. Tylianakis JM, Tscharntke T, Lewis OT. 2007 Habitat modification alters the structure of tropical host-parasitoid food webs. Nature 445, 202–205. (doi:10.1038/nature05429)
41. Bluthgen N, Menzel F, Bluthgen N. 2006 Measuring specialization in species interaction networks. BMC Ecol. 6, 9. (doi:10.1186/1472-6785-6-9)
42. Hill MO, Preston CD, Roy DB. 2004 PLANTATT—attributes of British and Irish plants: status, size, life history, geography and habitats. Abbots Ripton, UK: Centre for Ecology & Hydrology.
43. Gelman A, Su Y. 2014 arm: data analysis using regression and multilevel/hierarchical models. R package version 1.7–07. See http://CRAN.R-project.org/package=arm.
44. Falk S. 1991 A review of the scarce and threatened bees, wasp and ants of Great Britain. Research and Survey in Nature Conservation Report no. 35. Peterborough, UK: Nature Conservancy Council.
45. Ball S, Morris R. 2013 Britain's hoverflies: an introduction to the hoverflies of Britain. Princeton, NJ: Princeton University Press.
46. Gibson R, Knott B, Eberlein T, Memmott J. 2011 Sampling method influences the structure of plant–pollinator networks. Oikos 120, 822–831. (doi:10.1111/j.1600-0706.2010.18927.x)
47. Westphal C, et al. 2008 Measuring bee biodiversity in different habitats and biogeographic regions. Ecol. Monogr. 78, 653–671. (doi:10.1890/07-1292.1)
48. Corbet SA, et al. 2001 Native or exotic? Double or single? Evaluating plants for pollinator-friendly gardens. Ann. Bot. 87, 219–232. (doi:10.1006/anbo.2000.1322)
49. Comba L, Corbet SA, Barron A, Bird A, Collinge S, Miyazak N, Powell M. 1999 Garden flowers: insect visits and the floral reward of horticulturally-modified variants. Ann. Bot. Lond. 83, 73–86. (doi:10.1006/anbo.1998.0798)Abstract/
50. Neame LA, Griswold T, Elle E. 2012 Pollinator nesting guilds respond differently to urban habitat fragmentation in an oak-savannah ecosystem. Insect Conserv. Divers. 6, 57–66. (doi:10.1111/j.1752-4598.2012.00187.x)
51. Leong M, Kremen C, Roderick GK. 2014 Pollinator interactions with yellow starthistle (Centaurea solstitialis) across urban, agricultural, and natural landscapes. PLoS ONE 9, e86357. (doi:10.1371/journal.pone.0086357)

CHAPTER 8

The Influence of Garden Size and Floral Cover on Pollen Deposition in Urban Community Gardens

PETER A. WERRELL, GAIL A. LANGELLOTTO,
SHANNON U. MORATH, AND KEVIN C. MATTESON

8.1 INTRODUCTION

Many studies have shown the negative effects of pollen limitation on fruit or seed production in angiosperms (reviewed in Knight et al. 2005). For animal-pollinated plants, the effects of pollen limitation on fruit or seed production may result from lack of suitable pollinators (Bierzychudek 1981), a lack of co-flowering conspecific plants (Ågren 1996) or an abundance of heterospecific pollen (i.e. pollen from a different plant species). Heterospecific pollen deposition can reduce fruit or seed production of the flowering plant being pollinated, especially if the heterospecific pollen arrives before conspecific pollen (i.e. pollen from a different flower or a different plant of the same species) arrives (Galen and Gregory 1989; Caruso and Alfaro 2000). Though heterospecific pollen may not limit the amount of conspecific pollen deposited, it competes for limited stigmatic space

---

© Werrell, P.A. et al. 2009. The Influence of Garden Size and Floral Cover on Pollen Deposition in Urban Community Gardens. Cities and the Environment. 2(1):article 6. Creative Commons Attribution license (http://creativecommons.org/licenses/by/3.0/).

capable of hydrating conspecific grains. This has the same effect of decreasing the conspecific pollen load, in that space becomes less available to conspecific pollen that could potentially fill the stigma, germinate, and fertilize ovules. High conspecific pollen loads, on the other hand, are more likely to initiate fruit production (Bertin 1990) and increase seed production and weight (Winsor et al. 1987; Bertin 1990) in flowering plants.

Plant community structure is known to have effects on fruit production. However, it is sometimes unclear whether these effects are a direct result of the plant community, or indirectly mediated via heterospecific pollen deposition. For example, Bach and Hruska (1981) demonstrated that cucumber yield was highest when grown in low density monocultures, and was lowest when grown in high density polycultures. Although both density and diversity had an impact on yield, plant diversity had a larger effect on reproduction than did cucumber density. Although the authors attributed patterns in cucumber reproductive performance to competition for resources among plant species, it is possible that heterospecific pollen deposition also contributed to depressed yield in high density polycultures. However, the types of pollen (i.e. conspecific or heterospecific) deposited on cucumber stigmas was not examined in the study.

In addition to plant community structure, heterospecific pollen deposition on an insect pollinated species depends on pollinator abundance, activity and behavior. The generalist habits of many pollinator species (Waser et al. 1996) may play an important role in pollen limitation, and hence the reproductive success of plants (Galen and Gregory 1989). Generalist pollinators do not have a specialized relationship with one or a few flowering plant species within a particular genus or family. Thus, it is likely that promiscuous pollinators may deposit relatively large amounts of heterospecific pollen on the stigma of a given plant species. In this way, the floral community of the area immediately surrounding a flowering plant may affect the distribution of stigmatic pollen and serve as a major cause of conspecific pollen limitation.

Studies on heterospecific pollen transfer usually focus on the effect of the pollen load or pollen type on seed production and fruit size (Galen and Gregory 1989; Caruso and Alfaro 2000). These studies often include carefully controlled applications of different ratios of conspecific pollen, in which the amount of heterospecific pollen is known. Relatively few studies, by comparison, have examined how flowering plant abundance influences heterospecific pollen deposition on stigmas in the field. Furthermore, no study has yet explored the degree to which heterospecific pollen transfer occurs among plants within urban community gardens. Urban community gardens are an ideal setting for investigating how flowering plant abundance impacts conspecific versus heterospecific pollen deposition, and ultimately, fruit production. Because these gardens are often utilized by local residents of diverse ethnic and cultural heritage (Shinew et al. 2004), a wide variety of ornamental flowers, fruits, and vegetables are cultivated. Thus, plant abundance and plant community structure is generally quite variable from garden to garden.

We studied the degree to which plant abundance and plant community structure in urban gardens in East Harlem and the Bronx (New York City) affects pollen deposition on cucumbers (Curcurbitaceae: *Cucumis sativis*). Specifically, we measured the area within gardens occupied by non-cucumber, flowering plants to assess the potential for heterospecific pollen deposition. The area within gardens occupied by cucumber plants was also quantified, to assess the potential for conspecific pollen deposition. We expected that the abundance of heterospecific pollen deposited on cucumber flower stigmas would increase as the area within a garden occupied by non-cucumber flowering plants increased. Likewise, we expected that conspecific pollen deposition would increase as the area within a garden occupied by cucumber plants increased. Finally, both conspecific and heterospecific pollen deposition were expected to be highest in large, relative to small, gardens.

8.2 METHODS

Female flowers from cucumber (*C. sativis*) plants were sampled from three community gardens in the Bronx, NY and four community gardens in East Harlem, NY (Table 1). These seven gardens were chosen as study sites because they varied in several potentially important variables that may impact conspecific and heterospecific pollen deposition, such as total garden area, the total space occupied by plants in bloom (floral area) and the total area occupied by cucumber plants (cucumber area). In addition

Table 1. Pearson correlation coefficients, and associated P values, for the variables garden area (i.e. 'Garden Area'), area of a garden with flowering plants in bloom (i.e. 'Floral Cover'), and area of a garden planted with cucumbers (i.e. 'Cucumber Area'). P values are for the null hypothesis of no correlation among garden variables. Sample size is n=25 for Floral Area and Cucumber area, and n=29 for Garden Area.

	Garden Area	**Floral Cover**	**Cucumber Area**
Garden Area	1.00	0.96 P <0.0001	0.84 P<0.0001
Floral Cover		1.00	0.96 P<0.0001
Cucumber Area			1.00

to these potentially important independent variables, garden access, permission to place cucumber plants in the garden and permission to harvest existing flowers from cucumber plants that were already established in a garden also influenced our choice of study sites.

8.2.1 CUCUMBER PLANTS

We chose to examine pollen deposition on *C. sativis* flowers because cucumbers generally require insects to carry pollen from male flowers to female flowers in order to set fruit, although both parthenocarpy and, on rare occasion, self-pollination in the absence of insects have been known to occur (Gingras et at. 1999). In addition to requiring pollination to set fruit, cucumbers were especially well suited to this study because they can be successfully grown in pots in a manner that requires relatively little space.

In non-gynoecious varieties of cucumbers, male flowers outnumber female flowers about ten to one and open about ten days prior to females. Both male and females flowers produce nectar to attract pollinators. Flowers are usually open and receptive to pollination for about one day. Because cucumber flowers are a comparatively poor source of pollen or nectar, bees readily switch to other flowers present in the vicinity, when available (Delaplane and Mayer 2000). The characteristics of cucumber flowers, as well as the behavior of pollinators associated with cucumbers, suggest that heterospecific pollen may readily be deposited on the stigmas of cucumber flowers.

8.2.2 SAMPLING PROTOCOL

Samples of whole, female flowers (including ovaries) were collected from each of the community garden study sites between July 12, 2006 and August 1, 2006. In all but two gardens (La Casita Community and East Harlem Council), the cucumber plants from which flowers were collected were planted in raised beds and tended to by community gardeners. No attempt was made to identify the variety of these cucumber plants. Fertilization and watering regimes were not standard, and were determined by the gardener that tended the plot in which the cucumbers were grown. Soils and compost superficially appeared to be similar among beds and among gardens. However, no attempt was made to identify the source or characteristics of the soils in which these cucumbers were growing.

In the two gardens where cucumbers were not already present, or in which permission was not granted to collect flowers from growing cucumber plants, we placed potted cucumber plants into the gardens. Three 30 liter pots, with three plants per pot, were placed into each of these two gardens. Cucumber plants were sown in the glasshouse of Fordham University's Louis Calder Biological Field Station from Martha Stewart EverydayTM 'Picklebush' Pickling Cucumber brand seeds. In early May 2006, two seeds were planted per three inch pot, in a 1:1 ratio of soil and vermiculite. Three pellets of Osmocote slow-release fertilizer were added to each pot. Seedlings were transplanted (three per pot) into 26 L (7 gal.) pots filled with a 3:1 mixture of Miracle-GroTM Garden Soil for Flowers and Vegetables (3:1:2 N:P:K) and ML Peat Moss manufactured by Nerom Peat Inc. A 2.5 cm layer of river pebbles were placed into the bottom of the pot, to aid with drainage. Plants were placed in the gardens on July 21, 2006, and were watered to saturation three times a week until flowers were collected on August 1, 2006.

Female flowers were collected at the first sign of petal senescence to assure that flowers had the opportunity to be visited by pollinating bees. Three to five flowers were collected from each of the 7 gardens. Flowers were separately placed in vials with 70% ethanol, and were stored in a freezer at -20° C until acetolysis (to separate pollen from other organic material) was performed.

8.2.3 GARDEN VARIABLES

Because our garden study sites were relatively small and rectangular in shape, the area of all gardens was measured directly. Garden area was chosen as an independent variable in this study because the amount of vegetation as well as the number of pollinators was expected to vary with garden size.

The area of each flower bed within a garden was also measured. For the purposes of this study, a flower bed was defined as a discrete area, in which flowering plants were being deliberately grown and tended to, for the purposes of aesthetics and/or food production. During the time that cucumber flowers were being sampled within a garden, the percent space within each flower bed that was covered by noncucumber plants in bloom was visually estimated. The area within each flower bed covered by these blooming plants was calculated as the product of the flower bed area and our visual estimate of the amount of space occupied by plants in bloom, summed across all flower beds within a garden, for each garden. This value is referred to as 'floral cover'. Within each garden, the total area covered by cucumber plants was measured directly, and is referred to as 'cucumber cover'. Due to our inability to gain access to the Garden of Happiness, to estimate and measure floral cover and cucumber cover, these variables were not determined for this garden.

8.2.4 ACETOLYSIS AND SLIDE PREPARATION

Acetolysis, a technique adapted by G. Robinson of Fordham University from Erdtman (1960), was performed on collected flowers to dissolve all organic matter, except for the sporopollinen that composes pollen's outer layer (i.e. the exine). This procedure allowed for the separation of the pollen from the organic matter of the flower as well as the rest of the pollen grain which otherwise may obstruct view of dichotomous traits. Pollen contents from each sample were then mounted on slides, identified, and counted.

Acetolysis was carried out in 15 mL centrifuge tubes made of polypropylene that could resist reactivity with the reagents. The process consisted of a series of "washes" in which 7 mL of a given reagent was added, the sample was briefly vortexed and then centrifuged for ten minutes. The supernatant was then decanted and the next reagent was added. For each flower harvested, the stigma and the petals were removed from the ovary and included in the acid digest. The ovary was discarded, but the alcohol that each ovary was stored in was included in the digest, to include pollen that may have detached from the stigma during transportation. The first wash consisted of 5% KOH, followed by two washes in distilled water. Next, the sample was washed in glacial acetic acid, followed by an acetic acid mixture which consisted of a 9:1 ratio of acetic anhydride to sulfuric acid. Samples were then placed in boiling water for 5 minutes prior to centrifugation. Another wash in glacial acetic acid was performed, followed by two washes in distilled water. Samples were washed in 5%KOH once more, before being placed in boiling water for another 5 minutes. Centrifugation followed this step. Three more washes in distilled water were performed, followed by the final wash in 95% ethanol. The samples were then centrifuged for 20 minutes, to ensure that all pollen grains were forced into the pellet. After the final centrifugation, the supernatant was decanted and the pellet was left in a sterile hood until nearly dry (24-48 hours). Once the pellet had nearly dried, 40 µL of 95% ethanol was added and the solution was briefly mixed to homogenize the distribution of pollen within the ethanol. At this point, each sample was ready for slide preparation.

Five reference slides were prepared from each sample digested. Slides were prepared using 5 µL of ethanol/pellet solution, as well as one drop of molten glycerin jelly mounting medium with phenosafranin stain. The slides were examined using a compound microscope set at 100x total magnification. All pollen grains on each slide were counted, and their conspecificity or heterospecificity to cucumbers was noted.

To aid in determining whether field collected pollen grains were from cucumber plants or noncucumber plants, a voucher slide was prepared from cucumber flowers that were hand-pollinated under glasshouse conditions, void of insect pollinators. Pollen was taken directly off of the anthers of male cucumber flowers using a clean, fine hair paintbrush. Pollen grains were then transferred to the stigma of a recently opened female flower. The stigma was removed immediately after hand-pollination, and stained with basic fucsin before being transferred to and compressed on a clean slide.

Pollen grains on this voucher slide all presented a single morphology. Because the flower from which this sample was prepared was pollinated under controlled conditions, where the possibility for heterospecific pollen deposition was excluded, it was concluded that the pollen grains were conspecific to cucumbers. The morphology of these pollen grains as being those of *C. sativis* was further confirmed by comparison to a photo taken by Halbritter (2000). Grains from the voucher sample differed from grains prepared from acetolysis, in that basic fucsin stained the grains dark purple so as they were opaque, while acetolysis combined with the phenosafranin stain dyed cucumber grains pink and transparent. Nonetheless, in both sample types, the basic size and morphology of the cucumber pollen grains was evident.

Pollen grains were identified as either conspecific or heterospecific based on their size and their morphology, as confirmed by the voucher slide. Cucumber pollen grains range from 51-100 μm in diameter (Halbritter 2000), and are triangular-ellipsoid in shape, with three pores per grain, such that a single pore occupies each triangular angle. Heterospecific pollen grains were not identified to species, but instead were identified as those pollen grains whose size or morphology was visibly different from cucumber pollen grains.

8.2.5 STATISTICAL ANALYSES

Pearson's correlation coefficient was computed to assess the correlation of garden area, floral cover and cucumber area with one another. Because each of the three garden variables was positively and significantly correlated with one another (Table 1), the effect of these variables on pollen deposition was independently assessed.

Least squares regression was used to independently assess the influence of garden area, floral cover, and cucumber area within gardens on the mean number of conspecific pollen grains deposited on cucumber stigmas per garden. A companion set of least squares regressions was used to independently assess the influence of garden area, floral cover and cucumber area on the mean number of heterospecific grains deposited on cucumber stigmas per garden. The pollen counts from the five reference slides prepared from each flower were averaged prior to analysis. These data were blocked by garden, for each analysis. To meet the regression assumption of homogeneity of residual variance, all data were square root transformed prior to analysis. Because we conducted a total of six linear regressions, and to control for type I error, alpha was set to PM0.008 for rejection of the null hypothesis (Bonferroni adjustment for multiple comparisons). All analyses were performed using SAS v 9.0 (2002).

8.3 RESULTS

The urban gardens where this study was conducted varied in their total area (range = 181 to 1651 m^2), floral cover (range = 4.61 to 94.37 m^2) and cucumber area (range = 0.73 to 15.47 m^2). However, the area of gardens was more equitably distributed among garden study sites than were floral cover or cucumber cover (Table 2).

Garden area had a positive and significant effect on conspecific ($F_{1,22}$=33.30, P<0.0001) and heterospecific ($F_{1,22}$=9.12, P=0.0063) pollen deposition on cucumber stigmas (Figure 1). Floral cover had a positive and significant effect on conspecific ($F_{1,19}$=35.89, P<0.0001), but not on heterospecific, pollen deposition ($F_{1,19}$=1.58, P=0.22) on cucumber stigmas (Figure 2). Similarly, cucumber area had a positive and significant effect on conspecific pollen deposition ($F_{1,19}$=34.78, P<0.0001), but not on heterospecific pollen deposition ($F_{1,19}$=0.82, P=0.38) on cucumber stigmas (Figure 3). Relative to garden area and floral cover, cucumber area had the strongest effect on conspecific pollen deposition (regression coefficient =

Table 2. Name, location, size, and ownership of garden study sites located in New York, NY. Floral cover and cucumber cover were not determined in Garden of Happiness, due to issues with garden access.

Community Garden Name	Location	Garden Area (m²)	Flower bed Area (m²)	Floral Cover (m²)	Cucumber Cover (m²)
Los Amigos	326 Pleasant Ave, Harlem	181	37.84	7.32	1.29
Peaceful Valley	E. 117th St., Harlem	224	40.20	4.61	1.90
La Casita	223 E 119th St., Harlem	312	78.35	14.59	0.73
East Harlem Council	E. 117th St., Harlem	525	181.03	36.13	7.57
Fordham Bedford Lot Busters	2593 Bainbridge Ave. Bronx	1036	221.09	34.61	2.76
Garden of Happiness	2156 Prospect Ave., Bronx	1440	616.62	Not Determined	Not Determined
Tremont	Corner of E. Tremont Ave. and Lafontaine Ave., Bronx	1651	453.40	94.37	15.47

1.05; Table 3). Cucumber area explained roughly 66% of the variation in conspecific pollen deposition on cucumber stigmas ($r^2=0.66$; Table 3).

Because the concentration of data points towards the lower range of floral cover and cucumber area resulted in Tremont Community Garden having a large influence on the outcome of regression analyses, the effects of garden area, floral cover and cucumber area on pollen deposition were reanalyzed, with data from Tremont removed. Removal of this data influenced the outcome of regression analyses (Table 4). The effects of cucumber area ($F_{1,15}=3.99$, P=0.064) and floral cover ($F_{1,15}=2.81$, P=0.11) on conspecific pollen deposition were no longer significant with the data from Tremont removed. The effect of garden area on conspecific ($F_{1,18}=12.73$, P=0.002) and heterospecific ($F_{1,18}=17.03$, P=0.0006) pollen deposition remained significant, with the data from Tremont removed. The effects of cucumber area ($F_{1,15}=5.05$, P=0.04) and floral cover ($F_{1,15}=2.02$, P=0.18) on heterospecific pollen deposition remained non-significant (at P=0.008 to reject H_0) with the data from Tremont removed.

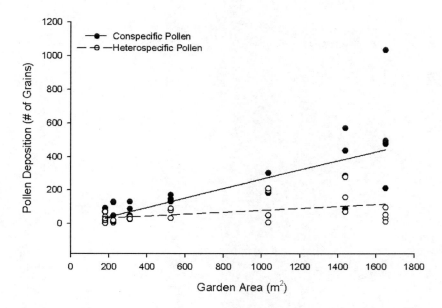

FIGURE 1: Mean number of conspecific and heterospecific pollen grains (± standard error bars) deposited on cucumber flowers, as a function of the area of the garden in which the cucumber flower was in bloom. The regression line modeling the effect of garden area on conspecific pollen deposition (y=0.01X+6.11) was significantly different from 0 (P<0.0001). Similarly, the regression line modeling the effect of garden area on heterospecific pollen deposition (y=0.002X+2.87)was significantly different from 0 (0.0063).

8.4 DISCUSSION

Because we were not able to estimate floral cover and cucumber cover in one of the larger gardens in this study (e.g. Garden of Happiness), we only had an estimate of these predictive variables for a single large garden. Consequently, most data were clustered towards the lower range for floral cover and cucumber cover, and the data from Tremont garden had a large

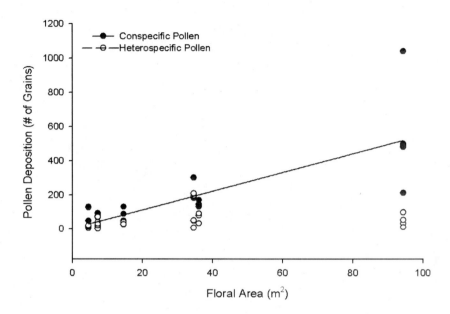

FIGURE 2: Mean number of conspecific and heterospecific pollen grains (± standard error bars) deposited on cucumber flowers, as a function of floral cover within the garden where the cucumber flower was in bloom. The regression line modeling the effect of floral cover on conspecific pollen deposition (y=0.16X+7.61) was significantly different from 0 ($P<0.0001$). There was no significant relationship between floral cover and heterospecific pollen deposition ($P<0.0401$; Bonferroni adjusted P to reject M0.008).

influence on the outcome of regression analyses. The results from this observational experiment should thus be interpreted with caution.

Pollen deposition, both conspecific and heterospecific grains, increased as garden size increased. This result was robust to the removal of the Tremont garden data. In addition, conspecific pollen deposition increased as the area of a garden planted with cucumbers increased. Unexpectedly, abundant floral cover (i.e. heterospecific plants) within a garden increased conspecific pollen deposition on cucumber plants.

That conspecific pollen deposition increases as floral cover increases suggests that heterospecific plants can have a positive effect on cucumber

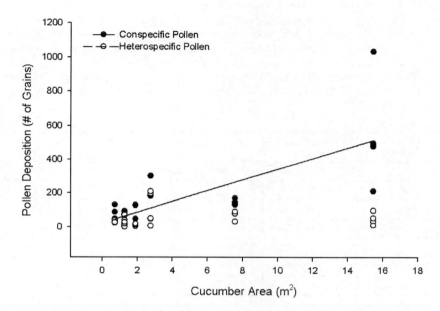

FIGURE 3: Mean number of conspecific and heterospecific pollen grains (± standard error bars) deposited on cucumber flowers, as a function of the area of cucumber plants growing within the garden where the sampled cucumber flower was in bloom. The regression line modeling the effect of cucumber area on conspecific pollen deposition (y=0.92X+0.38) was significantly different from 0 ($P<0.0001$). There was no significant relationship between cucumber area and heterospecific pollen deposition ($P=0.53$).

yield. A likely mechanism for this result is the positive effect of greater floral resources on pollinators, which may in turn have a positive effect on conspecific pollen deposition. In general, as floral abundance increases within an area, pollinator abundance and diversity increase (Potts et al. 2003; Fontaine et al. 2006; Herro 2006; Biesmeijer et al. 2006). It seems as if flowering plant abundance is important for attracting pollinators into the local vicinity of a garden. Once pollinators are attracted into a garden, cucumber plant abundance likely becomes an important factor dictating conspecific pollen deposition.

Table 3. Least squares regression results for the effect of garden area (i.e. 'Garden Area), area of a garden with flowering plants in bloom (i.e. 'Floral Cover'), and area of a garden planted with cucumbers (i.e. 'Cucumber Area) on conspecific, heterospecific and total pollen deposition on cucumbers. Prior to analysis, the data were square root transformed to meet the regression assumptions of homogeneous variance. To protect against Type 1 error, alpha was set to P$\leq$0.008 for rejection of the null hypothesis (Bonferroni adjustment for multiple comparisons). Those predictive variables that significantly influenced pollen deposition are marked with an asterisk(*).

Predictive Variable	Regression Line Equation	df	F value	P value	r^2
Conspecific Pollen Deposition					
Garden Area*	y=0.01X+6.11	1,22	33.3	<0.0001	0.64
Floral Cover*	y=0.16X+7.61	1,19	35.89	<0.0001	0.66
Cucumber Area*	y=1.05X+6.35	1,19	34.78	<0.0001	0.66
Heterospecific Pollen Deposition					
Garden Area*	y=0.002X+2.87	1,22	9.12	0.0063	0.50
Floral Cover	y=0.04X+3.21	1,19	1.58	0.2243	0.24
Cucumber Area	y=0.24X+2.92	1,19	0.82	0.3766	0.24

We hypothesize that the immediate area surrounding a given flower will have a large impact on the types of pollen deposited on cucumber stigmas, relative to the effects of plant community composition within the garden, as a whole. Monocultural patches have been shown to increase cucumber yield (Bach and Hruska 1981) which also suggests that if cucumber flowers are immediately surrounded by other cucumber flowers, more conspecific pollen will be deposited. Clumping groups of plants together, in species-specific patches, may optimize fruit and vegetable yield in urban gardens. Although this arrangement may seem obvious, in urban community gardens (where several gardeners independently manage small areas of the garden) fruit and vegetable plantings tend to be diffuse and scattered among garden plots, rather than clumped into single species beds. Whether such an arrangement indeed optimizes the effectiveness of insects as pollinators of these plants warrants further study.

Table 4. Least squares regression results for the effect of garden area (i.e. 'Garden Area), area of a garden with flowering plants in bloom (i.e. 'Floral Cover'), and area of a garden planted with cucumbers (i.e. 'Cucumber Area) on conspecific, heterospecific and total pollen deposition on cucumbers, with the data from Tremont Community garden excluded from the analysis. Prior to analysis, the data were square root transformed to meet the regression assumptions of homogeneous variance. To protect against Type 1 error, alpha was set to PM0.008 for rejection of the null hypothesis (Bonferroni adjustment for multiple comparisons). Those variables that significantly influenced pollen deposition are marked with an asterisk(*).

Predictive Variable	Regression Line Equation	df	F value	P value	r^2
Conspecific Pollen Deposition					
Garden Area*	y=0.01X+6.60	1,18	12.73	0.0022	0.47
Floral Cover	y=2.85X+2.94	1,15	69.60	0.0644	0.25
Cucumber Area	y=0.08X+7.97	1,15	1.27	0.3239	0.25
Heterospecific Pollen Deposition					
Garden Area*	y=0.01X+1.50	1,18	17.03	0.0006	0.52
Floral Cover	y=5.46X-6.99	1,15	5.05	0.0401	0.26
Cucumber Area	y=0.16X+2.66	1,15	2.02	0.1761	0.26

The number of bee visits required for optimal fruit set in cucumbers varies from study to study, and may be dependant on cucumber variety (Delaplane and Mayer 2000). However, multiple bee visits generally increases fruit set and the number of seeds per fruit (Collison 1976). Bumblebees are the most effective pollinators of cultivated cucumbers, although honey bees are also known to be effective (Gingras et al. 1999; Stanghellini et al. 1997, 2002). In urban gardens, sweat bees (*Lasioglossum sp.*) and bumble bees (*Bombus sp.*) are the most common visitors to cucumber flowers (Morath 2008; Langellotto unpublished data). Because foraging range generally scales with pollinator size (Gathmann and Tscharntke 2002), clumping plants into 'mini-monocultures' may enhance the effectiveness of smaller pollinators, such as the sweat bee.

Whether or not gardeners are able to clump their plants into 'mini-monocultures' is likely to be dictated by the total area of an individual garden. In gardens where more area was provided to individual gardeners (i.e. gardens with greater overall area) large patches of 'monoculture' were present, and larger amounts of conspecific pollen were deposited (Figs. 1 & 3). For example, gardeners working in the largest garden, the Tremont Community Garden, were able to plant cucumbers in monoculture patches averaging 2.58 m^2. Gardeners in the smallest garden, Los Amigos, only used patches averaging 0.65 m^2. Based on the results of this study, it may be beneficial for gardeners, especially those in smaller gardens, to work cooperatively and utilize the entire garden's available space to plant single monocultural patches for each crop, which could increase the amount of conspecific pollen received by flowers and increase yield.

In addition to serving as vital centers of social (Shinew et al. 2004) and civic (Schmelzkopf 1995) life in urban neighborhoods, community gardens can support local food production, and thus provide urban residents with access to a diversity of affordable produce (Baker 2004). This is particularly important in urban neighborhoods, where many community gardens were founded on vacant or abandoned lots in low to moderate-income neighborhoods (Pottharst 1995; Linn 1999). Local food production and access to a diverse array of quality and affordable produce is especially important in low income neighborhoods, where access to fresh food can be limited. For example, a survey of bodegas (i.e. small grocery stores) in the East Harlem neighborhood (where 4 of our study gardens were located) revealed that 40% failed to stock green vegetables and 26% failed to stock fresh fruit of any kind (Horowitz et al. 2004). Furthermore, quality and selection was variable in those stores that did stock fresh produce (Horowitz et al. 2004). Only 18% of East Harlem stores carried all foods recommended for a healthy diet compared to 58% of store in the prosperous Upper East Side (Horowitz et al. 2004). Studies that help improve the production of fruits and vegetables in urban community gardens may thus result in better access to healthy food choices.

REFERENCES

1. Ågren, J. 1996. Population size, pollinator limitation, and seed set in the self-incompatible herb, Lythrum salicaria. Ecology 77:1779-1790.

2. Bach, C.E. and A.J. Hruska. 1981. Effects of plant density on the growth, reproduction, and survivorship of cucumbers in monocultures and polycultures. Journal of Applied Ecology 18:929-943.
3. Baker, L.E. 2004. Tending cultural landscapes and food citizenship in Toronto's community gardens. Geographical Review 94:305-325.
4. Biesmeijer, J.C., S.P.M. Roberts, M. Reemer, R. Ohlemuller, M. Edwards, T. Peeters, A. P. Schaffers, S.G. Potts, R. Kleukers, C.D. Thomas, J. Settele, and W. E. Kunin. 2006. Parallel declines in pollinators and insect-pollinated plants in Britain and the Netherlands. Science 313:351-354.
5. Bertin, R.I. 1990. Effects of pollen intensity in Campsis radicans. American Journal of Botany 77:178-187.
6. Bierzychudek, P. 1981. Pollinator limitation of plant reproductive effort. The American Naturalist 117:838-840.
7. Caruso, C.M. and M. Alfaro. 2000. Interspecific pollen transfer as a mechanism of competition: Effect of Castilleja linariafolia pollen on seed set of Ipomopsis aggregata. Canadian Journal of Botany 78:600-606.
8. Collison, C.H. 1976. The interrelationships of honey bee activity, foraging behavior, climatic conditions, and flowering in the pollination of pickling cucumbers, Cucumis sativus L. Ph.D. Dissertation, Michigan State University, Lansing, MI.
9. Delaplane, K.S. and D.F. Mayer. 2000. Crop Pollination by Bees. CABI Publishing, Wallingford, UK and New York, USA. 352 pp.
10. Erdtman, G. 1960. The acetolysis method: a revised description. Svensk Botanisk Tidskrift 54:561-564.
11. Fontaine, C., I. Dajoz, J. Meriguet, and M. Loreau. 2006. Functional diversity of plant-pollinator interaction webs enhances the persistence of plant communities. Public Library of Science Biology 4:129-135.
12. Galen, C. and T. Gregory. 1989. Interspecific pollen transfer as a mechanism of competition: Consequences of foreign pollen contamination for seed set in the alpine wildflower, Polemonium viscosum. Oecologia 81:120-123.
13. Gathmann A. and T. Tscharntke. 2002. Foraging ranges of solitary bees. Journal of Animal Ecology 71:757-764.
14. Gingras, D., J. Gingras, and D. De Oliveira. 1999. Visits of honeybees (Hymenoptera: Apidae) and their effects on cucumber yields in the field. Journal of Economic Entomology 92:435-438.
15. Halbritter, H. 2000. Cucumis sativis. In: Buchner R. and M. Weber. PalDat – a palynological database: Descriptions, illustration, identification, and information retrieval. http://www.paldat.org/ (accessed 06/20/2006).
16. Herro, A. 2006. Bee and wildflower diversity decline together. World Watch 19:6.
17. Horowitz, C.R., K.A. Colson, P.L. Herbert, and K. Lancaster. 2004. Barriers to buying healthy foods for people with diabetes: evidence of environmental disparities. Journal of Public Health 94:1549- 1554.
18. Knight, T.M., J.A. Steets, J.C. Varmosi, S.J. Mazer, M. Burd, D.R. Campbell, M.R. Dudash, M.O. Johnston, R.J. Mitchell, and T.L. Ashman. 2005. Pollen limitation of plant reproduction: Pattern and process. Annual Review of Ecology, Evolution and Systematics 36:467-497.

19. Dudash, M.O. Johnston, R.J. Mitchell, and T. Ashman. 2005. Pollen limitation of plant reproduction: pattern and process. Annual Review of Ecology Evolution and Systematics. 36:467-497.
20. Linn, K. 1999. Reclaiming the sacred commons. New Village 1:42-49.
21. Matteson, K.C. 2007. Diversity and conservation of insects in urban gardens: theoretical and applied implications. Ph.D. Dissertation, Fordham University, Bronx, NY.
22. Morath, S.U. 2008. The effect of alternative floral resources on the pollination of cucumbers (Cucumis sativus) in New York City Community Gardens. M.S. Thesis, Fordham University, Bronx, NY.
23. Pottharst, K. 1995. Urban dwellers and vacant lots: partners in pride. Parks and Recreation 30:94-101.
24. Potts, S.G., B. Vulliamy, A. Dafni, G. Ne'eman, and P. Willmer. 2003. Linking bees and flowers: how do floral communities structure pollinator communities? Ecology 84: 2628-2642.
25. SAS. 2002. SAS/STAT user's guide. V 9.0. SAS Institute, Cary, North Carolina, USA.
26. Schmelzkopf, K. 1995. Urban community gardens as contested space. Geographic Review 85:364-381.
27. Shinew, K.J., T.D. Glover, and D.C. Parry. 2004. Leisure spaces as potential sites for interracial interaction: community gardens in urban Areas. Journal of Leisure Research 36:336-355.
28. Stanghellini, M. S., J. Tambrose, and J.R. Schultheis. 1997. The effects of honey bee and bumble bee pollination on fruit set and abortion of cucumber and watermelon. American Bee Journal 137: 386-391.
29. ———. 2002. Diurnal activity, floral visitation and pollen deposition by honey bees and bumble bees on field-grown cucumber and watermelon Journal of Apicultural Research 41: 27-34.
30. Waser, N. M., L. Chittka, M. V. Price, N. M. Williams, and J. Ollerton. 1996. Generalization in pollination systems, and why it matters. Ecology 77:1043-1060.
31. Winsor, J.A., L.E. Davis, and A.G. Stephenson. 1987. The relationship between pollen load and fruit maturation and the effect of pollen load on offspring vigor in Cucurbita pepo. The American Naturalist 129:643-656.

PART III

PLANNING ISSUES

CHAPTER 9

Bumble Bee Abundance in New York City Community Gardens: Implications for Urban Agriculture

KEVIN C. MATTESON AND GAIL A. LANGELLOTTO

9.1 INTRODUCTION

It is estimated that 15% of the world's food is produced within a variety of landscapes generally classified as 'urban' (Armar-Klemesu 2000). Urban agriculture is especially common in developing countries (van Veenhuizen 2000). However, crops are increasingly grown in industrialized nations as well, predominantly in community, residential and rooftop gardens (Lawson 2005). Vegetables and fruits grown in gardens and other urban green spaces provide food security for those living in poverty (Brown and Jameton 2000) and nutrition for many who live in neighborhoods that lack affordable sources of fresh produce (Horowitz et al. 2004).

In community gardens of New York City, a variety of plants are grown specifically for the edible fruits, seeds, or leaves that they yield. Successful fruit and seed production in many of these crops is dependent on bee

---

© Matteson, K.C. and Langellotto, G.A. 2009. Bumble Bee Abundance in New York City Community Gardens: Implications for Urban Agriculture. Cities and the Environment. 2(1):article 5. Creative Commons Attribution license (http://creativecommons.org/licenses/by/3.0/).

pollination (Klein et al. 2007); an ecosystem service that may be limited in the urban environment (Costanza et al. 1997). Honey bee hives are often placed into agricultural fields to supplement the pollination services for a variety of fruit-producing crops. In urban landscapes however, cultivated colonies of the European honey bee, *Apis mellifera* Linnaeus, 1758 (managed by recreational apiculturists), are a rare means of fostering crop pollination. As of March 2009, maintaining honey bee colonies is illegal in New York City, although a number of apiculturists nevertheless manage colonies in rooftop, community and private gardens throughout the five boroughs. In addition, some feral *A. mellifera* colonies can be found in city parks. While the presence of these colonies maintains a moderate abundance of *A. mellifera* workers in community gardens, pollination in urban gardens is likely more dependent on numerous 'wild' bees that naturally persist in heavily developed areas of the city (Matteson et al. 2008 and Figure 1, this paper).

Over 50 bee species have been documented within the community gardens of New York City (Matteson et al. 2008), including five species of bumble bee. The most abundant native bee is the common eastern bumble bee, *Bombus impatiens* Cresson 1863, which was the only bee observed in all community gardens sampled (N = 19) (Matteson et al. 2008) and which may be an especially important pollinator of crops in urban gardens (Figure 2). *Bombus impatiens* workers have been demonstrated to be effective alternates to *Apis mellifera* for pollination of greenhouse sweet peppers (Meisels and Chiasson 1997) and greenhouse tomatoes (Morandin et al. 2001) as well as field-grown blueberries (Stubbs and Drummond 2001), cucumbers and watermelon (Stanghellini et al. 2002). In addition, *B. impatiens* has been observed gathering pollen and/or nectar from a variety of crop flowers including cucumbers, tomatoes, eggplants, peppers, raspberries and more in New York City community gardens (Matteson, personal observations). Finally, in New York State, *B. impatiens* flies from April to November (with only *Apis mellifera* having a longer flight season) (Giles and Ascher 2006), suggesting that *B. impatiens* pollinates a variety of crops and other plants that flower throughout the growing season.

Although bumble bee workers in more natural landscapes have been found to forage several hundred meters from their nests (Dramstad 1996; Osborne et al. 1999; Walther-Hellwig and Frankl 2000), streets, buildings,

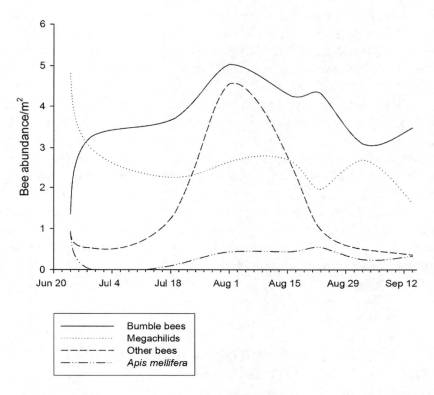

FIGURE 1: Relative abundance of four groups of bees in New York City community gardens from June to September 2005. Bee abundance was determined during 60 second observations of 1-m² quadrats placed in sunlit flower beds with at least 60% of flowers in bloom. Relative abundance per date is the average of all observations taken on that date across 18 community gardens in the Bronx and East Harlem. 'Other bees' include *Andrena*, *Mellisodes* and *Xylocopa* but not smaller bees in the genera *Hylaeus*, *Lasioglossum* or *Ceratina*.

car traffic and other hazards may limit bumble bee movements in urban landscapes. In order for *B. impatiens* bumble bees to effectively pollinate crop plants for food production, they must consistently visit individual urban gardens, or else effectively move among several garden sites to forage from and pollinate crop plants. However, the fragmented and dispersed nature of gardens and other green spaces within urban areas suggests that bumble bees may consistently forage within a single or a few gardens. A better understanding of bumble bee movement in urbanized landscapes may enable better management of pollinating species and ecosystem services they provide.

In this study, we investigated bumble bee abundance and movement within and between urban gardens. Specifically, we estimated the number of *B. impatiens* workers supported by individual gardens and evaluated the degree to which they were consistently found within a single garden, versus moved between adjacent gardens. In addition, we surveyed gardens in East Harlem and the Bronx (New York City), and compiled a list of edible crop plants that were being cultivated in these gardens. Using the literature, we determined the degree to which these crops depend upon bee pollination, and the degree to which bumble bees may foster pollination and food production in urban gardens.

9.2 METHODS

9.2.1 INCIDENCE AND POLLINATION DEPENDENT CROPS IN COMMUNITY GARDENS

There are over 700 community gardens in New York City (Matteson 2007). Between May and September of 2005, we surveyed crop plants grown in 19 community gardens located in the Bronx and East Harlem (Manhattan) in New York City. In order to represent the diversity of gardens in NYC, gardens were chosen that varied widely in size (range of 224 to 2188 m^2) and gardener management (amount of floral area, degree of disturbance, etc.). The mean area (910 m^2 ± 540 m^2, mean ± SD) of the 19 sampled gardens was similar to the mean size of all community gardens, across New York City (704 m^2 ± 856 m^2, mean ± SD) (Matteson 2007). Crops grown within community gardens often reflect the cultural heritage of the gardeners and the gardens sampled in this study were predominantly managed by gardeners of African and Latin American heritage. Therefore, there may be other crops not found during our survey, especially within New York

FIGURE 2: The development of many crops grown in community gardens benefits from pollination by bees. The common eastern bumble bee *Bombus impatiens* is shown here on an eggplant flower.

City community gardens managed by gardeners with other ethnic and cultural backgrounds.

We calculated the incidence of each crop as the number of gardens where the crop was grown, divided by the 19 surveyed gardens. In a recent review, Klein et al. (2007) classify the benefits of animal pollination for a variety of crops. For each crop, Klein et al. (2007) classified the 'positive impact by animal pollination' based on the reduction in crop yield when animal pollinators are absent as follows: *little*- absence of animal pollinators results in 0-<10% yield reduction (as determined by reductions in seed or fruit set, seed quality or fruit weight); *modest*- 10-<40% reduction; *great*- 40-<90% reduction; *essential*- J90% reduction. We classified crops in community gardens not included in Klein et al. (2007) as "*important*" if they were included in Corbet et al. (1991) or Morse and Calderone (2000).

9.2.2 BUMBLE BEE MARK-RECAPTURE

From 21 August through 12 September 2005, bumble bees were captured and marked in a subset of three community gardens in the Bronx (Fordham Bedford Lot Busters, Tremont Community Garden, Garden of Happiness) and three community gardens in East Harlem (Holy Rosary Garden, El Sitio Feliz/Union Settlement, El Gallo Social Club). The short study period precluded estimating birth rates, death rates or changes in population size throughout the season or between years. However, as part of a separate study, we measured relative abundance of bee groups in these gardens (including bumble bees, *Apis mellifera*, Megachilidae and other bees) from June to September in 2005. The results of this separate study (briefly presented here in Figure 1) indicate that bumble bee abundance in these community gardens (which included other bumble bee species in addition to *B. impatiens*) peaked in early August 2005 and declined slightly during the time period of the mark-recapture experiment in late August and September. Therefore, the estimated abundance presented in this paper can be interpreted as an underestimation of peak abundance of *B. impatiens* during one year in NYC community gardens.

All sampling took place on warm, sunny days between 10:00 and 18:00. Bees were captured with a hand-net and then carefully transferred into small glass vials which were placed in a cooler with ice. After approximately two minutes of cooling, the bees were inactive for a short time period (~30 seconds), making it possible to mark the dorsal thorax using a permanent paint pen (Uchida of America, Corp., Torrance, CA). In order to identify the garden in which each bumble bee was marked during later censuses, we used a different color pen for each garden site. After marking, bees were allowed to warm in the sunlight and fly away. We visited each of the six marking locations (gardens) as well as 12 other nearby gardens every 2-3 days, during which time we visually inspected all bumble bees for marks. Locations of all 18 gardens are reported in Matteson et al. (2008). In addition, maps of these gardens (and all community gardens in NYC) can be found by accessing http://www.oasisnyc.net/. The linear distance between the three marking locations and the other gardens visited in the Bronx ranged from 180 to 2970 m (mean distance = 1440 m).

In East Harlem, marking gardens were located between 240 and 1490 m from the other sampled gardens (mean distance = 830 m).

There are many formulas that estimate abundance of organisms within a focal location. Most of these are derivations of simple estimators that use the ratio of the total number of previously marked individuals to the number of individuals recaptured with marks. As a simple example, imagine that ten individuals are marked on the first day of a study. If on the second day eight individuals are captured, two of which have marks, then the estimate of abundance for that location would be: $(10 * 8)/2 = 40$ individuals. Because we conducted mark-recapture sampling over several occasions, we used Schumacher's method (Krebs 1989) to estimate worker populations in gardens. This method is similar to the above formula, but summed and averaged across several marking periods. To account for the potential effects of differences in garden size on our estimate of bumble bee abundance within gardens, we also calculated the number of bees per meter squared of garden area, by dividing our estimate of bumble bee abundance by the total area of a garden. There are several assumptions of the Schumacher method (and other mark-recapture methods). Specific to the calculations we used, it is assumed that animals are equally catchable and that there are no deaths, births, emigration or immigration within the population during the time frame of the study (Krebs 1989). Although our study was conducted over a short time period (~3 weeks), it is still likely that some individuals entered (via birth or immigration) or exited (via death or emigration) the population during the study.

9.3 RESULTS

9.3.1 INCIDENCE AND POLLINATION DEPENDENCE OF CROPS GROWN IN COMMUNITY GARDENS

On average, 23% of the area of the surveyed NYC community gardens was used for vegetable beds (range of 3% to 48%, N = 18) (Matteson 2007). Within these vegetable beds, we conservatively documented 25 crops (Table 1). Commonly grown crops included hot and sweet peppers, mints and other herbs, kale and collards, tomatoes and tomatillos, strawberries and cucumbers (Table 1). Although some crops were found in over three quarters of surveyed gardens, these may not provide the greatest yield if plants are small and not grown in mass. For instance, peach and apple trees (found in 61% of the sampled gardens) yield more fruit than sweet and hot peppers, which were grown in 100% of the sampled gardens.

Those crops from which fruits are harvested (e.g. cucumbers, strawberries, zucchini) are most likely to be directly affected by animal pollination. Specifically, the crops most likely to suffer reduced yield in the absence of animal pollinators include gourds such as pumpkins, squash and zucchini, cucumbers and fruits such as peaches, apples, plums and raspberries (Table 1). The harvest of crops from which edible leaves are consumed (e.g. kale, collards, herbs) may not be directly affected by animal pollination within gardens, because many gardeners buy new seeds each year. However, pollination may be important even for crops with edible leaves if gardeners allow plants to set seed and collect seeds for future planting.

9.3.2 BUMBLE BEE MARK-RECAPTURE

Bumble bees were abundant in gardens and were observed visiting flowers of 78% of pollination-dependent crops (Table 1). During the course of the mark-recapture experiment, a total of 229 *B. impatiens* workers were marked in six community gardens. Marking sessions in gardens typically lasted ~30 minutes during which time an average of 12 *B. impatiens* (range of 8 to 22; N = 7 marking periods) were captured and marked. Of those marked, 102 individual workers were recaptured (45%). Recapture rates in individual gardens ranged from 30% to 68% (Table 2). There were no captures of *B. impatiens* bumble bees in any gardens other than those in which they were originally marked.

Estimates of the number of *B. impatiens* using community gardens ranged from 46 to 164 workers (mean of 88) per garden (Table 2). These estimates of bumble bee abundance are surprisingly high considering the small size of these gardens (the six marking gardens had a mean area of 1320 m^2, range of 640 to 2188 m^2). Taking garden area into account resulted in estimates of 3 to 15 *B. impatiens* workers (mean of 8) per 100 m^2 of total garden area (Table 2). When omitting the area of gardens without flower beds (ornamental, crop or unmanaged), the estimated density during this time period increased to 6 to 29 *B. impatiens* workers (mean of 15) per 100 m^2 of garden floral area.

Table 1. Crops commonly grown in New York City community gardens and their dependence on animal pollination. Crops are listed by the percentage of gardens in which they were grown (out of 19 total gardens surveyed in the Bronx and East Harlem). Classification of 'positive impact by animal pollination' follows Klein et al. (2007), unless otherwise noted, and is based on the reduction in crop yield when animal pollinators are absent (as determined by seed or fruit set, seed quality or fruit weight). The category entitled 'Bumble bee visitation observed in NYC community gardens?' is based on informal observations conducted by the first author during five years of field work in these gardens.

Crops grown in NYC community gardens	Crop scientific name	% of gardens growing (N = 19)	Plant part harvested	Positive impact by animal pollination	Bumble bee visitation observed in NYC community gardens?
Bell pepper, Chile pepper	*Capsicum frutescens, C. annuum*	100	Fruit	Little	Yes
Mints, Oregano, Basil	*Mentha spp., Origanum vulgare, Ocimum basilicum*	100	Leaves	"Important"[a,b]	Yes
Kale/collards	*Brassica chinensis*	94	Leaves	"Important"[a,c]	Yes[d]
Tomato, Tomatillos	*Lycopersicon esculentum*	89	Fruit	Little	Yes[e]
Strawberry	*Fragaria spp.*	83	Fruit	Modest	No
Cucumber (Gherkin)	*Cucumis sativus*	78	Fruit	Great	Yes
Lettuce	*Lactuca sativa*	72	Leaves	"Important"[a,b]	Yes[d]
Cilantro/Coriander	*Coriandrum sativum*	67	Leaves/seeds	Great[a]	Yes
Beans	*Phaseolus spp.*	67	Fruit	Little	Yes
Peach	*Prunus persica*	61	Fruit	Great	No[g]
Apple	*Malus domesticus*	61	Fruit	Great	No[g]

Table 1. Continued.

Sunflower	*Helianthus annuus*	56	Seeds	Modest	Yes [f]
Broccoli	*Brassica oleracea*	44	Stalk, buds	"Important" [a,b]	No [d]
Eggplant	*Solanum melongena*	33	Fruit	Modest	Yes
Table grape/Vine grape	*Vitis vinifera*	28	Fruit	No increase	No
Okra/Gumbo	*Abelmoschus esculentus*	28	Fruit	Modest	Yes
Corn	*Zea mays*	22	Fruit	No increase	No [h]
Pumpkin, Squash, Zucchini	*Cucurbita maxima, C. mixta, C. pepo*	17	Fruit	Essential	Yes
Plum	*Prunus domestica*	11	Fruit	Great	No [g]
Raspberry	*Rubus idaeus*	11	Fruit	Great	Yes

a For seed production
b Source: Corbet et al. (1991)
c Source: Morse and Calderone (2000)
d Although kale/collards and lettuces are rarely allowed to go to flower in community gardens
e Very high bumble bee abundance and visitation. Bumble bees are important pollinators of tomatoes because they 'buzz-pollinate' (vibrate wings while visiting the flower) which facilitates the release of pollen from poricidal anthers.
f Very high bumble bee abundance and visitation. Two long-horned bees, *Melissodes agilis* and *M. bimaculatus* (Apidae), also were commonly observed visitors of sunflowers.
g These fruit trees flower early (April-May) and therefore are dependent on bees most active during this time period (*B. impatiens* flies during this time period but is less abundant). Andrenidae also are active during this period but few have been documented in these gardens (Matteson et al. 2008). *Apis mellifera, Bombus griseocollis,* flower flies (Syrphidae: Diptera) and other early pollinators may be of special importance for these crops.
h Wind-pollinated

Table 2. Garden marking sites, garden area, and the total number of bees marked and recaptured within New York City community gardens from 21 August 2005 through 12 September 2005. Estimated bee abundance was determined using Shumacher's method.

Community garden name	Garden area (m²)	Total number of bees marked	Number of bees recaptured	Percent of bees recaptured	Estimated bee abundance per garden (95% confidence interval)	Bee density per 100 m²
Fordham Bedford Lot Busters	1036	30	19	63%	46 (29 - 105)	4
El Sitio Feliz (Union Settlement)	1527	28	19	68%	50 (37 - 76)	3
Holy Rosary Garden	759	32	10	31%	60 (48 - 79)	8
El Gallo Social Club	640	27	8	30%	99 (72 - 157)	15
Tremont Community Garden	1651	45	23	51%	108 (80 - 167)	7
Garden of Happiness	1440	67	23	34%	164 (116 - 279)	11

9.4 DISCUSSION

Pollination by bees and other pollinators has the potential to increase production of several crops commonly grown in community gardens of New York City, including peaches, apples, strawberries, tomatoes, peppers, cucumbers and zucchini. Although gardeners tend to recognize the general role of bees in crop production, few realize the degree to which certain crops benefit from pollination by bees and other insects (Matteson, personal observation). Therefore, it is important to promote increased awareness of the specific benefits provided to humans by urban pollinators. Furthermore, while gardeners have traditionally focused gardening efforts on watering, composting, fertilizing and weeding of vegetable beds, an additional activity that may contribute to a productive garden is management of the garden to increase bee diversity or abundance. Inclusion of garden pollinator conservation under the auspices of a productive garden may be an effective means of fostering greater involvement in urban ecology and conservation.

In addition, it is important to increase awareness of pollinators other than the European honey bee (*Apis mellifera*), particularly in non-agricultural settings such as cities where there are few managed honey bee colonies. Over 220 bee species have been documented in the New York City limits (Giles and Ascher 2006) with 54 species found specifically within New York City community gardens (Matteson et al. 2008). Many of these species are known to be important pollinators (see discussion below) and many are more abundant than *A. mellifera* in this system (Matteson et al. 2008). Specifically, the relative abundance of bumble bees in these gardens was more than five times greater than *A. mellifera* (Figure 1).

Our estimates of bumble bee abundance were surprisingly high, particularly given the urban locality and small sizes of the surveyed gardens (range of 640 to 2188 m^2). Specifically, we estimated that florally rich community gardens may be utilized by over 100 bumble bee workers, with a density of 8 bumble bees per 100 m^2 of garden area. In comparison, grassland habitats in Sweden were found to have a mean density of less than 1 bumble bee per 100 m^2 (Öckinger and Smith 2007). Similarly, relatively fewer bumble bees (4 to 5 per sampling date) were found in 400 m2 plots within agricultural fields in England, UK (Carvell et al. 2004). This is not the only study to find an abundance of bumble bees in urban habitats. In a study of *Bombus terrestris* (Linnaeus, 1758), Goulson et al. (2002) found greater diversity of pollen and over all colony growth in suburban landscapes than in agricultural landscapes. In a genetic analysis, Chapman et al. (2003) estimated that urban cemeteries and public parks in London (each being roughly 1 ha in size) support over 50 separate bumble bee colonies and concluded that urban habitats support large bumble bee populations. The abundance of some bumble bees in urbanized landscapes may partially be due to the diversity and abundance of floral resources in gardens (Owen 1991) and other urban green spaces (Chapman et al. 2003).

We did not conduct supplementary hand pollination experiments or search vegetable beds for aborted fruits. Therefore, we cannot rule out the possibility that, despite the abundance of *B. impatiens* in these gardens, pollination by bees is a limiting service for crop production in these gardens. Nevertheless, our results suggest that there may be a sufficient abundance of bumble bees (in addition to other pollinating insects in urban gardens) to provide pollination services to many crops grown in community gardens. It is estimated that five bumble bee workers are needed to provide sufficient pollination for 100 m^2 of greenhouse tomatoes (Morandin et al. 2001), which is fewer than the minimum estimated worker abundance (6 per 100 m^2 of floral area) in these gardens. In addition, most community gardens are small relative to agricultural fields and few are intensively utilized for agricultural production, further suggesting that pollination services may not be limited in this setting.

Although some gardens were located within foraging range of each other (<500 m), no *B. impatiens* workers were found to move between gardens of their own accord in the mark-recapture experiment. We are not aware of any specific estimates of *B. impatiens* foraging range, but the maximum foraging range of four other bumble bee species in an agricultural landscape ranged from 449 m (for *B. pascuorum*) to 758 m (for *B. terrestris*) (Knight et al. 2005). While this suggests that *B. impatiens* may be capable of moving among gardens and other urban green spaces, optimal foraging theory suggests that bumble bees will gather the maximum amount of pollen attainable with minimum flight effort (Heinrich 1979). In addition, floral and patch constancy, whereby individual workers revisit the same flowers or area, is common in many bumble bee species and habitats (Bowers 1985; Heinrich 1979; Osborne and Williams 2001). *Bombus impatiens* is a generalist bumblebee (Heinrich 1979) and workers have been observed visiting both crop and ornamental flowers in these gardens. Because many ornamental garden flowers (e.g. marigolds, zinnias, coneflowers, sunflowers) bloom for relatively long periods, urban gardens may provide a relatively constant source of nectar and pollen. Similar to our results in the urban landscape, workers of *Bombus flavifrons* Cresson, 1863 in the Uinta Mountains of Utah were recaptured only in the meadow in which they were marked, despite proximity of the meadows to each other (Bowers 1985). It was concluded that the mountain meadows represented discrete systems of plant-pollinator interactions (Bowers 1985). This may also be the case for bumble bees in community gardens and other florally rich urban green spaces, at least over some time periods. Supporting this notion, a study in a Massachusetts suburb also found high levels of patch constancy of bumble bees, including *B. impatiens*, foraging on patches of flowering pepperbush (Bhattacharya et al. 2003).

We did not conduct a systematic search for bumble bee nests which may be inconspicuous even in heavily utilized garden habitats (Matteson, personal observation), particularly if located in tree cavities. Nevertheless, over the course of five years of data collection, no bumble bee nests were observed in these community gardens or reported to us by the gardeners that actively manage these sites. In addition, bumble bees were often observed to fly up and away from gardens after foraging on flowers within gardens, suggesting that bumble bee nests are located outside of gardens. Bumble bees are known to use tree cavities and rodent burrows for colony nesting sites (Kearns and Thomson 2001). Nesting sites in street trees or trees in other urban green spaces may be less likely to be disturbed by humans, relative to nests within gardens in burrows in the ground. Alternately, bumble bees may be dependent on larger urban parks for relatively undisturbed ground nesting sites (McFrederick and Lebuhn 2006). Several large city parks and green spaces (including the Bronx Zoo, the New York Botanical Garden, Crotona Park, Central Park and Marcus Garvey Park) were located between 100 and 700 m from the community gardens of this study. Therefore, depending on the foraging capabilities of *B. impatiens* in the urbanized landscape, workers may 'commute' from colonies located in parks or other urban green spaces (e.g. vacant lots, greenways, etc.) to forage in florally rich urban garden patches.

Several other insects, besides *B. impatiens*, may be important pollinators in urban community gardens of New York City. Although less abundant overall, *Bombus griseocollis* (DeGeer, 1773) is abundant earlier in the growing season (May-June, as opposed to *B. impatiens* which peaks from late June through August) and therefore may be an important pollinator of early flowering crops. In addition, three leaf-cutter bees (Megachilidae) were especially abundant in these gardens (Matteson et al. 2008). These include (in order of abundance in the community gardens), *Megachile centuncularis* (Linnaeus, 1758), *M. texana* Cresson, 1878 and the introduced alfalfa leaf-cutter bee, *M. rotundata* (Fabricius, 1793) (Matteson et al. 2008). Leaf-cutter bees are medium-sized bees that carry pollen on the ventral side of their abdomen, thereby easily transmitting pollen to female flowers. Small-bodied bees (*Lasioglossum*, *Hylaeus*, *Ceratina*) also were abundant in these gardens (Matteson et al. 2008) and New York City parks (Yurlina 1998) but may be less efficient pollinators on a per visit basis because they carry less pollen and are less likely to come into contact with anthers and/or stigmas (Kandori 2002). *Hylaeus spp.* (Colletidae) may be especially inefficient pollinators because they transport pollen internally (in their crop) and have relatively few body hairs and no external pollen-transmitting structures (Michener 2000). Nevertheless, 'inefficient pollinators' may still be important to the reproductive success of plants if the pollinators are extremely abundant (Olsen 1997) as is the case with these groups in NYC community gardens and parks. Finally, other insects such as butterflies, flies and some wasps may be important pollinators in this system. In particular, flower flies (Diptera: Syrphidae) were observed on a variety of flowers in these community gardens and were particularly abundant during cooler days when bees were less active (Matteson, personal observation). More studies, specifically linking abundance and diversity of urban pollinators to pollen movement among crop and other flowers, will add to our understanding of the ecosystems service of pollination within cities.

REFERENCES

1. Armar-Klemesu, M., 2000. Urban agriculture and food security, nutrition and health, pp 99-117. In Bakker, N., M. Dubbeling, S. Guendel, U. Sabel Koschella, and H. de Zeeuw (Eds). Growing Cities, Growing Food, Urban Agriculture on the Policy Agenda. DSE, Feldafing, Germany. http://www.ruaf.org/node/58 (accessed 06/08/2008).
2. Bhattacharya, M., R.B. Primack, and J. Gerwein. 2003. Are roads and railroads barriers to bumblebee movement in a temperate suburban conservation area? Biological Conservation 109:37-45.
3. Bowers, M.A. 1985. Bumble bee colonization, extinction, and reproduction in subalpine meadows in Northeastern Utah. Ecology 66:914-927.
4. Brown, K.H., and A.L. Jameton. 2000. Public health implications of urban agriculture. Journal of Public Health Policy 21:20-39.
5. Carvell, C., W.R. Meek, R.F. Pywell, and M. Nowakowski. 2004. The response of foraging bumblebees to successional change in newly created arable field margins. Biological Conservation 118:327-339.
6. Chapman, R.E., J. Wang, and A.F.G. Bourke. 2003. Genetic analysis of spatial foraging patterns and resource sharing in bumblebee pollinators. Molecular Ecology 12:2801-2808.
7. Corbet, S.A., I.H. Williams, and J.L. Osborne. 1991. Bees and the pollination of crops and wild flowers in the European community. Bee World 72:47-59.
8. Costanza, R., R. d'Arge, R.d. Groot, S. Farber, M. Grasso, B. Hannon, K. Limburg, S. Naeem, R.V. O'Neill, J. Paruelo, R.G. Raskin, P. Sutton, and M.v.d. Belt. 1997. The values of the world's ecosystem services and natural capital. Nature 387:253-260.
9. Dramstad, W.E., 1996. Do bumble bees (Hymenoptera: Apidae) really forage close to their nests? Journal of Insect Behavior 9:163-182.
10. Giles, V., and J.S. Ascher. 2006. A survey of the bees of the Black Rock Forest Preserve, New York (Hymenoptera: Apoidea). Journal of Hymenoptera Research 15:208-231.
11. Goulson, D., W.O.H. Hughes, L.C. Derwent, and J.C. Stout. 2002. Colony growth of the bumblebee, Bombus terrestris, in improved and conventional agricultural and suburban habitats. Oecologia 130:267-273.
12. Heinrich, B. 1979. Bumblebee Economics. Harvard University Press, Cambridge, Massachusetts, USA.
13. Horowitz, C.R., K.A. Colson, P.L. Hebert, and K. Lancaster. 2004. Barriers to buying healthy foods for people with diabetes: evidence of environmental disparities. American Journal of Public Health 94:1549-1554.
14. Kandori, I. 2002. Diverse visitors with various pollinator importance and temporal change in the important pollinators of Geranium thunbergii (Geraniaceae). Ecological Research 17:283-294.
15. Kearns, C.A., and J.D. Thomson. 2001. A Natural History of Bumblebees: A Sourcebook for Investigations. University Press of Colorado, Boulder, Colorado, USA. 120 pp.

16. Klein, A., B.E. Vaissière, J.H. Cane, I. Steffan-Dewenter, S.A. Cunningham, C. Kremen, and T. Tscharntke. 2007. Importance of pollinators in changing landscapes for world crops. Proceedings: Biological Sciences 274:303-313.
17. Knight, M.E., A.P. Martin, S. Bishop, J.L. Osbourne, R.J. Hale, R.A. Sanderson, and D. Goulson. 2005. An interspecific comparison of foraging range and nest density of four bumblebee (Bombus) species. Molecular Ecology 14:1811-1820.
18. Krebs, C.J. 1989. Ecological methodology. Harper and Row, Publishers, New York. 620 pp.
19. Lawson, L.J. 2005. City Bountiful: A Century of Community Gardening in America. University of California Press, Berkeley, California, USA. 363 pp.
20. Matteson, K.C. 2007. Diversity and conservation of insects in urban gardens: theoretical and applied implications. Dissertation, Fordham University, Bronx, New York. 208 pp.
21. Matteson, K.C., J.S. Ascher, and G.A. Langellotto. 2008. Bee richness and abundance in New York City urban gardens Annals of the Entomological Society of America 101:140-150.
22. McFrederick, Q.S., and G. Lebuhn. 2006. Are urban parks refuges for bumble bees Bombus spp. (Hymenoptera: Apidae)? Biological Conservation 129:372-382.
23. Meisels, S., and H. Chiasson. 1997. Effectiveness of Bombus impatiens Cr. as pollinators of greenhouse sweet peppers (Capsicum annuum L.). Acta Horticulturae 437:425-430.
24. Michener, C.D. 2000. The Bees of the World. Johns Hopkins University Press, Baltimore, Maryland, USA. 913 pp.
25. Morandin, L.A., T.M. Laverty, and P.G. Kevan. 2001. Bumble bee (Hymenoptera: Apidae) activity and pollination levels in commercial tomato greenhouses. Journal of Economic Entomology 94:462-467.
26. Morse, R.A.and N.W. Calderone. 2000. The value of honey bees as pollinators of U.S. crops in 2000. Bee Culture 128:1-15.
27. Öckinger, E. and H.G. Smith. 2007. Semi-natural grasslands as population sources for pollinating insects in agricultural landscapes. Journal of Applied Ecology 44:50-59.
28. Olsen, K.M. 1997. Pollination effectiveness and pollinator importance in a population of Heterotheca subaxillaris (Asteraceae). Oecologia 109:114-121.
29. Osborne, J.L., S.J. Clark, R.J. Morris, I.H. Williams, J.R. Riley, A.D. Smith, D.R. Reynolds, and A.S. Edwards. 1999. A landscape-scale study of bumble bee foraging range and constancy, using harmonic radar. Journal of Applied Ecology 36:519-533.
30. Osborne, J.L., and I.H. Williams. 2001. Site constancy of bumble bees in an experimentally patchy habitat. Agriculture, Ecosystems and Environment 83:129-141.
31. Owen, J. 1991. The Ecology of a Garden. The First Fifteen Years. Cambridge University Press, Cambridge, UK. 403 pp.
32. Stanghellini, M.S., J. Tambrose, and J.R. Schultheis. 2002. Diurnal activity, floral visitation and pollen deposition by honey bees and bumble bees on field-grown cucumber and watermelon. Journal of Apicultural Research 41:27-34.
33. Stubbs, C.S., and F.A. Drummond. 2001. Bombus impatiens (Hymenoptera: Apidae): An alternative to Apis mellifera (Hymenoptera: Apidae) for lowbush blueberry pollination. Journal of Economic Entomology 94:609-616.

34. van Veenhuizen, R. 2000. Cities farming for the future, In van Veenhuizen, 459 pp. R. (Ed.). Cities Farming for the Future, Urban Agriculture for Green and Productive Cities.RUAF Foundation, IDRC and IIRR, Phillipines. http://www.ruaf.org/node/961 (accessed 06/08/08).
35. Walther-Hellwig, K. and R. Frankl. 2000. Foraging habitats and foraging distances of bumblebees, Bombus spp. (Hym., Apidae), in an agricultural landscape. Journal of Applied Entomology 124:299-306.
36. Yurlina, M.E. 1998. Bee mutualisms and plant reproduction in urban woodland restorations. Dissertation, Rutgers, The State University of New Jersey, New Brunswick, New Jersey. 132 pp.

CHAPTER 10

Modification of a Community Garden to Attract Native Bee Pollinators in Urban San Luis Obispo, California

JAIME C. PAWELEK, GORDON W. FRANKIE, ROBBIN W. THORP, AND MAGGIE PRZYBYLSKI

10.1 INTRODUCTION

In recent years the popularity of gardening has increased. More people are growing their own food as a means of increasing personal access to more affordable, better-tasting, and healthier produce (Marsh 1998; Ferris et al. 2001; Lawson 2005; NGA 2009; MacVean 2009). In 2008, 36 million households grew vegetables, fruits, and herbs in residential gardens; this number is expected to grow 19% in 2009 (NGA 2009). Community gardens are an ever-increasing means of providing sustenance when lacking private access to land (Lawson 2005; MacVean 2009). An estimated one million households utilize community garden plots; an additional five million households have expressed interest in constructing local community plots (NGA 2009).

© Pawelek, J. et al. 2009. *Modification of a community garden to attract native bee pollinators in urban San Luis Obispo, California.* Cities and the Environment. 2(1):article 7. Creative Commons Attribution license (http://creativecommons.org/licenses/by/3.0/).

The benefits of gardens range from recreation to community activism to conservation of biodiversity (Martin and Mardsen 1999; Lawson 2005; Hunter and Hunter 2008; Tallamy 2009). Gardens, especially in urban areas where green spaces are becoming fewer and far between, can provide places where one can get back to nature and observe ecological processes and natural systems (Lawson 2005; Flores 2006). School gardens are also becoming more commonplace, and states like California have developed programs to encourage them (Lawson 2005). These then become places where children can learn about where their food comes from, how it comes to be there by learning about ecology and pollination, and learning about general nutrition (Flores 2006). Gardens also become venues for environmental education of local residents, places for biological and ecological research, and can improve neighborhoods by bringing people together and providing a sense of community (Martin and Mardsen 1999; Armstrong 2000; Lawson 2005; Matteson et al. 2008).

Until recently, little scientific study was given to the ecology of urban areas (Niemela 1999; Collins et al. 2000). Urban areas, in green spaces, gardens, and parks, can provide islands of habitat for native fauna, including small mammals, birds, and especially invertebrates (Frankie and Ehler 1978; Savard et al. 2000; Fetridge et al. 2008; Tallamy 2009). Increasingly, people are taking an interest in conserving native species by practicing habitat gardening for wildlife (Owen 1991; the Xerces Society 1998; Buchanan 1999; Frey 2001; Grissell 2001; Tait 2006; Frey 2009). With careful planning, urban residents can attract a large diversity of native species to their gardens (Owen 1991; Tommasi et al. 2004; Tait 2006; Fetridge et al. 2008; Matteson et al. 2008; Tallamy 2009), and thus can contribute to conservation of local fauna, especially when utilizing native plant species (Frey 2001; Grissell 2001; McIntyre and Hostetler 2001; McKinney 2002; Lowry 2007).

We propose that urban areas, with their diverse floral resources, can simultaneously provide food and habitat for a diversity of native bees, which are important garden visitors. Gardens can be designed and managed to successfully attract native bee species that will not only forage for pollen and nectar from flowers, but will also find spaces to nest, either in the ground or in existing cavities (Fetridge et al. 2008; Frankie et al. 2005, 2009a). In California there are over 1,600 native bee species (R.W. Thorp

Pers. Comm.), and almost 250 bee species (~15%) have been found to date in surveyed urban areas throughout the state (Frankie et al. 2009a). Further, existing gardens have the potential to be modified to become more pollinator-friendly. We tested this proposal in a community garden at Emerson Park in the city of San Luis Obispo, San Luis Obispo Co., California.

Our goal at Emerson Park was to diversify existing floral resources to make the garden more attractive to native bee species. We also wanted to record gardeners' responses to the modifications and assess their interest in learning how to garden for bees. We brought known bee attractive plants to the garden starting in 2007 and monitored them continually for growth, flowering, and attracted bees. We also monitored responses from local gardeners through personal communication, a questionnaire measuring interest in conserving native bee pollinators, and a focused interview.

10.2 MATERIALS AND METHODS

10.2.1 SITE DESCRIPTION

The Emerson Park Community Garden is located in San Luis Obispo, San Luis Obispo Co., California, which is almost halfway between San Francisco and Los Angeles. San Luis Obispo is slightly inland from the coast, but is still subject to coastal influences. The garden is located on the corner of Nipomo and Pismo Streets on land owned and managed by the Parks and Recreation Department of San Luis Obispo. The entire block is known as Emerson Park, which also includes an outside gym, playground, basketball court, large grassy field, and a Parks and Recreation building. The park is located in a residential neighborhood less than 2.4 km NE of Laguna Lake Park and Natural Reserve and 0.8 km E of Cerro San Luis Natural Reserve. The ~4,000 m^2 garden includes 29 plots which are managed and maintained by members of the local community (see Figure 1 for a picture of one gardener's plot).

The community garden began in 1997-98 on land that previously housed the Emerson School K-3. The school district managed it until the school closed in the early 1980's. In 1994 the city of San Luis Obispo purchased the property and began construction on the current Parks and

Recreation building in 1996. The land lay fallow between when the school closed and when the Parks and Recreation building was constructed. The garden was constructed in the exact location of the old school building. Although the garden started in 1997, by 2002 there were still only a small number of plots in use. From 2003 onward the garden received care and management of all the current 29 plots.

The garden plots are a combination of 17 large (~4.5m x 6m) and 12 small (~2m x 3m) plots. Prior to our addition of bee attracting plants the garden was utilized to grow vegetables, herbs, and a few ornamental flowers. In the early garden years (1997-2002) only a few plots were managed and most remained weedy for several years. Since 2003 the garden has been intensively managed and all plots have been in use. There were few weedy areas, and gardeners must work to keep their plots weed free to secure them for the entire year, or else they are given to someone else. As of the end of 2008, the three community gardens of San Luis Obispo had a waiting list of over 120 people.

Typical vegetables planted by most gardeners included tomatoes, lettuce, green beans, collard greens, Jerusalem artichokes, and corn. Ornamental flowers and herbs planted include rosemary, lavender, thyme, daffodils, nasturtium, sunflowers (*Helianthus annuus* vars.), Mexican sunflower, hollyhocks, and cosmos (Table 1). It is important to note that these plants were very sparse (~1 or 2 plants of each), and patch sizes were small (<0.5m^2), except sunflowers (*Helianthus annuus*), Mexican sunflower (*Tithonia rotundifolia*), and cosmos (*Cosmos bipinnatus*). One of the most attractive summer blooming flowers, cosmos, had been planted since the garden started in 1997.

10.2.2 GARDEN MODIFICATION

At the onset of the project in early-mid 2007, an assessment was made of existing plants in the garden that were known to attract bees (see lists in Frankie et al. 2005; http://nature.berkeley.edu/urbanbeegardens). Purpose of assessment was to determine the kinds of extant bees and if any plants could be used immediately to monitor bees, using the frequency count method described in Frankie et al. (2005). The evaluation indicated that

FIGURE 1: Main garden cooperator Barbara Smith's plot showing vegetables growing towards the back and patches of bee attracting plants, like *Penstemon heterophyllus* and *Coreopsis grandiflora*, growing towards the front of her plot.

only a few plants could be used to record bee diversity and abundance (Table 1). Of the pre-existing plants, the following are known to be consistently attractive to some native bees: rosemary (*Rosmarinus* sp.), lavender (*Lavandula* sp.), sunflowers (*Helianthus* spp.), Mexican sunflower (*Tithonia rotundifolia*), and cosmos (*Cosmos bipinnatus*). The two main criteria used to judge a plant's suitability were patch size and flower vigor. Plants also had to have consistent bee visitors, even if the numbers of visits were low. The garden was again surveyed in late summer and early fall of 2007 and records were made of additional floral resources in bloom and types of bees visiting them.

Table 1. Existing and added plant species to Emerson Park Garden from 2007-2009. Early Spr. = March-April, Lt. Spr.= April-May, Sum.=June-Aug., Fall=Sept.-Oct. cvs=cultivars Floral Resource: P=Pollen, N=Nectar

Scientific Name and Family	Flower Phenology	Floral Resource	Existing Plants	Added 2007	Added 2008	Added 2009
APIACEAE						
Foeniculum vulgare	Sum.-Fall	P/N	X			
ASTERACEAE						
Achillea millefolium[1]	Sum.	P				X
Aster chilensis cvs.[1]	Sum.-Fall	P/N		X		
Aster x frikartii	Sum.-Fall	P/N		X	X	
Bidens ferulifolia	Spr-Fall	P/N		X		
Calendula sp.	Sum.-Fall	P/N	X			
Centarea cineraria	Sum.	P/N	X			
Coreopsis grandiflora cvs.	Sum.-Fall	P/N		X	X	X
Coreopsis lanceolata	Sum.	P/N		X		
Cosmos bipinnatus[2]	Sum.-Fall	P/N	X			
Cosmos sulphureus	Sum.-Fall	P/N		X		
Echinacea purpurea	Sum.-Fall	P/N	X			
Encelia californica[1]	Early Spr.-Sum.	P/N			X	
Erigeron glaucus cvs.[1]	Lt. Spr.-Sum., Oct.	P/N		X	X	X
Erigeron karvinskianus	Lt. Spr.-Sum.	P/N	X			

Modification of a Community Garden to Attract Native Bee Pollinators

Table 1. Continued.

Gaillardia x *grandiflora* cvs.	Lt. Spr.-Fall	P/N	X				X
Gaillardia 'Oranges & Lemons'	Lt. Spr.-Fall	P/N		X		X	X
Grindelia hirsutula	Sum.-Fall	P/N		X			X
Grindelia stricta	Sum.	P/N			X		X
Helianthus annuus[1,2]	Sum.-Fall	P/N	X				X
Helenium 'Mardi Gras'	Sum.-Fall	P/N				X	
Helianthus tuberosus[2]	Sum.-Fall	P/N	X				X
Leucanthemum x *superbum*	Sum.	P/N	X				
Picris echioides	Lt. Spr.-Sum.	P/N	X				
Rudbeckia 'Gloriousa Daisy'	Died	P/N		X			
Rudbeckia hirta	Sum.	P/N	X			X	X
Solidago californica[1]	Sum.-Fall	P/N			X	X	
Tithonia rotundifolia[2]	Lt. Spr.-Sum	P/N	X				
BORAGINACEAE							
Borago officinalis	Sum.	N	X				
Echium candicans	Early Spr.-Lt.-Spr.	P/N	X				X
BRASSICACEAE							
Lobularia maritima	Lt. Spr.-Fall	P	X				
CONVOLVULACEAE							
Ipomoea tricolor	Sum.	N	X				

Table 1. Continued.

CUCURBITACEAE								
Cucurbita sp.	Sum.	P/N	X					
DIPSACACEAE								
Scabiosa atropurpurea	Sum.-Fall	P/N		X				
Scabiosa columbaria 'Black Knight'	Lt. Spr.-Sum.	P/N		X				
FABACEAE								
Psoralea pinnata Early	Spr.-Lt. Spr.	N				X		
HYDROPHYLLACEAE								
Phacelia californica[1]	Early Spr.-Sum.	P/N		X				
Phacelia tanacetifolia[1]	Lt. Spr.	P/N				X		X
LAMIACEAE								
Agastache 'Blue Fortune'	Sum.	N				X		
Calamintha nepetoides	Sum.-Fall	N						X
Caryopteris 'Hint of Gold'	Sum.-Fall	P/N						X
Caryopteris x clandonensis 'Summer Sorbet'	Sum.-Fall	P/N						X
Lavandula dentata var. candicans	Lt. Spr.-Fall	N				X		
Lavandula sp.[2]	Lt. Spr.-Fall	N	X					
Mentha sp.	Sum.-Fall	N	X					
Nepeta x faassenii	Lt. Spr.-Sum.	N		X				
Origanum sp.	Sum.-Fall	N	X					

Modification of a Community Garden to Attract Native Bee Pollinators

Table 1. Continued.

Species	Season	N/P			
Perovskia atriplicifolia	Sum.-Fall	N	X		X
Rosmarinus sp.	Fall-Early Spr.	N	X		
Rosmarinus officinalis 'De Force'	Early Spr.-Sum.	N		X	
Salvia brandegeei	Early Spr., Sum.-Fall	N		X	
Salvia chamaedryoides	Sum.-Fall	N	X		
Salvia 'Dara's Choice'	Lt. Spr.-Sum.	N		X	X
Salvia microphylla 'Hot Lips'	Sum.-Fall	N	X		X
Salvia 'Indigo Spires'	Sum.-Fall	N		X	X
Salvia leucantha	Fall	N	X		
Salvia uliginosa	Sum.-Fall	P/N		X	
Stachys byzantina	Sum.	N	X		X
Teucrium chamaedrys	Sum.	N	?		
Thymus sp.	Sum.-Fall	N	X		X
MALVACEAE					
Alcea rosea	Sum.-Fall	N	X		
PAPAVERACEAE					
Eschscholzia californica	Early Spr.-Lt. Spr.	P		X	X
POLYGONACEAE					
Eriogonum grande var. rubescens	Sum.-Fall	N	X		X

Table 1. Continued.

ROSACEAE					
Fragaria chiloensis[1]	Early Spr.-Lt. Spr.	P/N	X		
Rubus discolor	Lt. Spr.-Sum.	P/N	X		
SCROPHULARIACEAE					
Linaria purpurea	Sum.-Fall	N		X	
Penstemon heterophyllus cvs.[1]	Lt. Spr.-Sum., Oct.	N		X	
VERBENACEAE					
Aloysia triphylla	Sum.	N	X		
Vitex agnus-castus	Sum.-Fall	P/N			X
Species totals: 69			32	21	20

In spring of 2007 we began bringing bee attractive plants, including natives, non-natives, annuals, and perennials, to Emerson Community Garden. This site was added in 2007 to a California statewide survey currently being conducted by our labs at University of California, Berkeley and Davis (Frankie et al. 2009a). Previously, only the California Polytechnic State University Arboretum (Cal Poly) and a few residential gardens were monitored for native bees in San Luis Obispo, but this mainly provided spring/early summer information as it contained mostly California native plants, which have their greatest flowering at this time of year. Emerson Garden was selected as an additional site because it provided summer/fall opportunities for monitoring and sampling bees on non-native plant species (as well as a few natives). The statewide survey monitors 31 target plant types at 9 urban sites distributed widely from northern to southern California (Frankie et al. 2009a).

Since spring of 2007 we have brought 41 plant types, including cultivars, hybrids, and varieties, of which 19 are on the "target" plant list for the statewide survey. The remaining plant species were planted to generally increase diversity of bee attractive plants to the garden (Table 1). Based on results from the statewide survey, we have found that the more diverse gardens, with respect to plant material, also have the most diverse bees visiting them (Frankie et al. 2009a,b). Our findings indicate that predictive relationships exist between certain bee groups and certain plant types, and that this information can then be used to plan gardens. For example, California poppy (*Eschscholzia californica*) can expect to attract bumble bees (*Bombus* spp.), honey bees (*Apis mellifera*), and at least three species of sweat bees (*Halictus* spp.) throughout the state.

Seasonality was also considered when planning the bee garden. Bees need sources of nectar and/or pollen during the season in which they are foraging and provisioning nests (Tommasi et al. 2004; Wojcik et al. 2008; Frey 2009). With this in mind we selected plants that would successively bloom throughout the year (March-October) to provide these resources. Prior to our plant additions most of Emerson's plants bloomed from early summer to fall, so we incorporated spring flowers that would provide resources to early season bees.

A total of ~345 individual plants were brought to the garden during 2007-2009 with a survival rate of ~90%. Most were planted by our main cooperator in the garden, Barbara Smith, with our help and direction (Table 1). Plants were grouped in patches (~1.0m x 1.5m) in plots that had enough space to accommodate them. Large patches, rather than individual plants, are important because they offer more resources for bees (Isaacs et al. 2009). This allows them to forage longer in one place, which also allows for opportunity to observe and monitor them more easily. Gardeners with larger plots were more likely and willing to accept donations of bee plants, whereas some gardeners with smaller plots did not have extra room to spare, as the bee plants would have taken away from their limited space for growing vegetables. To date, 19 of 29 plots have welcomed the addition of bee plants.

10.2.3 PLANT ADDITIONS FROM 2007-2009

After initial assessment in mid 2007 we began bringing known bee attractive plants to the garden and incorporating them into plots where space was available. Some of the first plants brought to the garden in June 2007 included: *Linaria purpurea, Penstemon heterophyllus, Coreopsis grandiflora cultivars, Aster chilensis* 'Purple Haze', *Aster* x *frikartii, Bidens ferulifolia,* and *Perovskia atriplicifolia* (see Table 1 for complete list of plants). *Gaillardia* x *grandiflora* was already in the garden, but more plants were incorporated to increase patch size. Plants were sourced from local nurseries in the San Francisco Bay Area and San Luis Obispo, and were in either four-inch pots or one-gallon containers. A total of 129 individual plants representing 20 different types, including hybrids, cultivars, and varieties, were brought to the garden in 2007. Many of the plants, 13 of 20 types, were on the target plant list (Frankie et al. 2009a). Observations were made on flowering condition as they began to mature, as well as types of bees that began to visit them.

In 2008 we brought plants to the garden in January and continued through October. To diversify floral resources for early season bees we incorporated native spring flowering plants such as: *Encelia californica, Eschscholzia californica, Phacelia tanacetifolia,* and *Salvia brandegeei* (Table 1). We also added more plants of existing species to enhance patches or to replace plants that had not survived. Ten of 18 plant types introduced to the garden in 2008 were on the target list (Frankie et al. 2009a). In total ~125 individual plants were brought and planted in the garden in 2008.

In 2009, 17 plant types (~105 individual plants) were planted in the garden beginning in early spring, and most were incorporated into previous patches to increase patch size. Almost all of these had already been added to the garden previously, but there were a few new additions such as *Teucrium chamaedrys*, *Caryopteris clandonensis* 'Summer Sorbet', and *Vitex agnus-castus* (Table 1). Ten of 17 plant types brought to the garden were on the target list.

10.2.4 BEE MONITORING AND DATA COLLECTION FROM 2007-2009

In Emerson Park, bee data was collected through "frequency counts" as well as aerial netting, which was consistent with our methods for the statewide survey. Frequency counts are conducted by observing a patch of flowers, approximately $1.0\text{-}1.5m^2$, then counting the number of bees that make visits to the reproductive parts of the flowers within a period of three minutes (see methodology in Frankie et al. 2005, 2009a). Bees are identified to genera, and whenever possible to species, and counted as they enter and visit flowers within a given patch. After numerous replicated counts, usually on different patches over one or more growing seasons, a relative measure of attraction is established. We also record type of resource bees receive from the flower, either nectar, pollen, or both. Once counts are completed, collections of representative bee species are made. Collections are also made from non-target flowers that attract bees. Bees are transported to our lab at University of California, Berkeley, curated, labeled, and brought to R. Thorp at the University of California, Davis for identification.

Bee observations in the Emerson Garden began in late July of 2007, and frequency counts were performed on two plants at that time, *Cosmos bipinnatus* and *Helianthus annuus*, both of which were found in large enough patches for monitoring. Observations continued monthly through November of 2007, and frequency counts were performed again on the same plants in August and October. We chose to make limited collections of bees in 2007 to avoid depleting populations of bees that may have begun colonizing the garden.

In 2008 the garden was sampled for bees beginning in July and continued monthly through October. Bee collections and frequency counts (on nine plant types) began on plants in full flower and in large enough patches (1.0-1.5m^2), and included many that had been incorporated into the garden in either 2007 or earlier in 2008. Native spring flowers of 2008 had not yet developed to the point where bee counts or collections could be made. The garden was sampled 13 times between the dates of 21 July and 14 October.

In 2009 the garden was surveyed for bees (collections and frequency counts) beginning in May when many spring plants were in flower. Poor weather conditions contributed to the garden not being sampled earlier in the season. The garden was monitored at least twice monthly through the end of the growing season (late October).

10.2.5 EDUCATIONAL OUTREACH & SURVEY OF GARDENERS

During our visits to monitor plants and bees we regularly provided information to gardeners about conserving native bee pollinators and how to garden for them. We found that many people were unfamiliar with the different types of bees that occur in their gardens, and we were often able to show them diverse bees visiting their own flowers. One of us (GWF) gave an informal talk to about 10 gardeners in late August of 2007, which provided an overview of native bee ecology and our work to date on the California statewide survey.

Our main cooperator, Barbara Smith, took a strong interest in learning about bee gardening. She spread her knowledge to other curious gardeners at their monthly potluck dinners and encouraged them to donate parts of their plots to bee attracting flowers. She also directed them to our website (http://nature.berkeley.edu/urbanbeegardens), which is constantly being updated with new information about bees and preferred host plants.

To evaluate the environmental education aspect of our garden modification we distributed a questionnaire survey to all members of the community garden in January/February 2009 (see Appendix A). Our goal was to find out how much interest gardeners had in learning about native bees and if they wanted to learn more about gardening to attract them. A pre-test was done prior to distribution. The survey was sent by email to those who had access to computers and internet, with hard copies sent to the rest (see Appendix A). It included questions about how much time gardeners work in their plots, their main purpose for gardening, were they familiar with our project, and if they had donated space in their plots for bee plants. We also asked if they had visited our website, if they had noticed an increase in amount and diversity of bees in the garden, and if they would like to hear a presentation that would explain more about bees in their garden and how to attract and conserve them. All responses were received by the end of February.

Based on responses from the gardeners we followed up with a presentation in early March 2009 and asked the 13 gardeners present to participate in a focused interview in order to assess the presented information. We fielded questions from the gardeners that ranged from how bees find flowers to the cues that tell bees when to emerge from their nests. We then asked them a series of questions to find out if anyone had noticed an increase in bee activity in the garden; if they would like to join us on a walk through the garden to identify bees; if they would like signage in the garden to document our project; and if they thought the garden should have a mission statement that would acknowledge the project and newly added goals of the garden.

10.3 RESULTS

10.3.1 EXISTING GARDEN PLANTS: ATTRACTION TO BEES

Only five plant types met the selection criteria in the first garden assessment for plant and bee monitoring (see Table 1). Four of these, *Cosmos bipinnatus*, *Helianthus annuus*, *H. tuberosa*, and *Tithonia rotundifolia* had medium-large patches of vigorous flowers and were commonly (> 5 visits per 3 min. observation) attracting *Melissodes robustior* and honey bees on occasion (<3 visits per 3 min. observation). The fifth plant, *Lavandula* species, attracted honey bees and rarely (~1 visit per 4-5 observations) *Anthophora urbana*

(Table 1). All other potentially attractive bee plants were either in very small patches (< 0.5m^2), were small single specimens, or had poor flower quality. A few of these such as *Borago officinalis*, *Echinacea purpurea*, and oregano attracted honey bees on occasion. *Mentha* species attracted some honey bees and very few small bees, such as halictids and megachilids.

Other flowers that received visits by native bees were *Cosmos sulphureus*, *Salvia leucantha*, and *Gaillardia* x *grandiflora* cvs, though these were not found in large enough patch sizes or with enough vigorous flowering for monitoring. Bees observed visiting these flowers included the common *Melissodes robustior* and honey bee, as well as occasional to rare visits by *Anthophora urbana*, *Xylocopa tabaniformis orpifex*, and *Halictus* spp. Overall, the community garden of 29 plots in 2007 was considered largely unattractive to diverse bee species, especially natives, and this in turn was related to a lack of diverse and abundant floral resources (Frankie et al. 2005, 2009a).

10.3.2 PLANT ADDITIONS FROM 2007-2009: ATTRACTION TO BEES

The following added plants flowered in the first year, but were slightly attractive to honey bees only: *Bidens ferulifolia*, *Aster chilensis*, *Salvia* 'Indigo Spires', *Grindelia hirsutula*, and *Perovskia atriplicifolia*. However, *Solidago californica* was attractive to small bees, such as halictids, and rarely to honey bees. *Linaria purpurea* also began flowering the first year and was commonly observed drawing in *Anthophora urbana* and honey bees. *Salvia uliginosa* also flowered and attracted *Melissodes robustior*, *Xylocopa tabaniformis orpifex*, and honey bees.

In 2008 plants that received increased and measurable visitation by diverse native bees included *Bidens ferulifolia*, *Gaillardia* x *grandiflora*, *Salvia uliginosa*, *Linaria purpurea* and *Aster* x *frikartii*. For example, nine species of native bees were collected from *Aster* x *frikartii*, and five species were collected from *Gaillardia* x *grandiflora*. Other plants in the garden received increased levels of visitation, like *Cosmos bipinnatus* and

Lavandula spp., but these had not been added to the garden because they were already established.

Two native spring flowering plants that attracted new bees to the garden in 2009 were *Phacelia tanacetifolia* and *Salvia brandegeei*. Other plants found to be attractive to spring bees included *Coreopsis grandiflora*, *Grindelia hirsutula*, *Salvia uliginosa*, *Bidens ferulifolia*, and *Lavandula* spp. These flowers had been planted previously and are now established.

10.3.3 BEE MONITORING FROM 2007-2009

Numbers of bee taxa collected from original and added plant types from 2007 through 2009 are presented in Table 2. The most abundant bee in the garden in July was a long-horned bee (*Melissodes robustior*), which was frequently observed on *Cosmos bipinnatus*, *Helianthus annuus*, and *Tithonia rotundifolia*. Other native bees observed in the garden at this time were sweat bees (*Halictus* spp.), leaf cutting bees (*Megachile* spp.), and mining bees (*Anthophora* spp.), but all of these were rare and much less abundant than *M. robustior* and were found on *Lavandula* sp. and *Thymus* sp. Honey bees were also common in the garden and observed on *Echinacea purpurea*, *Lavandula* spp., *Borago officinalis*, and *Mentha* sp. Overall, bee diversity and abundance in the garden was low, with the exception of *M. robustior* and *A. mellifera*. The only new native bees observed later in the season were a very few carpenter bees (*Xylocopa* sp.), which were seen foraging on *Salvia leucantha*, *S. uliginosa*, and *S.* 'Indigo Spires'. *Melissodes robustior* remained the most common visitor in the garden until November (Table 2).

In 2008 we collected 21 bee species on 12 original and 10 added plant types from 2007/2008. One species, *Xylocopa tabaniformis orpifex*, was not collected, but was recorded, because it could be easily identified to species by all observers. Addition of this bee brought the total number of species to 22. Some bee species such as *Anthophora urbana*, *Apis mellifera* (honey bee), *Melissodes robustior*, and *Halictus tripartitus* had been collected/observed during the assessment phase in spring 2007, however, the vast majority of collected bee species in 2008 were considered new records to the garden. These four bee species are among the most common bees found throughout the state of California (Frankie et al. 2009a).

The most abundant bees in the garden, based on collections in 2008, were a long-horned bee (*Melissodes robustior*) and a sweat bee (*Halictus tripartitus*) (Table 2). *Melissodes robustior* was collected from 10 different plant species, seven of which were target plants, and *Halictus tripartitus* was collected on 14 plant species, nine of which were target plants. These two species along with a miner bee, *Anthophora urbana*, were present and collected each month from July to October. The honey bee, *Apis mellifera*, was also abundant in the garden and was a common and main visitor on many plants (Table 3), but not always collected, as it was easily identified and recorded.

Other bees collected and observed represent a diverse assortment of bees and include three species of cuckoo bees (*Triepeolus heururus*, *Xeromelecta californica*, and *Sphecodes* sp.) (Table 2). Cuckoo bees parasitize nests of other bees and thus rely on their hosts gathered floral resources for reproduction, as they do not build or provision their own nests. The squash bee, *Peponapis pruinosa*, a specialist on plants in the Cucurbitaceae family, was also present in the garden and frequently visited squash and pumpkin flowers.

Our previous sampling in greater San Luis Obispo, through 2007, revealed a total of 58 species in the area. Sampling from the Emerson Park garden in 2008 added eight new species to the area total. Sampling in the Cal Poly Arboretum also added eight new species, bringing the new total for San Luis Obispo to 74 for 2008.

The total number of collected bee species in 2009 was 31 (Table 2); four were new records for the San Luis Obispo area. Of those, 19 were new records for the garden and were attracted to six original and 13 added plant types from 2007-2009. Further, in contrast to the host plant associations of 2008, a higher percentage of bee species were collected from added plant types, which had been continually diversifying the garden over three years.

The increase in bee species from 2008 to 2009 is most likely the result of adding new diverse plant types to the garden (Frankie et al. 2009a) along with increased sampling effort in 2008 and 2009 compared to 2007. New genera (5) were also added to the list, which is another indication of increasing bee diversity (Table 2). Examples of notable increases include two *Andrena* species and three *Osmia* species that were recorded for the first time. These two genera are characteristic spring bees and are known to appear as California gardens mature with bee-attractive flowering plants (Frankie et al. 2005; Wojcik et al. 2008; Hernandez et al. 2009; Frankie and Pawelek unpub.). Three apid species, *Anthophora curta* and two spring *Bombus* species were recorded for the first time in 2009. Prior to 2009, *Bombus* were extremely rare in the garden, although in the nearby arboretum of California Polytechnic State University *Bombus melanopygus* and *B. vosnesenskii* were common on native plant species. Finally, numbers of small bees in the genera *Hylaeus* and *Lasioglossum* increased noticeably in 2009. From the total of 31 collected bee species in 2009, 24 were collected from added plant types only; seven from original types. Of the 19 bee species recorded for the first time in 2009, 16 were collected from added plants only (Table 2).

Plants that received the highest diversity in bee visitation, from collections and frequency counts, are shown in Table 3. Eight of the added plant types were more attractive than the originals, that is, being visited by more bee species, except for *Lavandula* spp., which had the most diversity with seven species. In its first year of flowering, *Phacelia tanacetifolia*, which is known to attract a wide diversity of bees (Frankie et al. 2009a), was visited by seven species. Of the original plant types, *Foeniculum vulgare* and *Calendula* sp. are considered weedy, but are still attractive to a variety of small bees. Overall and consistently, most added plant types had noticeably higher bee species diversity than established original plants in the garden (Table 3).

The total number of bee species recorded in the garden since the modification began in 2007 stands at 40 species in 17 genera. Total numbers of bee taxa recorded to date in all of San Luis Obispo are 78 species in 30 genera, 5 families.

Table 2. Number of bee taxa collected from added and original plant types, 2007 – 2009. The first number represents total number of bees collected and the numbers in parenthesis reflect the number of bees collected from added and original plants, respectively. Greater sampling effort in 2008-2009 compared to 2007.

Bee Species	2007	2008	2009
ANDRENIDAE			
Andrena cerasifolii			1 (0,1)
Andrena anguistitarsata			1 (1,0)
APIDAE			
Anthophora curta			7 (1,0)
Anthophora urbana	4 (0,1)	12 (5,2)	3 (2,1)
Apis mellifera †	Several Observed	2 (0,2)	4 (4,0)
Bombus crotchii			1 (1,0)
Bombus melanopygus			1 (1,0)
Bombus vosnesenskii		1 (0,1)	6 (6,0)
Ceratina acantha		7 (2,1)	6 (3,2)
Ceratina nanula		1 (0,1)	
Melissodes robustior	7 (0,2)	33 (6,4)	14 (5,0)
Peponapis pruinosa		4 (0,2)	
Triepeolus hetururus *		1 (0,1)	
Xeromelecta californica *		1 (0,0)	1 (1,0)
Xylocopa tabaniformis orpifex			4 (2,1)
COLLETIDAE			
Colletes hyalinus gaudialis			1 (1,0)
Hylaeus mesillae		4 (2,2)	
Hylaeus polifolii			3 (1,0)
Hylaeus punctatus †		2 (1,0)	4 (1,0)
Hylaeus rudbeckiae		1 (1,0)	12 (6,0)
HALICTIDAE			
Halictus farinosus			1 (1,0)
Halictus ligatus		2 (0,0)	
Halictus tripartitus	1 (0,1)	43 (8,6)	13 (4,1)
Lasioglossum incompletum			3 (2,0)

Table 2. Continued.

Lasioglossum sisymbrii			2 (1,0)
Lasioglossum tegulariforme		1 (1,0)	
Lasioglossum (Dialictus) sp. 3			1 (1,0)
Lasioglossum (Evylaeus) sp. 3			1 (1,0)
Sphecodes sp. *		1 (0,1)	
MEGACHILIDAE			
Megachile angelarum	2 (0,1)		2 (1,1)
Megachile concinna †		1 (1,0)	2 (2,0)
Megachile fidelis			1 (1,0)
Megachile frugalis			1 (1,0)
Megachile gentilis		1 (1,0)	
Megachile montivaga		2 (0,1)	2 (1,1)
Megachile perihirta		1 (0,1)	
Megachile rotundata †		5 (2,0)	2 (1,0)
Osmia californica			1 (1,0)
Osmia coloradensis			6 (3,0)
Osmia cyanella			1 (1,0)
Total species collected	5	21	31
Total genera collected	5	13	14

(0,0) = No Host Label; † Non-native bee species; *Cuckoo Bee;.
Total no. of species collected in garden = 40 (17 genera)

10.3.4 SURVEY RESULTS

We received completed surveys from 18 gardeners, seven through email and 11 hard copies. Almost 95% (17 out of 18) wanted to hear a presentation on our work so we made another, more formal, presentation to all interested gardeners during the first week of March 2009. Half the gardeners had visited our website before receiving the survey and had found the information presented useful. Only two of 18 people did not make their

Table 3. Number of bee taxa collected from added and original plant types, 2007 – 2009. The first number represents total number of bees collected and the numbers in parenthesis reflect the number of bees collected from added and original plants, respectively. Greater sampling effort in 2008-2009 compared to 2007.

Original plant types[1]	Total number bee species collected/counted[3]	Main bee groups[4]
Lavandula spp.	7	Hb, Aurb, Meg
Cosmos bipinnatus	4	Mel, Hb
Borago officinalis	4	Hb, Hal, B
Helianthus annuus[2]	3	Mel, Hb
Salvia 'Hot Lips'	3	Xylo, Hal, sb
Tithonia rotundifolia	3	Mel, Hb, Hal
Foeniculum vulgare	3	Hal, Hyl, Hb
Calendula sp.	2	Hal
Added plant types[1]		
Gaillardia x grandiflora cvs	11	Hb, Mel, sb
Salvia uliginosa	11	Hal, Xylo, Hb, B
Aster x frikartii	9	sb, Mel, Meg
Bidens ferulifolia	9	Mel, Hal, sb
Coreopsis grandiflora cvs	8	Mel, Osm, sb
Phacelia tanacetifolia[2]	7	B, sb, Hb
Solidago californica[2]	6	Hal, sb, Hb
Grindelia stricta[2]	5	Mel, Hb, Hal
Grindelia hirsutula[2]	4	Mel, Hal, sb
Linaria purpurea	4	Aurb, Meg, Hb

[1] Includes cultivars
[2] Plants native to California
[3] From aerial netting and frequency counts, 2007-2009
[4] Left to right: highest to lowest bee frequency on plant types.
Main Bee Group Codes: Aurb=*Anthophora urbana*; B=*Bombus*; Hal=*Halictus*; Hb=Honey bee; Hyl=*Hylaeus*; Meg=Megachile; Mel=*Melissodes*; Osm=*Osmia*; sb=small bee; Xylo=*Xylocopa*

plot available to the bee plant project, and all but one liked the concept of adding selected flowers to attract native bee pollinators.

Only three people had noticed increased bee activity in the garden, although others said they just started to become aware after looking at our website. Everyone was in agreement that a walk through the garden with us would be helpful so that they could see and learn to identify some of the bees visiting their flowers. They also thought the idea of an educational sign and a new mission statement for the garden would be helpful in promoting it as a pollinator friendly vegetable garden. In July of 2009 the gardeners met and developed a mission statement that reflected their participation in our project. Their mission statement is as follows: "The Emerson Community Organic Gardeners in collaboration with Dr. Gordon Frankie at the University of California, Berkeley are participating in a native bee study by establishing native bee attractive plants and habitat to conserve and increase (or restore) native bees and other pollinators." They have also come to a consensus that they will not do any excessive tilling or use any pesticides or herbicides that may damage native bee populations in the garden. Several gardeners have started planting their own bee plants in their plots since hearing the presentation and visiting the website (B. Smith Pers. Comm.).

10.4 DISCUSSION

Design or modification of a garden to attract bees is possible if correct plants are chosen and managed throughout the growing season. Bee-attractive plant materials were incorporated in patches in the Emerson garden through time to provide seasonal resources of nectar and pollen. Increased diversity of plant materials added to the garden is believed to have contributed to increased diversity of native bee species observed and collected in the garden from 2007 to 2009.

Our findings from the statewide survey suggest that there are predictable relationships; that is, certain flowers will attract mostly the same types of bees no matter where they are found in the state (Frankie et al. 2009a,b). Thus, by adding more plants having predictable relationships, this should increase bee diversity and eventually abundance. Our 2009 bee-plant findings at Emerson provide support for this hypothesis. The general pattern of increasing plant diversity of known bee plants has allowed for early stage development of bee habitat gardening at Emerson (see relevant 15 year garden study by Owen 1991).

The number of bee species collected in the Emerson garden has increased each year since 2007, along with increased sampling effort, and we expect this number to further increase as the study continues in 2010 and beyond. It is probable that the most common bee species (*Melissodes robustior*, *Halictus tripartitus*, and *Anthophora urbana*) were already established in the garden because some of their host plants were found in the garden before modification. Honey bees came from outside the garden, as Emerson does not have any established colonies. Presence of cuckoo bees in the garden indicates that a food web is beginning to form and that more complex relationships are developing. The three species of cuckoo bees (Table 2) recorded in the garden are most likely associated with the three most common bees in the garden, but specific host records are not known for some of the species collected so only generalizations can be made (R.W. Thorp Pers. Comm.). The garden added 12 new species to our list of bees in San Luis Obispo, which is encouraging, because this site is located ~ 4.8 kilometers from our other study site at the Cal Poly Arboretum, which has a diverse inventory of flowering plants from California and other parts of the world.

The diversity of bee species could have been higher if we had used additional collecting methods such as pan traps (Wojcik et al. 2008; Hernandez 2009) and other interception devices. These methods, however, would not have provided floral host information for collected bees, which were needed to meet our goals.

The ongoing drought in California (2007 to present, http://www.water.ca.gov/drought/) may have also affected diversity and abundance levels of bees at Emerson garden as these conditions are believed to impact bee development and emergence. Less than optimal climatic conditions are known to cause some bee species to hold over in their nests for more than a year (R. Thorp and G. Frankie, unpub). Bee numbers are expected to increase when the drought breaks and conditions become more favorable for their reproduction and survival.

If bee-attracting plants in the garden are managed and encouraged each year, overall diversity and abundance of native bees is likely to continue to increase. We have observed this trend in our experimental bee garden in Berkeley, California (Wojcik et al. 2008; Hernandez et al. 2009), and in other gardens throughout the state, such as Descanso Gardens near Pasadena, and a cemetery garden in Sacramento. We increased the floral diversity at those sites, to varying degrees, continued monitoring bees for the last four years, and have seen a steady increase in the diversity of bees at each site (Frankie et al. 2009a).

In addition to the community garden in San Luis Obispo we have also created and modified other gardens in the state with the goal of attracting native bee pollinators. We have worked with school gardens in Marin and San Francisco Counties, home gardens in Ukiah (Mendocino Co.) and Soquel (Santa Cruz Co.), and the University of California Santa Cruz Arboretum (Frankie et al. 2009b). With the decline of managed honey bee populations due to colony collapse disorder (CCD), native bees and other pollinators have received more attention creating increased interest in gardening to attract and conserve pollinators in other areas as well. There are two major pollinator gardens in the planning stages now – the Pollinator Park in Guelph, Canada (http://www.pollinator.ca/guelph/), and the Honey Bee Haven Garden in Davis, California (http://entomology.ucdavis.edu/news/honeybeehavenwinner.html). Also, a honey bee sanctuary called the Melissa Garden in Healdsburg, California was started in the fall of 2007 and designed by Kate Frey, a garden designer focusing on habitat gardening for insects and birds (Frey 2009).

Educating gardeners at Emerson Park added another level to our project. By giving presentations and utilizing surveys we were able to evaluate gardeners' interest and merge the human component with the science. Without their interest we would not have had the space to incorporate the new bee attractive plants, as their cooperation was essential. After two years of our project the gardeners developed their own mission statement and based on our recommendations have been planting their own bee plants.

The importance of cooperators cannot be overlooked or underappreciated when beginning a project of this type. We have cooperators at all our sites throughout the state and have found that it is crucial to form relationships with "lead gardeners" as well as home owners and garden managers, as they will be our main contact for future work. We rely heavily on lead gardeners and other cooperators to manage plants we bring to the gardens. Lead gardeners also help by keeping us informed about the type of audience we are working with and their interests. They are also essential in maintaining project momentum and they often educate and promote our work to others.

Environmental education is an extremely important part of our work as we expect to transmit information from scientific research to interested individuals and groups in the public sector. Often this is not the case as there can be a division between scientific research and what is communicated to the public. The important point is for scientists to learn how to package technical information into userfriendly language - both verbal and written (Jacobson 1999; Vergano 2009).

At the national level, several NGO organizations and U.S. governmental agencies are involved in promoting pollinators, especially bees, and habitat gardening. Three prominent NGO institutions are leading the way: North American Pollinator Protection Campaign (www.nappc.org), National Wildlife Federation (www.nwf.org), and Xerces Society (www.xerces.org). At least five governmental agencies including the National Park Service, the U.S. Forest Service, the Bureau of Land Management, the U.S. Fish and Wildlife Service, and the USDA, including NRCS (Natural Resources Conservation Service), have new mandates to promote awareness, protection, and conservation of pollinators (www.nappc.org). Additionally, other groups such as landscape designers have expressed interest and have the ability to collaborate with the scientific community to promote insect conservation in urban areas (Hunter and Hunter 2008).

These habitat gardens have the potential to be used for many purposes and can be a great meeting ground for communication of ideas. Habitat gardens for pollinators may serve as conservation of genetic reserves for the future as well (Owen 1991). With the results of our work in the Emerson Park garden we think that is it possible that more gardens could be modified and designed with the goal of attracting and conserving wildlife, especially pollinators (Frankie 2009a,b).

REFERENCES

1. Armstrong, D. 2000. A survey of community gardens in upstate New York: Implications for health promotion and community development. Health & Place 6:319-327.
2. Buchanan, C. 1999. The Wildlife Sanctuary Garden. Ten Speed Press, Berkeley, CA. 224 pp.
3. Collins, J.P., A. Kinzig, N.B. Grimm, W.F. Fagan, D. Hope, J. Wu, and E.T. Borer. 2000. A New Urban Ecology. American Scientist 88:416-425.
4. Ferris, J., C. Norman, and J. Sempik. 2001. People, Land, and Sustainability: Community Gardens and the Social Dimension of Sustainable Development. Social Policy & Administration 35(5):559-568.
5. Fetridge, E.D., J.S. Ascher, and G.A. Langellotto. 2008. The Bee Fauna of Residential Gardens in a Suburb of New York City (Hymenoptera: Apoidea). Annals of the Entomological Society of America 101(6):1067-1077.
6. Flores, H.C. 2006. Food not Lawns: How to Turn Your Yard into a Garden and Your Neighborhood into a Community. Chelsea Green Publishing Company. White River Junction, VT. 334 pp.
7. Frankie, G.W. and L.E. Ehler. 1978. Ecology of insects in urban environments. Annual Review of Entomology 23:367-387.
8. Frankie, G.W., R.W. Thorp, M. Schindler, J. Hernandez, B. Ertter, and M. Rizzardi. 2005. Ecological Patterns of Bees and Their Host Ornamental Flowers in Two Northern California Cities. Journal of the Kansas Entomological Society 78(3):227-246.
9. Frankie, G.W., R.W. Thorp, J. Hernandez, M. Rizzardi, B. Ertter, J.C. Pawelek, S.L. Witt, M. Schindler, V. Wojcik. 2009a. Native bees are a rich natural resource in urban California gardens. California Agriculture 63(3):113-120.
10. Frankie, G.W., R.W. Thorp, J.C. Pawelek, J. Hernandez, and R. Coville. 2009b. Urban Bee Diversity in a Small Residential Garden in Northern California. Journal of Hymenoptera Research 18(2):368- 379.
11. Frey, K. 2001. The Pleasures of a Habitat Garden. Pacific Horticulture 62(3):20-26.
12. Frey, K. 2009. The Melissa Garden: A Sanctuary and Season of Honeybees. Pacific Horticulture 70(3):29-34.
13. Grissell, E. 2001. Insects and Gardens: In Pursuit of a Garden Ecology. Timber Press, Inc. Portland, OR. 345 pp.
14. Hernandez, J. 2009. Bee visitation (Hymenoptera: Apoidea) in a newly constructed urban garden in Berkeley, California. Apidologie (Submitted).
15. Hunter, M.C. and M.D. Hunter. 2008. Designing for conservation of insects in the built environment. Insect Conservation and Diversity. 1(4):189-196.
16. Isaacs, R., J. Tuell, A. Fiedler, M. Gardiner, and D. Landis. 2009. Maximizing arthropod-mediated ecosystem services in agricultural landscapes: the role of native plants. Frontiers in Ecology and the Environment 7(4):196-203.
17. Jacobson, S.K. 1999. Communication Skills for Conservation Professionals. Island Press, Washington, D.C. and Covelo, CA. 351 pp.

18. Lawson, L.J. 2005. City Bountiful: A century of community gardening in America. University of California Press, Berkeley and Los Angeles, CA. pp. 363.
19. Lowry, J. L. 2007. The Landscaping Ideas of Jays: A Natural History of the Backyard Restoration Garden. University of California Press. Berkeley and Los Angeles, CA. 280 pp.
20. MacVean, M. 2009 Jan. 17. Victory gardens growing in popularity. San Francisco Chronicle. Sect F:4.
21. Marsh, R. 1998. Building on traditional gardening to improve household food security. Food, Nutrition and Agriculture 22:4-14.
22. Martin, R. and T. Mardsen. 1999. Food for Urban Spaces: The Development of Urban Food Production in England and Wales. International Planning Studies 4(3):389-412.
23. Matteson, K.C., J.S. Ascher, and G.A. Langellotto. 2008. Bee Richness and Abundance in New York City Urban Gardens. Annals of the Entomological Society of America 101(1):140-150.
24. McIntyre, N.E. and M.E. Hostetler. 2001. Effects of urban land use on pollinator (Hymenoptera: Apoidea) communities in a desert metropolis. Basic and Applied Ecology 2:209-218.
25. McKinney, M.L. 2002. Urbanization, Biodiversity, and Conservation. BioScience 52(10):883-890.
26. NGA. 2009. National Gardening Association. Impact of Home and Community Gardening in America. http://www.gardenresearch.com/home?q=show&id=3126 (accessed 08/05/2009).
27. NAPPC. 2009. North American Pollinator Protection Campaign. See website at www.nappc.org and www.pollinator.org.
28. Niemela, J. 1999. Is there a need for a theory of urban ecology? Urban Ecosystems 3:57-65.
29. Owen, J. 1991. The ecology of a garden: The first fifteen years. Cambridge University Press, Cambridge. 403 pp.
30. Savard, JP. L., P. Clergeau, and G. Mennechez. 2000. Biodiversity concepts and urban ecosystems. Landscape and Urban Planning 48:131-142.
31. Tait, M. 2006. Wildlife Gardening for Everyone. Think Publishing, London, UK. 288pp.
32. Tallamy, D.W. 2009. Bringing Nature Home. Timber Press, Portland, OR. 358 pp.
33. Tommasi, D., A. Miro, H.A. Higo, and M.L. Winston. 2004. Bee diversity and abundance in an urban setting. The Canadian Entomologist 136:851-869.
34. Vergano, D. 2009 Aug. 24. Science needs great communicators. USA Today. Sect 5:D.
35. Wojcik, V.A., G.W. Frankie, R.W. Thorp, and J. Hernandez. 2008. Seasonality in Bees and Their Floral Resource Plants at a Constructed Urban Bee Habitat in Berkeley, California. Journal of the Kansas Entomological Society 81(1):15-28.
36. The Xerces Society and The Smithsonian Institution. 1998. Butterfly Gardening: Creating Summer Magic in Your Garden. Sierra Club Books, San Francisco. 228 pp.

PART IV

URBAN HOME AND COMMUNITY GARDENING

CHAPTER 11

Urban Home Gardens in the Global North: A Mixed Methods Study of Ethnic and Migrant Home Gardens in Chicago, IL

JOHN R. TAYLOR AND SARAH TAYLOR LOVELL

11.1 INTRODUCTION

The home food garden represents a major lacuna in the rapidly expanding academic literature on urban agriculture in the developed world. A recent review of the peer-reviewed literature on community gardens, for example, identified 46 studies of such gardens in the United States[1]. A comparable search on Google Scholar for studies of US home food gardens yielded only five results, including: two quantitative analyses of the spatial distribution of urban food gardens, including home gardens, in Chicago, Illinois[2] and Madison, Wisconsin[3]; a socio-demographic analysis of survey data from rural, suburban and urban households with food gardens in the state of Ohio[4]; a qualitative study of Vietnamese home gardeners in Louisiana[5]; and a study of households participating in a home gardening program in San Jose, CA[6]. What do we know about home food gardens

---

© *Cambridge University Press 2014. Urban Home Gardens in the Global North: A Mixed Methods Study of Ethnic and Migrant Home Gardens in Chicago, IL.* Renewable Agriculture and Food Systems, Volume 30, Special Issue 01, February 2015. DOI: http://dx.doi.org/10.1017/S1742170514000180. Creative Commons Attribution licence (http://creativecommons.org/licenses/by/3.0/).

suggests they make a substantially larger contribution to the total area of urban food production than the public sites of urban agriculture, e.g., community gardens, farms and school gardens, that have garnered more attention[2,3]. Taylor and Lovell[2], for example, found that the total area of larger home gardens in Chicago visible in aerial images in Google Earth exceeded that of all other urban agriculture sites combined (158,876 versus 105,305 m^2). With the addition of smaller gardens not visible in aerial images, this number can be expected to be much higher.

We define the 'urban home food garden' (UHFG) as a garden managed by a single household on owned, rented or borrowed land, either on the same property as the residence or on adjacent land such as a vacant lot, tree lawn or right of way. Outdoor home food gardening may occur in the ground, in raised beds or in containers on built surfaces. The UHFG may provide food—including vegetables, fruit and culinary herbs—for not only the household but also for the larger community through the gifting, sale or barter of garden production. The lack of research on UHFGs in the North is puzzling and may, we hypothesize, stem from multiple factors, including the very diversity of the UHFG and its functions and the relative inaccessibility of backyard UHGFs to researchers who wish to sample and study them[7].

Our current research program seeks to address this gap in the literature—and ultimately to offer guidance to non-governmental organizations (NGOs), policymakers and other researchers—by exploring the social–ecological or socio-natural effects of home food gardening using a mixed methods research approach. Our methodology combines qualitative social science methods (in-depth interviews and participant observation) with qualitative and quantitative natural science methods (botanical surveys, garden mapping, and the physical and chemical analysis of soil properties) as a way of developing a better understanding of the relationship between the lived experiences of gardeners and the biophysical characteristics and processes of their gardens.

Our research program is informed by the more extensive academic literature on community gardens in the Global North and home gardens in the South and rural North. Community gardens are reported to contribute to household and community food security, community development and resilience and the reproduction of ecological knowledge through communities of practice. Home gardens in the South also purportedly contribute to food security, subsidize household food budgets, enhance household nutrition, furnish urban livelihoods, and conserve crop and native plant biodiversity[7]. At a broad scale, we ask, do UHFGs in the North have these same effects? If so, how? Through what interactions of the human and the biophysical?

Based on a review of the literature on community gardens and on home gardens in the South and rural North, we have developed an extensive set of research questions and hypotheses about the effects or properties of home food gardens in the urban North, reported in a previous paper[7]. In this paper, we begin to address a subset of these questions and hypotheses through an analysis of data from a study of home gardens in Chicago, IL. This work is ongoing; data were collected in the summer and fall of 2012 and 2013 from a purposive sample of 31 African American, Chinese-origin and Mexican-origin households with home gardens. In a third round of data collection in 2014, the sample will be expanded to include more gardeners, more ethnic groups and more neighborhoods, and research questions will focus on urban agrobiodiversity, including its cultural role and the processes through which it is maintained. Future publications will present an extended, comparative analysis of the dynamics of home gardening across groups.

11.2 STUDY SITE AND FOCAL POPULATIONS

The project focuses on three populations—African American, Chinese-origin and Mexican-origin households with gardens—in three areas on the south side of Chicago, IL. Covering more than 606 km², Chicago is the third most populous city in the United States, with a current population of almost 2.7 million human inhabitants[8], a dramatic decline from a high of over 3.6 million in 1950. The study areas were selected based on the ethnic composition of their populations (Table 1). The majority of residents of Study Area 1 are African American; Study Area 2 has a large Chinese-origin population and encompasses Chicago's Chinatown, while the majority of residents of Study Area 3 are Latino, primarily of Mexican descent. (The neighborhoods constituting the three areas are not identified, to protect the confidentiality of study participants in this and future publications, and are identified in the rest of the paper as Study Area 1, 2 or 3.) Previous research has revealed important differences in the spatial distribution of UHFGs in the city: single-plot vacant lot gardens are more prevalent in African American-majority neighborhoods, while on-lot garden density is greatest in neighborhoods with high proportions of Chinese immigrants[2]. Mexican-origin households were included as a focal population because persons of Mexican descent constitute the largest Latino group in the city.

11.3 METHODS

A purposive sampling strategy was used because of the lack of research on UHFGs in the North. Smaller purposive samples and a mixed methods research approach employing qualitative methods from the social sciences permit the in-depth investigation of garden-related patterns and processes, garden-centered social networks and the meaning of garden-related practices from the perspective of the gardener. Such an approach can be a productive prelude to quantitative surveys with representative random samples, allowing the researcher to determine the lay of the land before embarking on a large-scale study.

The authors' dataset of larger UHFGs in Chicago—developed through manual aerial image analysis in Google Earth—was used initially to identify households with UHFGs in the selected areas. All households with large UHFGs in these areas were contacted by mail, and non-responding households were visited in person. In addition, smaller food gardens were identified through fieldwork—by driving and walking up and down neighborhood streets and alleys—and were added to the recruitment effort. From each area, an ethnically homogeneous sample was selected. A screener was used to ensure that samples represented the targeted ethnic group and diverse family structures and included lower income households (those with a total gross household income of less than twice the US Poverty Guideline). Gardens of diverse types and sizes were also sought.

Data collection began in 2012 with ethnobotanical surveys. To characterize the ecological context of food gardens within the larger residential

Table 1. Characteristics of the study areas selected for a mixed methods study of African American, Chinese-origin and Mexicanorigin households with home food gardens in Chicago, IL.

	Study area 1 (African American sample)	Study area 2 (Chinese-origin sample)	Study area 3 (Mexican-origin sample)
Housing[1] (%)			
Single family	20–25	25–30	25–30
Owner occupied	30–35	45–50	45–50
Income[1]			
Mean household income	$20–30,000	$40–50,000	$40–50,000
< Poverty level (%)	40–45	20–25	20–25
< 2× poverty level (%)	65–70	40–45	50–55
Race/ethnicity[2] (%)			
White, non-Hispanic	0–5	25–30	5–10
African American, non-Hispanic	95–100	0–5	0–5
Asian, non-Hispanic	0–5	45–50	5–10
Hispanic	0–5	20–25	85–90
Foreign born[1] (%)	0–5	30–35	45–50
Food insecure[3] (%)	40–45	15–20	10–15

Note: Ranges are given to mask the identities of the study areas.
[1] US Census Bureau (2010), 2005–2009 American Community Survey 5-year estimates.
[2] US Census Bureau (2010), 2010 Census.
[3] Greater Chicago Food Depository (2011), Food insecurity rates for Cook County communities.

landscape, all cultivated plants on the lot were inventoried. Garden inventories and maps were updated during subsequent garden visits during the 2012 growing season. Two or three in-depth, hour-long interviews were conducted with the household's primary gardener, often in the garden itself, which permitted the interviewer to observe the gardener's interactions with both plants and people in the garden and with passersby on city streets, alleys and sidewalks. Repeated visits to gardens during the growing season permitted: (1) the establishment of rapport with gardeners from minority groups; (2) the documentation of seasonal changes in crop plant assemblages and other dynamic social or ecological processes; and (3) the collection of detailed information from gardeners on a wide range of topics, including gardening practices, participation in gardening activities, garden history, garden-centered social networks and personal history. The household's primary food preparer—who was often also the primary gardener—was also interviewed. For each household, three soil samples to a depth of 30 cm were collected systematically from each garden area once during the growing season, in August or September. The samples were analyzed for texture, nutrients, pH, soil organic matter and heavy metals. The rate of water infiltration was measured in three locations in each garden area using a single ring infiltrometer. Gardens were re-inventoried in the summer of 2013, and gardeners were re-interviewed, when possible, about changes in their garden since the previous year.

11.4 RESULTS AND DISCUSSION

11.4.1 SAMPLE CHARACTERISTICS

The socio-demographic characteristics of the 31 gardeners (10 Mexican-origin, 10 Chinese-origin and 11 African American) recruited for the study varied across ethnic groups (Table 2). As a whole, African American and Chinese-origin gardeners were older than Mexican-origin gardeners, who were more likely to have young children at home than the other two groups. The Mexican-origin and African American samples were roughly divided between men and women, while only one of the Chinese-origin gardeners was male. The majority of the African American gardeners (10 of 11) were homeowners and longtime residents of the neighborhood; duration of residence and home ownership were mixed for the other two groups. Because of the study's focus on ethnic gardeners and the greater popularity of gardening among older adults[9], almost all sample members were internal or international migrants. Of the 11 African American gardeners, seven—between the ages of 61 and 87—had migrated to Chicago as teenagers or young adults from rural areas or small towns in three southern US states, Alabama, Arkansas and Mississippi, as part of the Great Migration of African Americans from the American South to North. Only one of the

Table 2. Characteristics of the gardeners and gardens selected for a mixed methods study of African American, Mexican-origin and Chinese-origin households with home food gardens in Chicago, IL.

	Study area 1 (African American sample)	Study area 2 (Chinese-origin sample)	Study area 3 (Mexican-origin sample)
Gardener characteristics			
Sample size	11	10	10
Gender ratio (M:F)	5:6	1:9	5:5
Race/ethnicity	African American	Chinese-origin	Mexican-origin
Age range	Late 40s to late 80s	Late 40s to early 80s	Early 30s to late 70s
Foreign born	1 (9%)	9 (90%)	10 (100%)
Household income <2× poverty level	5 (45.5%)	3 (30%)	5 (50%)
Garden characteristics			
Mean food production area	61.7m^2	52.2m^2	40.4m^2
Location			
Single family lot	4 (36.3%)	3 (30%)	0 (0%)
Multifamily lot	2 (18.2%)	6 (60%)	6 (60%)
Vacant lot	5 (45.5%)	1 (10%)	4 (40%)
Plant diversity			
Mean food plant richness (taxa/garden)	16.3	14.4	8.6
Mean flowering plant richness (taxa/garden)	17.7	4.4	6.3

Chinese-origin gardeners was US born; the others were immigrants from southern China. All of the Mexican-origin gardeners grew up in towns or rural areas in central to southern Mexico.

11.4.2 GARDEN TYPOLOGIES

Garden location and structure varied across study areas (Table 2 and Fig. 1). As expected, vacant lot gardens were most common in Study

Area 1. Of the 11 African American gardens, five occupied vacant lots, four of which were former building sites that were being gardened in usufruct (n=2) or were owned (n=2) by residents of adjacent buildings. The fifth lot had never been developed but had been owned and gardened continuously by the same family since the 1930s. The remaining six gardens were located in the backyards of single-family houses or 'family buildings', i.e., two or three flat buildings in which members of the same family occupy all apartments. Four of the gardens of Mexican-origin households were on vacant lots, all former building sites; one lot was owned by the gardener, and the other three lots were gardened in usufruct. In general, on-lot gardens in Study Area 3 occupied more marginal spaces—including front yards and fence lines—because the backyards of the multifamily buildings in which gardeners in the study resided are often shared, multifunctional spaces accommodating the needs of multiple households, often including small children. The gardens of Chinese-origin households exhibited a unique layered structure consisting of a ground layer of leafy crops overtopped by vigorous vining crops—typically winter or hairy melon (*Benincasa hispida*) and bitter melon (*Momordica charantia*)—supported by trellises constructed from found lumber and branches. Only one garden in the Chinese-origin sample was on vacant land, which was privately owned and was gardened in usufruct by a recent immigrant from China. The gardens of Chinese-origin households were located primarily in the backyards of single-family dwellings, multifamily buildings or family buildings, with secondary growing areas in front yards and side yards. Food production in front yards is more extensive in Chinatown than in any other neighborhood in Chicago, but front yard gardens may be less culturally acceptable outside the ethnic enclave. A Chinese-origin gardener living on an ethnically mixed block outside Chinatown reported that her non-Chinese-origin neighbor objected to her front yard garden, characterizing it as messy.

Below we present an evaluation of our hypotheses about the properties and effects of UHFGs in the Global North, based on our published review of the literature on community gardens and on home gardens in the South and rural North[7].

FIGURE 1: Examples of home food gardens of African American (top left), Mexican-origin (bottom left) and Chinese-origin (right) households in Chicago, IL.

11.5 PROPERTIES AND EFFECTS OF THE GARDEN: AN EVALUATION OF HYPOTHESES

Below we present an evaluation of our hypotheses about the properties and effects of UHFGs in the Global North, based on our published review of the literature on community gardens and on home gardens in the South and rural North[7].

11.5.1 HYPOTHESIS 1

UHFGs make a substantial contribution to household food budgets and to community food systems.

The contribution of home gardens to the local food system was difficult to determine quantitatively for two reasons. Gardeners were asked to weigh all garden production during the 2012 growing season using a scale provided by the project. However, non-compliance was high, even among gardeners who appeared to be committed to the project. While garden production could be estimated from average yield statistics and the area or number of plants of each crop grown, as has been done in some studies of community gardens10, the resulting estimates are likely to be unreliable because of the large variation in growing conditions—and apparent plant productivity—observed in the sampled gardens. Soils were highly heterogeneous with widely varying nutrient levels. Furthermore, buildings and vegetation shaded all gardens but to varying degrees. Shading, the effects of which have not been investigated for most vegetable crop species, may have a large impact on yields[11].

Although production could not be measured directly or estimated, average food garden area (51.8 m^2) was relatively large compared to the area of a standard city lot (290 m^2). Gardens ranged in size from 2.4 to 201.3 m^2. Not surprisingly, given the large area of some gardens, some informants reported that their gardens made a substantial contribution to their household food budgets. One African American gardener, for example, claimed that she seldom bought vegetables during the growing season except for those she did not grow herself, including white potatoes, sweet potatoes and corn. Freezing produce from the garden was a common way for African American and Mexican-origin gardeners to preserve the harvest. For the former, preserving food they grew or purchased from farms outside the city and even stores represented a continuation of their parents' practice of putting up food for the winter in the rural South. One informant remarked, 'I never had to go hungry [as a child] because my father and mother, they were thrifty farmers, and they made sure during the summer they prepared for the winter'. Her neighbor added, 'Well when...chicken goes on sale or stuff...you'll be there [at the grocery store] because you don't want it to run out before you get there, and you buy more than what you need, maybe a two-month supply for your family'.

11.5.2 HYPOTHESIS 2

UHFGs contribute to local food systems beyond the household through the barter, gifting or sale of food.

African American, Mexican-origin and Chinese-origin gardeners all said they shared food with neighbors, friends, family or even strangers. Only one gardener, of Mexican origin, reported selling produce—primarily *pápalo* (*Porophyllum ruderale*), a strongly aromatic herb popular in the Mexican state of Puebla—from his garden. In Chinatown, however, older women who had been observed working in their backyard gardens were also observed selling produce at a transient, informal market on a neighborhood street corner. When one of these women was later approached in her garden and asked about selling vegetables on the street corner, she denied doing so. Some home gardeners—particularly migrant gardeners—may be reluctant to admit to selling produce from their gardens, which is not explicitly permitted in the city's zoning ordinance, leading to the underreporting of sales. African American gardeners, though, seemed to find the idea of selling garden produce to be almost morally repugnant. As one gardener remarked, 'I'm so goodhearted, I just hate to sell anything like that. But there's money in that too. But the collard greens, if I go out there and pick them, I could sell them. But I just feel like I'm supposed to give them. I can't set no price for nobody'.

In Study Area 1, vacant lot gardens make a larger contribution to the local food system through gifting than do on-lot UHFGs. One gardener reported that 10–12 households received food from his vacant lot garden, while another reported she gave food—apparently substantial amounts—to anyone who asked, and even to those who did not: 'There was a group of ladies I was giving some to over on P_ Street up there when I was taking the train to work. I walked through there every day, and one year we had so much I was like, I've got to give this stuff away because once you've harvested it you've got to do something with it. I had so many tomatoes and cucumbers I just put them in bags, put them in the truck, and said, hey y'all, get some of this'. For African American gardeners, sharing food from the garden may represent a continuation of Southern traditions of hospitality and community care, traditions which one elderly gardener referenced when discussing her chores on her parents' farm in Mississippi: 'We had about ten cows we had to milk every morning before we went to school. And people who didn't have cows, they would send gallon buckets up to where we were milking the cows, and my mother would say give this one a gallon of milk and that one a gallon of milk. She has four babies, and this one has so many. That's the way we would share with others'.

11.5.3 HYPOTHESIS 3

Home gardens contribute to local food systems by making culturally acceptable foods readily accessible through culture-specific assemblages of plant species and varieties.

(See Table 3.) African American gardeners from the rural American South often recalled fondly the gardens and diverse food crops their parents had grown: 'We would plant rows and rows of sweet potatoes, a whole field of sweet potatoes, just sweet potatoes. We raised peanuts and made our own peanut butter. All of the gardening that we did I could do…Corn, tomatoes, okra, string beans, all kinds of peppers, eggplant. We grew Brussels sprouts, squash, zucchini, white potatoes, onions, garlic; we had so many things—snow peas, three or four varieties of string beans actually'. Childhood memories of gardens influenced the composition of the food crop assemblages found in contemporary gardens. As one informant remarked when asked how he decided what to grow in his garden each year, 'I'm from Alabama, and during that time that I was down there my father used to grow everything, you know, like vegetables, greens, you name it, corn, cotton, you name it. My father he did it and I was raised up doing that and once I got up here [I got] into the garden'. The unique suite of crop plants found in these gardens support Southern foodways, or what one informant called 'country cooking,' which historically have been strongly influenced by African American cooks[12]. Collard, mustard and turnip greens were a prominent feature of these gardens, and some gardeners also allowed 'poke sallet' (*Phytolacca americana*), a weedy native perennial species spread by birds, to grow in their gardens to add to their greens.

Table 3. Assemblages of unique food crops observed in the home gardens of African American, Mexican-origin and Chinese-origin households in Chicago, IL.

African American	Mexican-origin	Chinese-origin
Black-eyed pea (*Vigna unguiculata* subsp. *unguiculata*)	Amaranth, green (*Amaranthus* sp.)	Amaranth, green and red (*Amaranthus* sp.)
Collards (*Brassica oleracea* Acephala Group)	Chilies—10+ varieties (*Capsicum* sp.)	Bitter melon (*M. charantia*)
Kale (*Brassica oleracea* Acephala Group)	Epazote (*D. ambrosioides*)	Bunching onion (*Allium fistulosum*)
Mustard greens (*Brassica juncea* cvs)	'*Frailes*' (unidentified)	Chinese broccoli (*Brassica oleracea* Alboglabra Group)
Okra (*Abelmoschus esculentus*)	*Hierba buena* (*Mentha spicata* subsp. *spicata*)	Chinese cabbage (*Brassica rapa* subsp. *chinensis*)
Poke sallet (*P. americana*)	*Hoja santa* (*P. auritum*)	Chinese celery (*Apium graveolens*)
Sweet potato (root) (*Ipomoea batatas*)	Lambsquarters (*C. album*)	Chinese lettuce (*Lactuca sativa* cvs)
Turnip (top and root) (*Brassica rapa* subsp. *rapa*)	*Pápalo* (*P. ruderale*)	Chinese mustard (*Brassica juncea* cvs)
	Sugarcane (*Saccharum* sp.)	Chrysanthemum, edible (*Glebionis coronaria*)
	Tropical corn (*Zea mays* subsp. *mays*)	Mustard spinach (*Brassica rapa* var. *perviridis*)
		Garlic chives (*Allium tuberosum*)
		Lemongrass (*Cymbopogon* sp.)
		Malabar spinach (*Basella alba*)
		Perilla (*Perilla frutescens*)
		Pomegranate, dwarf (*Punica granatum* var. *nana*)
		Sweet potato (leaves) (*Ipomoea batatas*)
		Watercress (*Nasturtium officinale*)
		White and yellow cucumber (*Cucumis sativus* cvs)
		Winter/hairy melon (*B. hispida*)
		Yardlong bean (*Vigna unguiculata* subsp. *sesquipedalis*)
		Yu choy sum (*Brassica rapa* var. *parachinensis*)

Mexican-origin gardeners also grew a suite of unique crops, including chilies (*Capsicum sp.*) and herbs. The composition of that assemblage, like that of African American gardeners, was also influenced by ethnic foodways and the plants that migrant gardeners or their relatives had cultivated in Mexico. At least ten varieties of chilies were identified growing in gardens; the majority were common varieties purchased as plants from commercial sources [big box stores (e.g., Home Depot), supermarkets and a local flea market called 'Swap-O-Rama'] but others were grown from seed procured from friends or relatives in the neighborhood, in other US states and in Mexico. Herb plants integral to regional Mexican cooking were also grown in gardens, including *pápalo* (*P. ruderale*), *epazote* (*Dysphania ambrosioides*), the tropical herb *hoja santa* (*Piper auritum*) and an unidentified species called '*frailes*' by the gardener. *Pápalo* was grown from seed from multiple sources, including neighbors and friends and relatives in Mexico. Some gardeners grew tropical corn from seed imported from Mexico. This photoperiod-sensitive plant fails to bear ears in Chicago; instead, gardeners harvested its wide leaves to make a type of tamale known as a corunda popular in the Mexican state of Michoacán. Like the African American gardeners who harvested self-sown pokeweed from their gardeners, one Mexican-origin gardener allowed the weedy annuals green amaranth, or pigweed (*Amaranthus sp.*), and common lambsquarters (*Chenopodium album*), to grow in his garden for culinary use.

Gardeners of Chinese descent grew the largest assemblage of unique crop plants with origins in the Global South, including diverse leafy and vining crops integral to their layered gardens and successional, seasonal plantings. Bitter melon (*M. charantia*) and winter or hairy melon (*B. hispida*) are key components of this culture-specific assemblage, with even small gardens accommodating these vigorously vining plants. Winter melon in particular was a prized food crop, cosseted by gardeners, who supported the large fruit with plastic bags and straw baskets, and occasionally stolen by non-gardeners, according to one informant.

11.5.4 HYPOTHESIS 4

Gardens conserve (agro)biodiversity.
A diversity of food crops minimizes the impact of crop failure in agricultural systems[13], while flowering and other ornamental plants provide valuable ecosystem services—including pollination services and habitat for insect predators of plant pests[14]—that potentially enhance the productivity and sustainability of those systems. Three measures of diversity were calculated to compare food crop and flowering plant diversity across study areas: richness (total number of taxa), taxa per square meter of total garden area (excluding lawn area) and similarity (the proportion of common crops between two sites or groups of sites). In aggregate, African American gardens demonstrated the highest food plant richness, with an average of 16.3 food crops per garden, and Mexican-origin gardens the lowest, with only 8.6 crops per garden. The average richness of Chinese-origin gardens was 14.4 crops. When normalized for total garden area, crop plant diversity was quite similar across all three groups of gardens: 0.38 versus 0.38 versus 0.30 crops m^{-2} for African American, Mexican and Chinese-origin gardens, respectively.

With a Sørensen–Dice similarity index (S_{SD}) of 0.47, the aggregate food crop assemblages of African American and Mexican-origin gardens were more similar to each other than either was to the aggregate crop plant assemblage of Chinese-origin gardens (S_{SD}=0.21 for both comparisons). Surprisingly, gardens in Study Area 1, the most economically disadvantaged area in the study, exhibited the highest diversity of ornamental flowering plants, with an average of 17.7 species per garden compared to 4.4 and 6.3 species per garden in the Chinese- and Mexican-origin gardens, respectively. The average number of flowering species per square meter of total garden area was almost equal in the African American and Mexican-origin gardens, 0.49 and 0.51, respectively, and much lower in the Chinese-origin gardens, 0.13. The implications of low floral diversity for the productivity of the gardens of Chinese-origin households warrant further investigation.

Although we attempted to characterize food plant diversity at the variety level, gardeners often could not remember what varieties they had planted and appeared to make little or no distinction at the infraspecific (within species) level. The following exchange was typical of discussions about crop varieties:

Interviewer: What kind of carrots do you grow?
Informant: I don't know. Do you know when I buy them I just buy them.
Interviewer: How do you pick out which ones?
Informant: The first pack I see I just buy them.

Across gardens, infraspecific diversity appeared to be low. Most African American gardeners, for example, reported planting one variety of collards, 'Georgia', and a handful of conventional tomato varieties, including 'Beefsteak', 'Early Girl', 'Roma', 'Better Boy' and 'Big Boy'. Mexican-origin gardeners planted the same tomato varieties as African American gardeners. The infraspecific diversity of cross-pollinating Chinese vegetable crops grown from saved seed, such as winter gourd and bitter melon, could not be determined from the data collected. Differentiating between the varieties grown in home gardens would require phenotypic evaluation in a common garden or genomic analysis.

Low infraspecific diversity has implications for the overall productivity of the UHFG. With a narrow genetic base, the food crops grown in urban gardens may be vulnerable to disturbances such as disease outbreaks or, with climate change, highly variable weather conditions. Urban growing environments are also highly heterogeneous[11] and are often of marginal quality compared to agricultural land outside the city. Because of a lack of research on the performance of crop plants in these environments, it is unknown whether the varieties currently grown by urban gardeners are equally productive across environments or whether gardeners might be better served by varieties adapted to particular niches in the urban landscape, e.g., shady gardens, gardens with well drained or poorly drained soils.

11.5.5 HYPOTHESIS 5

Diverse factors and processes influence garden plant richness and, consequently, the contributions of the UHFG to urban systems.

While some quantitative studies suggest landscape diversity could be greater for affluent households (a so-called 'luxury effect' of access to greater resources)[15], in our finer grained qualitative study we found that other factors and processes contribute to the development and maintenance of diversity in the home food garden and its landscape context. The unpredictability of environmental conditions and crop plant performance, for example, may prompt gardeners to diversify the crops they grow. As one African American gardener—who had earlier commented on the unpredictability of Chicago's weather—remarked, 'Every year you're not going to have a good crop for certain things but you just keep on because you will get something, and so this year looks like I'm going to have a good crop of tomatoes'. The African American gardeners with the highest ornamental flowering plant diversity in their gardens acquired their plants from neighbors, fellow garden club members, plant salvage or plant 'giveaways' sponsored by NGOs or government agencies. One African American gardener with few economic resources—and no automobile—but high social capital was particularly adept at mobilizing that capital to enlarge her collection, even recruiting the drug dealer across the street to ferry her to and from a plant giveaway in his luxury car. African American gardeners' longer duration of residence in their homes may also account for the high diversity of ornamental plants in their gardens, allowing them to accumulate perennial species over 40 or more years in some cases.

11.5.6 HYPOTHESIS 6

Gardens rely heavily on external inputs, undermining their sustainability.

While Kortright and Wakefield[16] found that most home food gardeners in their Toronto-based study practiced organic cultural methods—possibly an effect of provincial restrictions on cosmetic pesticide use—that was not the case in our study. The use of synthetic fertilizers, including water-soluble fertilizers such as Miracle-Gro™, was common, and the use of synthetic pesticides purchased from big box stores or local garden centers was not uncommon. One African American gardener, for example, reported applying a pre-emergent herbicide and fertilizer to his garden each spring. Even those gardeners who did not use synthetic fertilizers applied bagged organic matter to their gardens, e.g., composted cow manure, purchased at supermarkets or big box stores. No gardeners used cover crops. Only one had a compost pile. Gardeners did practice other passive forms of nutrient cycling, including burying kitchen and garden waste in their gardens. However, many gardeners reported throwing garden waste in the municipal trash at the end of the growing season. Soil testing guided the application of neither fertilizer nor organic matter. Not even the sole master gardener in the study sample had ever had her soil tested for nutrients.

Gardeners relied heavily on other inputs external to the local community, including water, seeds and plants, though Chinese-origin gardeners were less reliant on external inputs of seeds and plants than African American or Mexican-origin gardeners. The majority of the crops they grew were direct seeded, obviating the need for purchased plants, and they saved seeds from crops such as bitter melon, long bean and winter melon. While seemingly benign, the use of commercial seeds and plants may have negative social and ecological consequences. As Calvet-Mir et al.[17] found in rural villages in Vall Fosca in the Catalan Pyrenees of Spain, reliance on the market for seeds and plants can lead to reduced agrobiodiversity, a loss of social–ecological knowledge and the breakdown of social networks. It can also stymie the development of locally adapted varieties. At the same time, the ready availability of commercial seeds and plants may be enabling for urban gardeners who may lack the time, land or horticultural knowledge to produce their own seeds or transplants[7].

11.5.7 HYPOTHESIS 7

Gardening practices and external inputs influence the chemical and physical properties of garden soils, which may be a source of ecosystem services and disservices.

Urban garden soils are highly heterogeneous not only because of disturbance from initial development and construction but also because of the activities of gardeners. Like garden flora, garden soils were assembled from diverse sources. Gardeners filled the foundations of demolished buildings with materials scavenged from alleyways. They augmented the 'native' soil of their gardens with soil, compost and manure purchased in bulk or as bagged goods. They reported scavenging soil and organic matter from locations including an old stable, a forest preserve, construction sites and even the grounds of a former tuberculosis sanitarium.

They also applied organic and synthetic fertilizers to their soils, and in the majority of gardens surveyed nutrients were not limiting. Phosphorus and potassium levels often far exceeded levels required for optimal plant growth. While 25 ppm of phosphorus is an optimum level for vegetable gardens[18], sample concentrations ranged from 36 to 1076 ppm and averaged 263 ppm across the 31 gardens in the study. Concentrations of potassium ranged from 40 to 1236 ppm and averaged 231 ppm; 200 ppm is the recommended level for vegetable gardens[18]. Phosphorus and potassium levels were significantly higher in Chinese-origin gardens than in Mexican-origin or African American gardens, and the phosphorus and potassium concentrations of samples from the former gardens were strongly correlated ($R^2=0.63$), suggesting a common source of both nutrients in these gardens, most likely synthetic fertilizers. We hypothesize that Chinese-origin gardeners believe that very high levels of soil nutrients are necessary to sustain their apparently highly productive gardens. However, at high levels, phosphorus concentrations may inhibit plant growth. In addition, phosphorus, which has low solubility in water but adsorbs strongly to soil particles, may pollute stormwater through the erosion of those particles from bare garden soils. Stormwater pollution from gardens may be particularly problematic in Chinatown, which has a high proportion of impervious surface and where food gardens appear to constitute the largest pervious land cover type.

Gardeners' practices may mitigate the environmental impact of overfertilization by improving stormwater infiltration in garden soils, an important ecosystem service. Infiltration rates for urban soils have been reported to be highly variable19, and initial infiltration rates for our Chicago garden soils ranged from 0.07 to 30.0 cm min^{-1}. On average, however, rates were quite high across all three groups of gardens, ranging from 4.3 cm min^{-1} in Chinese-origin gardens to 5.4 cm min^{-1} in the African American gardens. Gardeners' application of organic matter and frequent tillage of garden soils, both of which increase soil porosity, may account in part for these high average infiltration rates. The percentage of soil organic matter was relatively high across all garden sites, ranging from 2.9% to 13.4% with an average value of 6.4%. Almost all gardens (n=29) were weed and mulch free, with the top stratum of bare soil frequently disturbed by hand cultivation or rototilling. Several African American gardeners planted their crops on bare ridges of soil and reported hoeing soil from the area between crop rows onto the ridges over the course of the growing season, practices they traced to their Southern roots. While high infiltration rates may mitigate the impact of excess garden nutrients on stormwater quality by reducing the erosion of phosphorus-laden soil particles from bare garden soil, they also potentially increase the leaching of water-soluble nutrients such as nitrates into groundwater.

11.5.8 HYPOTHESIS 8

Soil contamination could pose a threat to food safety and human health and undermine the UHFG's contribution to local food systems.

None of the gardeners in our study had previously tested their soil for lead (or for nutrients or other heavy metals), and only two gardeners were cognizant of the potential health risk posed by contaminated soil. Only one gardener employed compost-filled raised beds for food production, a common mitigation technique in community gardens. All other gardens were in ground, in 'native', unmitigated soil. EPA lead levels varied widely across garden soil samples, from 60 to 992 ppm, but study area averages were uniformly high, between 337 and 363 ppm. (Concentrations of other heavy metals were highly correlated with lead levels.) Those averages were much lower than the mean value of 2180 ppm reported by Shinn et al.[20] for 62 residential properties in a four-block area of Chicago, comparable to the mean value of 395 ppm reported by Kay et al.[21] for 57 samples from city-owned land and higher than the mean value of 224 ppm reported by Witzling et al.[22] for in-ground community garden plots in the city. The risk that lead-contaminated soil poses to the health of gardeners and their families is uncertain, with a wide range of maximum safe levels proposed in the literature[22]. Research suggests that the uptake of soil lead by vegetable crops may be weak[23,24]. Inhalation or consumption of contaminated soil particles, though, represents another exposure pathway. For 27% of the soil samples collected in our study, the lead concentration exceeded the EPA's hazard threshold of 400 ppm of lead in bare soil in children's play areas[25]. The frequent cultivation of garden soil that we observed may therefore result in increased exposure of gardeners and their families to lead in the form of contaminated dust or soil particles directly ingested or adhering to garden produce.

11.6 CONCLUSION

Our work with African American, Mexican-origin and Chinese-origin gardeners in Chicago suggests that UHFGs in the Global North share a number of beneficial effects that have been reported in the literature for community gardens and for home gardens in the South. UHGFs in the North strengthen community self-reliance and resilience by contributing produce from unique, culture-specific assemblages of food plants to local food systems through the gifting and, to a lesser extent, the sale of food. Gardens are also sites of cultural reproduction, which may enhance resilience at the household level, where values, practices and ethnic identity are resources that help individuals cope with crisis and trauma[26]. We found significant differences in gardener demographics, gardening practices, garden morphology, flowering plant diversity and food plant assemblages across ethnic groups. Future publications based on the data examined in this report will explore these differences and their implications for urban socio-natural systems in greater detail.

UHFGs in the Global North may also serve as reservoirs of (agro)biodiversity. In this study we found that a number of processes and factors other than household income—the so-called luxury effect of greater access to resources—contributed to the biodiversity of residential lots with food gardens. However, while overall plant diversity was high in some gardens, particularly African American gardens, floral diversity was low in others, notably the gardens of Chinese-origin households, and many gardeners grew a narrow range of commercial cultivars from purchased seed or plants. Low flowering and crop plant diversity may have negative implications for garden productivity and the contribution of the UHFG to local food systems. At the same time, ethnic gardeners—particularly Chinese-origin gardeners—who save the seeds of open-pollinated varieties of traditional crop plants may be preserving agrobiodiversity with origins in the Global South. Measuring the infraspecific diversity of these crops, however, requires research beyond the scope of the present project.

Although most of the impacts of gardening were positive, we found that the gardeners in this study relied heavily on external inputs, including seeds, plants, water, organic matter and synthetic fertilizers and pesticides to produce food. The sustainability of these inputs is questionable and their use reduces household and community self-reliance. While gardeners compost some garden waste on site, much of it enters the municipal waste stream, contributing to regional landfills and leaving open nutrient cycles within the garden. Gardeners import nutrient-rich compost and fertilizers from outside the garden, and a lack of careful nutrient management may contribute to urban stormwater pollution. Furthermore, contamination of unmitigated home garden soils poses a potential threat to the health of gardeners and their families, though in the case of lead the ingestion or inhalation of contaminated soil particles may present a greater risk to human health than the uptake of lead by crop plants.

Clearly, UHFGs in the Global North have the potential to make a substantial contribution to urban systems at the level of the household and larger scales. Our research, however, suggests a need for material support and outreach to fully realize that potential. Access to material resources was a concern for gardeners in our study and may be an even greater issue for the neighborhood residents not included in this study who wish to garden but do not. Some gardeners in the study expressed an interest in acquiring more land for recreational gardening or for small-scale farming, which is currently not permitted in residential districts in Chicago. Others remarked on the high cost of seeds, plants and other gardening supplies and lamented the loss of public or private distribution programs of free vegetable seeds and plants.

Gardeners in our study demonstrated an interest in learning more about gardening. While their practices were informed by traditional agroecological knowledge associated with their place of origin, those practices were malleable. They were further shaped by practical knowledge gained through gardening in Chicago, by the popular media, and by their interactions with gardening friends and neighbors and staff at garden centers and big box stores. Gardeners also frequently had questions for researchers about pest control, nutrient management and the cultivation of particular crop plants. All of these findings suggest a need for and receptiveness to increased outreach to home gardeners—particularly underserved minority gardeners—by the extension and research communities.

In addition to material and informational resource limitations, the biophysical environment potentially constrains the productivity and sustainability of urban production systems[27] including the home garden. Our research suggests that home gardeners could make valuable and willing partners in designed experiments[28] and participatory research programs with the goal of developing culturally appropriate, productive, sustainable and safe models of food production for the home garden. Gardeners in our study were curious about ecological processes in the food garden, formulating and testing hypotheses about garden phenomena, such as the failure of plants to thrive. With their inquisitiveness about the biophysical world and knowledge of urban food production practices, gardeners such as these could serve as co-researchers in university-sponsored research projects. As co-researchers, gardeners would help shape research goals and methods, and collect data in their own home gardens, which would function as experimental replicates in, for example, multilocational field trials of new food plant cultivars bred for urban conditions.

Through these strategies—increased outreach and material support for home gardening and participatory research programs addressing the social and biophysical limitations to urban food production—the promise of home food gardens as a source of social and ecological benefits can be fully realized in the urban Global North.

REFERENCES

1. Guitart, D., Pickering, C., and Byrne, J. 2012. Past results and future directions in urban community gardens research. Urban Forestry & Urban Greening 11:364–373.

2. Taylor, J.R. and Lovell, S.T. 2012. Mapping public and private spaces of urban agriculture in Chicago through the analysis of high-resolution aerial images in Google Earth. Landscape and Urban Planning 108(1):57–70.
3. Smith, V.M., Greene, R.B., and Silbernagel, J. 2013. The social and spatial dynamics of community food production: A landscape approach to policy and program development. Landscape Ecology 28(7):1415–1426.
4. Schupp, J.L. and Sharp, J.S. 2012. Exploring the social bases of home gardening. Agriculture and Human Values 29(1):93–105.
5. Airriess, C.A. and Clawson, D.L. 1994. Vietnamese market gardens in New Orleans. Geographical Review 84(1):16.
6. Gray, L., Guzman, P., Glowa, K.M., and Drevno, A.G. 2014. Can home gardens scale up into movements for social change? The role of home gardens in providing food security and community change in San Jose, California. Local Environment 19(2):187–203.
7. Taylor, J.R. and Lovell, S.T. 2014. Urban home food gardens in the Global North: Research traditions and future directions. Agriculture and Human Values 31(2):285–305.
8. U.S. Census Bureau 2011. U.S. Census Bureau delivers Illinois' 2010 Census population totals 2011. Available at Web site http://2010.census.gov/news/releases/operations/cb11-cn31.html (cited November 21, 2011).
9. National Gardening Association. 2009. The impact of home and community gardening in America 2009. Available at Web site http://www.gardenresearch.com/files/2009-Impact-of-Gardening-in-America-White-Paper.pdf (accessed March 15, 2012).
10. Vitiello, D. and Nairn, M. 2009. Community Gardening in Philadelphia: 2008 Harvest Report. University of Pennsylvania Planning and Urban Studies, Philadelphia.
11. Wagstaff, R. and Wortman, S.E. 2014. Crop physiological response across the Chicago metropolitan region: Developing recommendations for urban and peri-urban farmers in the North Central US. Renewable Agriculture and Food Systems (online ahead of print):1–7.
12. Harris, J.B. 2011. High on the Hog: A Culinary Journey from Africa to America. Bloomsbury Publishing, New York, USA.
13. Thrupp, L.A. 2000. Linking agricultural biodiversity and food security: The valuable role of agrobiodiversity for sustainable agriculture. Internal Affairs 76(2):283–297.
14. Andersson, E., Barthel, S., and Ahrné, K. 2007. Measuring social–ecological dynamics behind the generation of ecosystem services. Ecological Applications 17(5):1267–1278.
15. Cook, E.M., Hall, S.J., and Larson, K.L. 2012. Residential landscapes as social–ecological systems: A synthesis of multi-scalar interactions between people and their home environment. Urban Ecosystems 15(1):19–52.
16. Kortright, R. and Wakefield, S. 2011. Edible backyards: A qualitative study of household food growing and its contributions to food security. Agriculture and Human Values 28(1):39–53.

17. Calvet-Mir, L., Calvet-Mir, M., Molina, J.L., and Reyes-García, V. 2012. Seeds exchange as an agrobiodiversity conservation mechanism: A case study in Vall Fosca, Catalan Pyrenees, Iberian Peninsula. Ecology and Society 17(1):29.
18. Rosen, C.J., Bierman, P.M., and Eliason, R.D. 2008. Soil Test Interpretations and Fertilizer Management for Lawns, Turf, Gardens, and Landscape Plants. University of Minnesota Extension, St Paul, MN.
19. Pitt, R. and Lantrip, J. 2000. Infiltration through disturbed urban soils. In James, W. (ed.). Applied Modeling of Urban Water Systems, Proceedings of the Conference on Stormwater and Urban Water Systems Modeling, February 1999, Toronto, Ontario. CHI, Guelph, Ontario, Canada. p. 1–22.
20. Shinn, N.J., Bing-Canar, J., Cailas, M., Peneff, N., and Binns, H.J. 2000. Determination of spatial continuity of soil lead levels in an urban residential neighborhood. Environmental Research 82(1):46–52.
21. Kay, R.T., Arnold, T.L., Cannon, W.F., and Graham, D. 2008. Concentrations of polycyclic aromatic hydrocarbons and inorganic constituents in ambient surface soils, Chicago, Illinois: 2001–2002. Soil & Sediment Contamination 17(3):221–236.
22. Witzling, L., Wander, M., and Phillips, E. 2011. Testing and educating on urban soil lead: A case of Chicago community gardens. Journal of Agriculture, Food Systems, and Community Development 1(2):167–185.
23. Attanayake, C.P., Hettiarachchi, G.M., Harms, A., Presley, D., Martin, S., and Pierzynski, G.M. 2014. Field evaluations on soil plant transfer of lead from an urban garden soil. Journal of Environmental Quality 43(2):475–487.
24. McBride, M.B., Simon, T., Tam, G., and Wharton, S. 2013. Lead and arsenic uptake by leafy vegetables grown on contaminated soils: Effects of mineral and organic amendments. Water, Air, Soil Pollution 224(1):1–10.
25. Environmental Protection Agency. 2001. Lead. Identification of dangerous levels of lead. Final rule, 40 CFR Part 745. EPA, Washington, DC.
26. McCubbin, L.D. and McCubbin, H.I. 2005. Culture and ethnic identity in family reslience. In Ungar, M. (ed.). Handbook for Working with Children and Youth: Pathways to Resilience across Cultures and Contexts. Sage Publications, Thousand Oaks, CA. p. xxxix, 511.
27. Wortman, S.E. and Lovell, S.T. 2013. Environmental challenges threatening the growth of urban agriculture in the United States. Journal of Environmental Quality 42(5):1283–1294.
28. Felson, A.J. and Pickett, S.T. 2005. Designed experiments: New approaches to studying urban ecosystems. Frontiers in Ecology and Environment 3(10):549–556.

CHAPTER 12

Community Gardens as Contexts for Science, Stewardship, and Civic Action Learning

MARIANNE E. KRASNY AND KEITH G. TIDBALL

12.1 INTRODUCTION

The word learning generally brings to mind students acquiring a set body of information or content that is generalisable rather than related to a specific environment or other learning context. So, for example, students who are ecologically literate should acquire content related to the fundamental principles of ecology, including how biotic and abiotic factors interact to influence species distributions, ecological processes at varying scales, ecological models, and evolutionary theory (Jordan et al. 2009).

Whereas such content may be learned in a classroom, interactive or socio-cultural theories suggest that science and other learning occurs through the participation of the learner in the social and bio-physical processes taking place in a particular environment or context (Bandura 1977; Sfard 1998; Rogoff et al. 2003; Wenger 2003; Gauvain 2005; Illeris 2007).

© Krasny, M. and Tidball, K. 2009. Community gardens as context for science, stewardship and advocacy learning. Cities and the Environment. 2(1):article 8. Creative Commons Attribution license (http://creativecommons.org/licenses/by/3.0/). Used with the permission of the authors.

Drawing from the work of Bandura (1977) and Wenger et al. (2002), interactive theories focus on imitation of and interaction with skilled practitioners, and moving from a novice to skilled participant in a community of practice. For example, a young person might become increasingly skilled as a member of a community gardening community of practice through interaction with the environment and with more experienced gardeners during the act of gardening. Such communities of practice are characterized by a "joint enterprise" (e.g., gardening and associated social and cultural practices), "mutual engagement" that binds members together, and a "shared repertoire" of tools, language, and stories (Wenger 1998).

Whereas both cognitive and interactive views of learning focus on changes in individual learners, researchers working within the context of natural resources management have used the term social learning to describe changes that transpire among a group of stakeholders engaged in adaptive co-management of watersheds and other social-ecological systems (Blackmore 2007). Thus, social learning is defined as a collaborative process among multiple stakeholders aimed at addressing management issues in complex systems (Schusler et al. 2003; Blackmore et al. 2007; Pahl-Wostl et al. 2007). Although Wenger and other socio-cultural theorists use the term social learning to refer to individual learning as a result of interaction or participation, for the purposes of this paper we use the term interactive to refer to theories emphasizing learning as interaction or participation focusing on individual learners, and social learning to refer to learning among a group of natural resources management stakeholders.

Community gardens are distinctive in their ability to integrate food production with environmental stewardship and civic engagement. Environmental stewardship takes the form of restoring neglected and degraded plots of land, and civic engagement includes building relationships, collaboratively mobilizing resources for advocacy and to promote neighborhood well-being, and coming together to share and celebrate cultural traditions (Saldivar and Krasny 2004; King 2008; Campbell and Wiesen 2009). From the perspective of learning, community gardening can be considered as a rich community of practice integrating multiple activities and skills, and thus presents unique opportunities for multiple types of learning. Such opportunities include learning as acquisition of science content, learning as interaction or participation in planting, social, and cultural practices, and social learning among a group of gardeners to address management and policy issues.

While recognizing that community gardening provides ongoing opportunities for learning among adult gardeners, our purpose in this article is to outline more specifically how educational programs designed around community gardening might foster multiple types of learning among youth. To accomplish this purpose, we first present a brief overview of the Garden Mosaics intergenerational community gardening education program and of the learning theory underlyin this program. Next we examine evidence for multiple types of learning among youth in Garden Mosaics. We finish our discussion by showing the relationship of multiple forms of learning to the rich community gardening context and to the larger social-ecological system. At this time, our evidence for learning is based on surveys, interviews, and artefacts or products produced by participants (e.g., Gardener Stories and Action Project reports posted to the program website). Because our empirical evidence is limited, our intent is not to make definitive claims about the impacts of Garden Mosaics or other community gardening education programs. Rather our objective is to use learning theory and our own experience to stimulate thinking about community gardening educational strategies that may meet multiple learning, community, and environmental goals, and about how one might assess the outcomes of such programs.

12.2 GARDEN MOSAICS

Garden Mosaics is an intergenerational educational program taking place in urban community gardens across the United States (U.S.) and in other countries, which seeks to "connect youth and elders to investigate the mosaics of plants, people, and cultures in gardens." The youth participants, ranging in age from 9-18 years, engage in Garden Mosaics largely through out-of-school programs, including science enrichment, environmental education, youth action, gardening, and youth employment. These programs are sponsored by faith-based organizations, summer camps, community development corporations, half-way houses, 4-H, and community centers. Originally developed at Cornell University in collaboration with non-profit greening groups in cities across the U.S., Garden Mosaics is now housed with the American Community Gardening Association. The majority of funding for Garden Mosaics came from the National Science Foundation (NSF), although the U.S. Department of Agriculture and other agencies and foundations also contributed (Krasny et al. 2005).

The Garden Mosaics youth activities integrate learning from the "traditional" or practical knowledge of community gardeners with learning from science resources produced at Cornell University. Community gardeners in the U.S. come from all walks of life, and include immigrants from developing countries and African-Americans with roots in the rural southern states. Similarly in South Africa and other countries, community gardeners are often immigrants or internal migrants to cities with rural, agricultural backgrounds. Through Garden Mosaics, these gardeners share with youth the ways in which they have adapted agricultural practices from their homeland to highly urbanized settings. During their imscience investigations including the Gardener Story, Garden Inventory, Neighborhood Inventory, and Weed Watch, youth in Garden Mosaics interview gardeners and collect data on vegetables, weeds, soils, and the role of gardens in their community. Drawing on what they learn in these investigations, and in short-term learning activities outlined in the program's Science Pages, youth conduct Action Projects to enhance their community. Submitting the results of the imscience investigations and Action Projects to the program website provides opportunities for youth to share their learning. Thus the program activities are designed to facilitate science learning, intergenerational mentoring, cultural understanding, and community action (Textboxes 1 and 2). These goals are reflected in the multiple online and print resources, including illustrated Science Pages in English, Spanish, and other languages, a program manual, a training DVD for educators, and an interactive digital learning tool focusing on global agricultural biodiversity (www.gardenmosaics.org).

Over the first four years of the program, approximately 1200 educators, 14,000 youth, and 2500 elder gardeners from cities across the U.S. participated in Garden Mosaics activities. Currently the materials are available for free online and for purchase, and groups such as the American Community Gardening Association and Cornell Cooperative Extension continue to incorporate Garden Mosaics activities into new educator workshops and

> **Textbox 1.** Garden Mosaics Learning Activities.
>
> *i-m-science investigations, in which youth conduct research on gardens and their community.*
>
> - Neighborhood Exploration, in which youth explore the assets of their community using spatial images, interviews, and observations conducted while walking around their neighborhood;
> - Gardener Story, which entails interviewing a gardener about the connections of planting practices to cultural traditions;
> - Community Garden Inventory, in which participants list the activities and benefits community gardens provide for their neighborhood; and
> - Weed Watch, designed to collect data about weed problems and control methods in urban gardens.
>
> *Action Projects, in which youth apply what they have learned in their i-m-science investigations to enhancing their neighborhood or local gardens.* Example Action Projects include youth building a handicap-accessible raised bed, planning a neighborhood garden festival, donating produce to food kitchens, creating a plant sculpture in a garden, or sharing what they have learned with younger children.
>
> *Short-term inquiry* and other learning activities ranging from jeopardy games focused on food crops to blog exchanges with youth overseas.

ongoing after-school youth and school programs. The overwhelming majority of Garden Mosaics participants are urban minority and immigrant youth and adults; more recently we also are conducting Garden Mosaics programs in communities impacted by military deployment.

12.3 LEARNING THEORY SUPPORTING COMMUNITY GARDENING EDUCATION

We initially designed the Garden Mosaics program based on science inquiry learning principles (National Research Council 1996; 2000) and on

> **Textbox 2.** Example Garden Mosaics Youth Program.
>
> **Garden Mosaics Youth Program: Sacramento CA**
> In Sacramento, youth interviewed Hmong community gardeners about what they were growing and the cultural relevance of their plants. The youth compiled a list of insects in the gardens with both the English and Hmong names. They also learned that there was a long waiting list for plots at the community garden, so they designed a new community garden for elders and youth next to their high school.
>
> **Garden Mosaics Youth Program: Bronx, NY**
> In the Bronx, Abraham House provides housing and services for first-time offenders and their families. The youth in their summer program conducted an interview of "Pablo" at the nearby Bronx Cultural and Community Garden, and posted what they had learned on the Gardener Story database. Abraham House staff and Cornell graduate student Alexey Kudryavtsev worked together to guide the youth in inventorying weed problems, and entering their data on the Weed Watch database. The youth created a poster of their Weed Watch activities, which they presented at the annual meetings of the Weed Science Society of America. Later the youth used a blog to share their garden and neighborhood activities with youth conducting Garden Mosaics activities in Tomsk, Siberia.

ideas about the importance of "free choice" (Falk and Dierking 2002) or out-of-school settings for learning, such as community gardens. However, through our engagement in this and related civic ecology education programs (Krasny and Tidball 2009a), we developed a broader understanding of the potential role that learning theory may play in designing community gardening education programs. Underlying the science inquiry movement are individualist theories of learning, including behaviorist, cognitive, and constructivist psychology, which describe learning as an internal activity characterized by acquisition of knowledge and skills that may be transferred across contexts. However, community gardens, where there is an existing community of practice as well as a rich context for learning that integrates gardening, social interactions, advocacy, and cultural diversity, lend themselves to theories that describe learning as an outcome of interaction with the social and bio-physical environment (Illeris 2007). Such theories variously emphasize learning as moving from an inexperienced to skilled member of a community of practice (Lave and Wenger 1991; Wenger et al. 2002; Rogoff et al. 2003); the larger social, cultural and historical contexts of learning (sociocultural theory, Lemke 2001); learning as embedded in the more immediate social and environmental context (situated learning, Brown et al. 1989); the importance of reciprocal interactions among learners' behaviors, capabilities, and environment (social learning, Bandura 1977); and learning taking place through interactions of the learner with other components of an activity system (activity theory, Engestrom et al. 1999). However, all these interactive theories have in common their ability to help us think about alternatives to cognitive conceptions of learning as an individual activity with little reference to the social and environmental context.

In applying Lave and Wenger's (1991) notion of learning as changing participation in communities of practice to youth education, questions arise as to how to structure the learning experience to foster more skillful participation. In an empirical study comparing environmental learning among high school students in classrooms and community-based organizations, Hogan (2002) found that without proper mentoring and scaffolding by adults, students who were placed in a community environmental organization failed to achieve all the desired learning outcomes related to environmental stewardship and advocacy. In contrast, Bouillion and Gomez (2001) described a sequence of progressively more complex learning experiences for primary school students in Chicago focused on riverbank restoration, which resulted in both learning outcomes for the participants and improvements in the local community and ecosystem. Thus, rather than simply placing a young person in a community garden and expecting learning to transpire, this research suggests that opportunities for interacting with experienced adults who actively model the practices, coach novices, and provide scaffolding are needed to enable a young person to move from being an observer of a practice such as scientific research, gardening, or resource management, to a peripheral participant (someone who participates but has not yet mastered the practice), to a full or skilled participant (Brown et al. 1989; Rogoff et al. 2003; Gauvain 2005).

Much of the literature emphasizing learning as interaction has been in science education, suggesting that students learn science through participating in authentic science research communities (Brown et al. 1989). Citizen science programs, in which young people collect data that contribute to larger scientific studies, are one means of situating learning in authentic scientific practice (Krasny and Bonney 2005). Krasny and Tidball (2009a) have suggested that learning may also be situated in authentic natural resources management practices, such as community gardening, community forestry, and watershed restoration. These authors use the term civic ecology to refer to these small-scale, self-organized stewardship practices that integrate environmental and social values in cities and other peopled landscapes; this term also reflects the linked social and ecological systems implications of urban participatory environmental restoration and management initiatives (Tidball and Krasny 2007; Krasny and Tidball In Press). Community gardening and other civic ecology practices often emerge from the actions of local residents wanting to make a difference in the social and natural environment of their community, and is recognizable when both people and the environment benefit measurably and memorably from these actions. Thus, civic ecology practices can be considered as one form of adaptive comanagement, which integrates the participatory processes of collaborative resource management, with ongoing learning through experimentation inherent to adaptive management (Plummer and FitzGibbon 2007; Armitage et al. 2008b). Whereas adaptive co-management often is imposed by state agencies or other organizations, in the case of community gardens, this management practice has a tradition of self-organization and emergence, or being initiated by stakeholders within the community (c.f., Ruitenbeek and Cartier 2001).

Situating learning in community gardening and other civic ecology practices has several potential positive outcomes related to environmental and science learning. First, concern has been raised about the negative tone of environmental education that focuses on pollution and other environmental problems, whereas civic ecology education situates learning in positive expressions of community engagement and environmental stewardship. Moreover, youth may be motivated by the opportunity to contribute as valued members of a community (Olitsky 2007) and by seeing how their actions lead to changes in their environment (Chawla 2008). Finally, Aikenhead (1996), Jegede and Aikenhead (1999), and Fakudze (2004) have suggested that integrating the knowledge of parents and other local adults into a science education program, such as is possible through a community gardening education program, may serve as a means for immigrant and other youth who may not be exposed to western scientific ways of thinking at home to "cross borders" between the subcultures of family/community and western science/science education. Through integrating the knowledge of community members, educational activities may become more relevant and more readily understood, and thus may reduce a feeling of alienation among minority and immigrant students (Moll et al. 1992; Aikenhead 1996).

Researchers working within the context of natural resources and adaptive co-management have expanded on the notion of individual learning as participation in a community of practice, to suggest that learning also may be an organizational or group process that is an outcome of specific forms of participation in resource management (Armitage et al. 2008b). They have described social learning as the process by which stakeholder interactions go beyond participation to concerted action that brings about policy change, or more generally a collaborative process among multiple stakeholders aimed at addressing management issues in complex systems (Schusler et al. 2003; Keen et al. 2005; Blackmore 2007; Ison et al. 2007; Mostert et al. 2007; Pahl-Wostl et al. 2007; Plummer and Armitage 2007; Plummer and FitzGibbon 2007; Fernandez-Gimenez et al. 2008). The ability to take concerted action depends on gaining adequate knowledge through experiential processes of learning-by-doing or more intentional experimentation directed at understanding the impact of a management practice or responding to changes in the social-ecological system, as well as through discussion and reflection (Armitage et al. 2008b). Thus social learning within adaptive co-management is characterized by inclusion and integration of multiple stakeholders, perspectives, and knowledge systems; experimentation and observation; a social-ecological systems orientation; interaction and negotiation; and reflection on and evaluation of results (Plummer and FitzGibbon 2007). Finally, evidence of social learning includes shared action (e.g., "experiments undertaken"), modifications in practice on the basis of knowledge gained and reflection, and questioning of management system routines, norms, and protocols (Armitage et al. 2008b).

In much of the adaptive co-management literature, social learning entails researchers and managers designing a specific set of participatory decision-making and learning experiences for stakeholders, such as simulation modeling (Pahl-Wostl and Hare 2004), participatory mapping (Ison et al. 2007), or search conferences (Schusler et al. 2003). In the community gardening context, social learning may emerge in concert with ongoing management and advocacy efforts among gardeners, such as when gardeners use their experiential knowledge of the outcomes of community gardening to collectively advocate for protection of their gardens against the threat of development. Other instances of social learning are focused more on resource management rather than advocacy, and include an adaptive learning component (Armitage et al. 2008a). For example, volunteer efforts to restore degraded prairie and savannah habitats in Chicago provide a case study of how, through a series of informal planting and land management experiments (e.g., controlled burns to suppress invasive species), lay people and scientists were able to continually improve upon means of managing their social and biophysical environment (Stevens 1995; Jordan 2003; Moskovits et al. 2004).

12.4 EVIDENCE OF LEARNING IN GARDEN MOSAICS PROGRAMS

We turn next to evidence from Garden Mosaics for learning related to science content, stewardship, and civic action, drawing from the three learning perspectives described above: learning as acquisition (cognitive or acquisition theories), learning as participation (socio-cultural or interactive theories), and learning among a group of stakeholders directed at changing management practice (social learning within a natural resources management context). In our initial attempts to directly measure science learning outcomes of Garden Mosaics programs, the program director (Krasny), her graduate student (Doyle), and the outside program evaluator (Thompson) encountered challenges related to limited literacy levels and range in age among participants, resistance to paper and pencil tests among youth in out-of-school educational settings, and wide variation in activities implemented among programs at different sites. We then turned to more active measures of youth learning (e.g., drawings) as well as to indirect measures such as interviews and surveys of educators, the methods and results for which are reported in the three sub-sections below. Thus the evidence we present is preliminary and more rigorous studies would be needed to justify further claims about the types of learning that occur through intergenerational community gardening education programs.

12.4.1 SCIENCE LEARNING: LEARNING AS ACQUISITION AND INTERACTION

Consistent with the goals of our funder (NSF), our original goal for Garden Mosaics was acquisition of science content and inquiry skills by youth through hands-on activities. These activities included taking measurements on social and bio-physical phenomena and interaction with knowledgeable adults within an urban, ethnically diverse, gardening context. We used postprogram interviews with youth, pre/post-program drawings by youth and youth-generated lists of garden components, post-program educator surveys, and examination of reports of imscience investigations generated by youth to provide evidence of science learning.

During the pilot phase of Garden Mosaics, a graduate student conducted 30 open-ended interviews with a convenience sample of 28 participating youth from six cities, asking about how they benefited from the program. Although youth cited learning about soils, plants, and gardening as a benefit, this science learning outcome was mentioned less often than other benefits, ranking after gardening skills, learning from and developing relationships with elder gardeners, academic/research skills such as writing and measuring, and teamwork/ responsibility, and appreciation for the value of gardens (Krasny and Doyle 2002).

In the garden drawing activity also conducted during the early phases of the program, the outside program evaluator asked each youth in five different summer programs in low income, minority, urban neighborhoods in New York City and Pennsylvania to draw a garden before and after their involvement in Garden Mosaics summer programs. The evaluator then coded the drawings for presence of the following elements: trees, grass, flowers, fruits and vegetables, plant roots, soil, organized planting (beds, rows, etc.), row labels, paths, fences, watering mechanisms, weather elements, structures (casitas, sheds, etc.), animal life, people, and garden tools. Nineteen out of 23 youth who completed the pre- and post-drawings included at least one new element in their end of program drawing, with the mean number of new elements per drawing varying by site and ranging from 1.3 to 3.8. Fruits and vegetables were the most commonly included drawing element at both times. Grass, soil, weather, and flowers also frequently were included at both times, although there was a large decrease in the percent of drawings including flowers after the program, consistent with the fact that most of the gardens contained vegetables rather than flowers. Elements that tended to appear more frequently at the end of the program included water, organized planting, weather, grass, trees, and animals (Thompson 2004).

In an attempt to discern youth understanding of gardens as ecosystems, in particular garden inputs and outputs, the outside evaluator asked youth at the five sites who had completed the garden drawings the following questions before and after the program: "What does a garden need to grow and thrive?" and "What does a garden give back to you?" Eighty-eight and 94% of the lists completed after the program included at least one new input and output respectively, and 60% of the input and 75% of the output lists were longer following the program. There was little change in the frequency with which an item was listed at both times. Sun, water, soil, and air were the most frequently mentioned inputs, with seeds, care, and a person/gardener also common. On output lists, food and flowers were by far the most frequently listed garden items at both times; youth had difficulty imaging other garden outputs (Thompson 2004).

After several years of program implementation, a Cornell graduate student familiar with Garden Mosaics conducted an online survey of all educators for whom we had records of participation in Garden Mosaics training workshops or short Garden Mosaics presentations at professional conferences, and/or who had received the Garden Mosaics training DVD. Of the 696 email invitations mailed to educators, 105 were undeliverable, and 303 educators responded (response rate = 44%). Of educators who attended a workshop and received a DVD, 44% implemented the program, compared to 43% of those who only attended workshops, 20% who only received the DVD, and 13% who attended a short presentation of Garden Mosaics at professional conferences (Kudryavtsev 2006).

A subset of educators who responded to the online survey answered an open-ended question about what they felt was the greatest impact of the Garden Mosaics program on youth. Responses to this question were coded manually by the program director (Krasny). Given our original science learning focus in educator trainings and in the Garden Mosaics curricular materials, it is not surprising that science learning was listed most frequently as a program impact for youth. However, other impacts also were cited, including motivation to learn and awareness of the role of community gardens in the neighborhood (Table 1).

Whereas not all participants in the imscience investigations posted reports on the Garden Mosaics website, and thus these reports do not provide evidence of the learning of a representative sample of Garden Mosaics participants, they do suggest the types of learning that may occur when a group leader guides youth in this aspect of the program. For example, Gardener Stories posted online suggest that youth in some programs learned about gardeners' planting practices, backgrounds, and cultural traditions; the Community Garden Inventory results suggest that youth learned about activities, plants, and structures that occur in the gardens, and thus what the garden contributes to the surrounding community; the Neighborhood Exploration results suggest that the youth learned about their community's assets and needs; and the Weed Watch data sheets suggest that youth learned about weed species, growth, problems, and control methods.

In short, through our program evaluation and online databases, we have evidence to suggest that community gardening education programs have the potential to enhance understanding of science content among youth participants and to engage youth in the process of data collection and presentation of results. Interactive learning theories would suggest that interaction with elders and with the garden environment was important to this learning, whereas cognitive theories would emphasize acquiring content through factual resources such as the Science Pages.

Table 1. Educator responses to open-ended survey question: "Briefly describe greatest impact of Garden Mosaics on Youth." (n = 66 educators, some educators reported multiple impacts).

Youth Impact	Number of Responses	Example Educator Response
Science concepts	13	Connecting broad ecological concepts with on-site school garden.
		Students saw a connection between the health of the soil (we examined organisms in soil and compost) and what can grow there.
		Participants were able to identify the garden plots in a better way, at the same time they learned and/or practiced their east, south, north and west in order to learn about directions.
Awareness of gardens and gardens' contributions to community	12	Made students more aware of gardens and how they can reflect culture and experiences.
		Greater awareness of role gardens can play in creating a sustainable urban environment.
General learning and exposure	11	New material for my kids.
		Hands-on, collaborative learning experience.
Motivation to learn	9	The look of learning and the fact that they get it.
		An excitement for science was developed.
Awareness of source of food	5	Understanding where food comes from.
Connection to nature	6	They experienced the satisfaction and calming influence of working in a garden.
Self-empowerment, sense of achievement	5	Sense of achievement in growing.
		Students felt empowered and successful.
		Recognition of power to control surroundings.
Contributions to community	4	Gave them an opportunity to beautify their community and learn about land caretaking.
		They learned that they are part of the community and whatever they do has an impact on it.
Learning from elders	4	Realize that scientist is a broad definition, includes elders w/ knowledge.
		Youth got a lot of learning from Gardeners.
Working together	2	The students have an appreciation for … working together as a team.
Multicultural understanding	1	Multicultural understanding.
Stayed out of trouble	1	They stayed out of trouble
Science inquiry	1	Enhanced learning into scientific inquiry.

12.4.2 STEWARDSHIP: LEARNING AS PARTICIPATION IN A COMMUNITY GARDENING COMMUNITY OF PRACTICE

Through our work implementing Garden Mosaics in the United States, Canada, and South Africa, our vision expanded from community gardens as sites for science learning to encompass community gardening as a form of emergent, asset-based, resource management in cities (Tidball and Krasny 2007). This enabled us also to broaden our view of the educational potential of community gardens to encompass increasingly skilled levels of participation in urban resource management or stewardship, and to apply theories about interactive learning and adaptive co-management to a consideration of how youth might learn through participation in these stewardship communities of practice. Thus in addition to plant science and food security, which is the focus of many backyard and school gardening education programs, community gardening education programs may focus more broadly on the practice of coupled socialecological resource management in urban systems.

Through participating in the ongoing community gardening activities under adult guidance, youth may have gained competence as members of the community gardening community of practice. Whereas our evaluation did not focus specifically on more skilled levels of participation, reports of accomplishments of individual programs written by our outside evaluator (Thompson 2004; Krasny 2007), and Action Project reports posted to the website (c.f., Textbox 2, www.gardenmosaics.org), provided some evidence of youth becoming engaged in such a community of practice. Activities of the community gardening community of practice in which youth participated included gardening alongside elders, social and cultural events, harvest festivals, and educational events for other youth and community members. The fact that the youth cited forming relationships with gardeners as a benefit of their participation in Garden Mosaics suggests that, in addition to the gardening "joint enterprise," mutual engagement characterized this community gardening community of practice. The Gardener Stories and Garden Inventories posted online indicate that youth and gardeners also may have developed a shared repertoire of gardening language and stories (Wenger 1998).

Further, evidence from two evaluation studies showed that forming relationships with youth was an important outcome of participation in the program for community gardeners, reinforcing the notion that mutual engagement was created through the Garden Mosaics activities. In the online educator survey conducted by Kudryavtsev (2006), 20 of the 53 educators who responded to an open-ended question about the greatest impact of the program for gardeners talked about gardeners engaging and sharing knowledge with youth (Table 2). Similarly, in openended interviews with four gardeners during the pilot phase of the program, common responses to questions about program outcomes included forming relationships with youth and interaction with youth and others (Krasny and Doyle 2002).

12.4.3 CONCERTED ACTION: SOCIAL LEARNING AMONG GROUPS

Through the Action Projects, young people also became part of stakeholder groups taking concerted action to enhance the environment, a process referred to as social learning by scholars of natural resources management (Blackmore 2007). Action Projects were described in reports posted by the youth groups online and in accomplishment reports completed by educators. These projects included New York City participants who worked with community leaders, gardeners and other adults to turn an abandoned lot into a new garden; former gang members in Harlem who launched a local foods awareness and environmental justice campaign; youth in Philadelphia who conducted soil tests, made recommendations to the gardeners for improving the soil, and arranged for delivery of free compost to the garden to improve the soil quality; and Boston youth who donated the harvest from their plots to a women's shelter and food kitchen (Krasny 2007). These projects tended to involve hands-on environmental stewardship and community actions, rather than advocacy for a particular resource management policy as has been described in the adaptive co-management social learning literature (Blackmore et al. 2007; Pahl-Wostl et al. 2007; Plummer and FitzGibbon 2007). Whereas the environmental education literature also has focused on engagement in the policy process through such approaches as action competence (Jensen and Schnack 1997), a recent

Table 2. Educator responses to open-ended survey question: "Briefly describe greatest impact of Garden Mosaics on Gardeners." (n = 52 educators, some educators reported multiple impacts).

Gardener Impact	Number of Responses	Example Educator Response
Opportunity to interact with youth	20	The one gardener involved in this project appeared happy to share his knowledge with students and he seemed proud to show the 'fruits' of his labor.
		Increased personal vitality due to interaction with youth and renewed sense of purpose.
		City kids are not scary to work with when everyone is interested in plants!
Share knowledge with/ teach youth	9	Sharing their knowledge with the students and helping the students in their research.
		Being able to share the how's and why's of gardening with youth.
New information/ skills	7	Learned new ways to create food source.
		New materials, new ideas.
Learn about science	5	Realization of the science involved in gardening.
		Understanding of basic science, composting, connections.
Practical	4	Brought food home to their families and friends.
Learn about youth	3	Understanding that children could grasp gardening concepts and enjoy it!
Personal growth	3	Feel valued and included.
Tie to nature	2	Nature and elderly.
		Environmental awareness.
Building community	1	Community building.

study by Schusler et al. (2009) describes a broader suite of strategies for engaging youth in environmental action, encompassing both stewardship and policy activities.

According to Plummer and FitzGibbon (2007), social capital may be an outcome of the deliberation processes involved in social learning, and both social learning and social capital are linked to stakeholder engagement in adaptive co-management. The Garden Mosaics findings about the importance of the interactions with youth to the gardeners (Krasny and Doyle 2002; Krasny 2007) would suggest that youth and adults formed trusting relationships, which along with participation in civic activities such as community gardening, are aspects of social capital (Putnam 1995). In addition to their importance in adaptive co-management, social learning and social capital may enhance the resilience of a city neighborhood or other social-ecological system, or the capacity of such systems to respond to ongoing and catastrophic disturbances and conflict (Walker and Salt 2006).

12.5 COMMUNITY GARDENS AS SITES FOR LEARNING

Boyer and Roth (2006) have differentiated between school classrooms and out-of-school "heterogeneous" learning environments, which because of their variable and changing cultural, bio-physical and social environment, offer multiple opportunities for learning not available in classrooms. Community gardens, with their diversity of plants, cultures, and management and governance practices, can be considered as heterogeneous learning environments offering multiple possibilities for learning focused on science, stewardship, and advocacy. For example, the plants and insects offer opportunities for students to observe and perform experiments and thus acquire content knowledge related to pollination, whereas the community gardening practice, including planting, tending plants, and collaboratively developing rules related to plot allocation and pesticide use, allow opportunities for youth to become increasingly more skilled as members of a civic ecology community of practice (Krasny and Tidball 2009a). Further, through engaging with other gardeners in implementing and advocating for garden and neighborhood improvements, young people may become part of stakeholder groups engaging in concerted action.

Thus, our observations and evaluations of the Garden Mosaics program suggest that community gardens may provide opportunities for science content learning through both acquisitional and interactive processes, for learning as participation in communities of practice that integrate social, food security, and environmental outcomes, and for social learning as concerted action among a group of stakeholders. By providing opportunities to engage in multiple forms of learning, community gardens may expand on learning opportunities available in other informal science education settings such as museums and botanic gardens, which may focus more narrowly on science content. Further, community gardens are unique among both traditional (e.g., museum) and civic ecology (e.g., community forestry, wetland habitat restoration) learning contexts because of the cultural diversity represented by immigrant, minority, and other gardeners, and the related diversity of types of knowledge and planting practices.

Thus, community gardening provides opportunities for learning that addresses multiple societal goals, including creating a populace that is scientifically literate, that practices resource stewardship, and that is engaged in civic life. However, a number of challenges present themselves in facilitating such educational programs. These include providing the guidance and scaffolding that are necessary for youth to become more skilled members of community gardening communities of practice, and working within an informal educational infrastructure that includes myriad small, non-profit organizations and government agencies in which communication channels and networks are less clearly defined than in the formal, school educational system.

Although not covered here, community gardening education also has the potential to foster outcomes of interest to environmental educators and health practitioners. These include environmentally responsible behaviors, opportunities for unstructured time in nature, positive youth development, understanding of linkages between global and local food security, and gardening skills themselves (Krasny 2009). Recently, the National Forum on Children and Nature recognized community gardening as a best practice for connecting youth with nature (The Conservation Fund 2008).

12.6 CONCLUSION

Viewing learning as the result of interactions among individuals and the social and biophysical components of their environment provides an opportunity to explore the role of education in a larger social-ecological system. Interestingly, both interactive and social learning theories borrow terms from ecology, including references to learning as an emergent property arising out of interactions that are only partially controlled by the facilitator or teacher, and as fostering changes in the learner and the environment through a series of feedback loops and other interactions (Boyer and Roth 2006; Chawla 2008; Tidball and Krasny, 2009). Thus, an understanding of interactive and social learning is useful in considering how a civic ecology practice, such as community gardening, might foster outcomes not only for individuals, but also for the larger social-ecological system. For example, youth engaged in a community gardening education program such as Garden Mosaics form connections with adults, and reinforce and enhance the contributions adult community gardeners make to their community. Such contributions can include fostering biological and cultural diversity and ecosystem services, such as food, pollination, and sites for reconnecting with nature. This suggests that, in addition to examining the outcomes of community gardening education programs for individual and groups of participants, further research could examine the role of such programs in the larger socialecological system. In short, the question arises from the work described in this paper: What are the impacts of community gardening education not only on individual learning, but also on ecosystem services, social capital, and biological and cultural diversity, and thus on the sustainability and resilience of urban social-ecological systems (c.f., Folke et al. 2002)?

REFERENCES

1. Alberti, M., and J. Marzluff. 2004. Ecological resilience in urban ecosystems: linking urban patterns to human and ecological functions. Urban Ecosystems 7:241–265.
2. Barbosa, O., J. A. Tratalos, P. R. Armsworth, R. G. Davies, R. A. Fuller, P. Johnson, and K. J. Gaston. 2007. Who benefits from access to green space? A case study from Sheffield, UK. Landscape and Urban Planning 83(2–3):187–195.
3. Benedict, M. A., and E. T. McMahon. 2006. Green infrastructure: linking landscapes and communities. Island Press, Washington, D.C., USA.
4. Bjerke, T., and T. Ostdahl. 2004. Animal-related attitudes and activities in an urban population. Anthrozoös 17(2):109–129.
5. Bolin, B., S. Grineski, and T. Collins. 2005. The geography of despair: environmental racism and the making of South Phoenix, Arizona, USA. Human Ecology Review 12(2):156–168.
6. Bolund, P., and S. Hunhammar. 1999. Ecosystem services in urban areas. Ecological Economics 29(2):293–301.
7. Boone, C. G., G. L. Buckley, J. M. Grove, and S. Chona. 2009. Parks and people: an environmental justice inquiry in Baltimore, Maryland. Annals of the Association of American Geographers 99(4):767–787.

8. Bullard, R. D. 2000. Dumping in Dixie: race, class, and environmental quality. Third edition. Westview Press, Boulder, Colorado, USA.
9. Clark, W. A. V. 1991. Residential preferences and neighborhood racial segregation: a test of the Schelling segregation model. Demography 28(1):1–19.
10. Clergeau, P., G. Mennechez, A. Sauvage, and A. Lemoine. 2001. Human perception and appreciation of birds: a motivation for wildlife conservation in urban environments of France. In J. M. Marzluff, R. Bowman, and R. Donnelly, editors. Avian ecology and conservation in an urbanizing world. Kluwer Academic, Norwell, Massachusetts, USA.
11. Cutts, B. B., K. J. Darby, C. G. Boone, and A. Brewis. 2009. City structure, obesity, and environmental justice: an integrated analysis of physical and social barriers to walkable streets and park access. Social Science and Medicine 69(9):1314–1322.
12. Dallimer, M., K. N. Irvine, A. M. J. Skinner, Z. G. Davies, J. R. Rouquette, L. L. Maltby, and K. J. Gaston. 2012. Biodiversity and the feel-good factor: understanding associations between self-reported human well-being and species richness. BioScience 62(1):47–55.
13. Dickinson, J. L., B. Zuckerberg, and D. N. Bonter. 2010. Citizen science as an ecological research tool: challenges and benefits. Annual Review of Ecology, Evolution, and Systematics 41(1):149–172.
14. Duryea, M. L., G. M. Blakesiee, W. G. Hubbard, and R. A. Vasquez. 1996. Wind and trees: a survey of homeowners after Hurricane Andrea. Journal of Arboriculture 22(1):44–50.
15. Elith, J., and J. Leathwick. 2007. Predicting species distributions from museum and herbarium records using multiresponse models fitted with multivariate adaptive regression splines. Diversity and Distributions 13(3):265–275.
16. Elith, J., S. J. Phillips, T. Hastie, M. Dudík, Y. E. Chee, and C. J. Yates. 2011. A statistical explanation of MaxEnt for ecologists. Diversity and Distributions 17(1):43–57.
17. Evans, K. L., S. E. Newson, and K. J. Gaston. 2009. Habitat influences on urban avian assemblages. Ibis 151:19–39.
18. Ewing, R. 1999. Best development practices: a primer. Smart Growth Network, Butte, Montana, USA.
19. Fuller, R. A., K. N. Irvine, P. Devine-Wright, P. H. Warren, and K. J. Gaston. 2007. Psychological benefits of greenspace increase with biodiversity. Biology Letters 3(4):390–394.
20. Germaine, S. S., S. S. Rosenstock, R. E. Schweinsburg, and W. S. Richardson. 1998. Relationships among breeding birds, habitat, and residential development in Greater Tucson, Arizona. Ecological Applications 8(3):680–691.
21. Glaeser, E., and J. Vigdor. 2012. The end of the segregated century: racial separation in America's neighborhoods, 1890-2010. Civic Report No. 66. Manhattan Institute, New York, New York, USA.
22. Gobster, P. H. 1998. Explanations for minority "underparticipation" in outdoor recreation: a look at golf. Journal of Park and Recreation Administration 16(1):46–64.
23. Gobster, P. H. 2001. Visions of nature: conflict and compatibility in urban park restoration. Landscape and Urban Planning 56:35–51.

24. Gobster, P. H. 2002. Managing urban parks for a racially and ethnically diverse clientele. Leisure Sciences 24(2):143–159.
25. Graham, C. H., and R. J. Hijmans. 2006. A comparison of methods for mapping species ranges and species richness. Global Ecology and Biogeography 15(6):578–587.
26. Hernandez, P. A., C. H. Graham, L. L. Master, and D. L. Albert. 2006. The effect of sample size and species characteristics on performance of different species distribution modeling methods. Ecography 29(5):773–785.
27. Hope, D., C. Gries, W. Zhu, W. F. Fagan, C. L. Redman, N. B. Grimm, A. L. Nelson, C. Martin, and A. Kinzig. 2003. Socioeconomics drive urban plant diversity. Proceedings of the National Academy of Sciences USA 100(15):8788–8792.
28. Horwitz, P., M. Lindsay, and M. O'Connor. 2001. Biodiversity, endemism, sense of place and public health inter-relationships for Australian inland aquatic systems. Ecosystem Health 7:254–265.
29. Hough, M. 1989. City form and natural process. Routledge, London, UK.
30. Iverson, L. R., and E. A. Cook. 2000. Urban forest cover of the Chicago region and its relation to household density and income. Urban Ecosystems 4:105–124.
31. Jennings, V., C. J. Gaither, and R. S. Gragg. 2012. Promoting environmental justice through urban green space access: a synopsis. Environmental Justice 5(1):1–7.
32. Jerolmack, C. 2008. How pigeons became rats: the cultural-spatial logic of problem animals. Social Problems 55(1):72–94.
33. Jim, C. Y., and H. H. T. Liu. 1997. Storm damage on urban trees in Guangzhou, China. Landscape and Urban Planning 38:45–59.
34. Kessel, A., J. Green, R. Pinder, R. Wilkinson, C. Grundy, and K. Lachowycz. 2009. Multidisciplinary research in public health: a case study of research on access to green space. Public Health 123(1):32–38.
35. Kinzig, A. P., P. Warren, C. Martin, D. Hope, and M. Katti. 2005. The effects of human socioeconomic status and cultural characteristics on urban patterns of biodiversity. Ecology and Society 10(1):23.
36. Kruskal, J. B. 1964. Multidimensional scaling by optimizing goodness of fit to a nonmetric hypothesis. Psychometrika 29:1–27.
37. Kuo, F. E., W. C. Sullivan, R. L. Coley, and L. Brunson. 1998. Fertile ground for community: inner-city neighborhood common spaces. American Journal of Community Psychology 26(6):823–851.
38. Kuo, F. E. 2001. Coping with poverty: impacts of environment and attention in the inner city. Environment and Behavior 33(1):5–34.
39. Kuo, F. E., and W. C. Sullivan. 2001. Environment and crime in the inner city: does vegetation reduce crime? Environment and Behavior 33(3):343–367.
40. Landry, S. M., and J. Chakraborty. 2009. Street trees and equity: evaluating the spatial distribution of an urban amenity. Environment and Planning A 41:2651–2670.
41. Loss, S. R., G. L. Hamer, E. D. Walker, M. O. Ruiz, T. L. Goldberg, U. D. Kitron, and J. D. Brawn. 2009a. Avian host community structure and prevalence of West Nile virus in Chicago, Illinois. Oecologia 159(2):415–424.
42. Loss, S. R., M. O. Ruiz, and J. D. Brawn. 2009b. Relationships between avian diversity, neighborhood age, income, and environmental characteristics of an urban landscape. Biological Conservation 142(11):2578–2585.

43. MacGregor-Fors, I., and J. E. Schondube. 2011. Gray vs. green urbanization: relative importance of urban features for urban bird communities. Basic and Applied Ecology 12(4):372–381.
44. Mateo, R. G., T. B. Croat, Á. M. Felicísimo, and J. Muñoz. 2010. Profile or group discriminative techniques? Generating reliable species distribution models using pseudo-absences and target-group absences from natural history collections. Diversity and Distributions 16(1):84–94.
45. McCune, B., and J. B. Grace. 2002. Analysis of ecological communities. MjM Software Design, Gleneden Beach, Oregon, USA.
46. McCune, B. and M. J. Mefford. 2011. PC-ORD. Multivariate analysis of ecological data. Version 6.0. MjM Software, Gleneden Beach, Oregon, USA.
47. McPherson, E. G., D. Nowak, G. Heisler, S. Grimmond, C. Souch, R. Grant, and R. Rowntree. 1997. Quantifying urban forest structure, function and value: The Chicago Urban Forest Climate Project. Urban Ecosystems 1:49–61.
48. McPherson, E. G., J. R. Simpson, Q. Xiao, and C. Wu. 2011. Million Trees Los Angeles canopy cover and benefit assessment. Landscape and Urban Planning 99(1):40–50.
49. MEA. 2005. Millennium ecosystem assessment: ecosystems and human well-being. Island Press, Washington, D.C., USA.
50. Melles, S., S. Glenn, and K. Martin. 2003. Urban bird diversity and landscape complexity: species-environment associations along a multiscale habitat gradient. Conservation Ecology 7(1):5.
51. Mielke, P. W. 1991. The application of multivariate permutation methods based on distance functions in the earth-sciences. Earth-Science Reviews 31(1):55–71.
52. Miller, J. R. 2005. Biodiversity conservation and the extinction of experience. Trends in Ecology and Evolution 20(8):430–434.
53. Miller, J. R., and R. J. Hobbs. 2002. Conservation where people live and work. Conservation Biology 16(2):330–337.
54. Nowak, D., E. Crane, and J. Stevens. 2006. Air pollution removal by urban trees and shrubs in the United States. Urban Forestry and Urban Greening (4):115–123.
55. Oksanen, J., F. G. Blanchet, R. Kindt, P. Legendre, P. R. Minchin, R. B. O'Hara, G. L. Simpson, P. Solymos, M. H. H. Stevens, and H. Wagner. 2011. Vegan: community ecology package. Version 2.0-2. Oulun Yliopisto, Finland.
56. Pearson, R. G., C. J. Raxworthy, M. Nakamura, and A. T. Peterson. 2007. Predicting species distributions from small numbers of occurrence records: a test case using cryptic geckos in Madagascar. Journal of Biogeography 34:102–117.
57. Phillips, S. J., R. P. Anderson, and R. E. Schapire. 2006. Maximum entropy modeling of species geographic distributions. Ecological Modelling 190(3-4):231–259.
58. Phillips, S. J., and M. Dudík. 2008. Modeling of species distributions with Maxent: new extensions and a comprehensive evaluation. Ecography 31(2):161–175.
59. Phillips, S. J., M. Dudík, J. Elith, C. H. Graham, A. Lehmann, J. R. Leathwick, and S. Ferrier. 2009. Sample selection bias and presence-only distribution models: implications for background and pseudo-absence data. Ecological Applications 19(1):181–197.
60. Pickett, S. T. A., M. L. Cadenasso, J. M. Grove, P. M. Groffman, L. E. Band, C. G. Boone, and M. A. Wilson. 2008. Beyond urban legends: an emerging framework

of urban ecology, as illustrated by the Baltimore Ecosystem Study. BioScience 58(2):139–150.
61. Pineda, E., and J. M. Lobo. 2009. Assessing the accuracy of species distribution models to predict amphibian species richness patterns. Journal of Animal Ecology 78(1):182–190.
62. Pyle, R. M. 1978. The extinction of experience. Horticulture 56:64–67.
63. Sekercioglu, C. H. 2002. Impacts of birdwatching on human and avian communities. Environmental Conservation 29(3):282–289.
64. Sekercioglu, C. H., G. C. Daily, and P. R. Ehrlich. 2004. Ecosystem consequences of bird declines. Proceedings of the National Academy of Sciences USA 101(52):18042–18047.
65. Strohbach, M. W., D. Haase, and N. Kabisch. 2009. Birds and the city: urban biodiversity, land use, and socioeconomics. Ecology and Society 14(2):31.
66. Taylor, A. F., F. E. Kuo, and W. C. Sullivan. 2002. Views of nature and self-discipline: evidence from inner city children. Journal of Environmental Psychology 22(1-2):49–63.
67. Troy, A., and J. M. Grove. 2008. Property values, parks, and crime: a hedonic analysis in Baltimore, MD. Landscape and Urban Planning 87(3):233–245.
68. Troy, A. R., J. M. Grove, J. P. O'Neil-Dunne, S. T. Pickett, and M. L. Cadenasso. 2007. Predicting opportunities for greening and patterns of vegetation on private urban lands. Environmental Management 40(3):394–412.
69. Turner, W. R., T. Nakamura, and M. Dinetti. 2004. Global urbanization and the separation of humans from nature. BioScience 54(6):585–590.
70. Tyrväinen, L., K. Mäkinen, and J. Schipperijn. 2007. Tools for mapping social values of urban woodlands and other green areas. Landscape and Urban Planning 79(1):5–19.
71. Ulrich, R. S. 1984. View through a window may influence recovery from surgery. Science 224(4647):420–421.
72. UNPFA [United Nations Population Fund]. 2011. State of the world population 2011: people and possibilities in a world of 7 billion. http://www.unfpa.org/swp
73. U.S. Census Bureau. 2009. A compass for understanding and using American Community Survey data: what researchers need to know. U.S. Government Printing Office, Washington, D.C., USA.
74. Wenny, D. G., T. L. DeVault, M. D. Johnson, D. Kelly, C. H. Sekercioglu, D. F. Tomback, and C. J. Whelan. 2011. The need to quantify ecosystem services provided by birds. The Auk 128(1):1–14.
75. Whelan, C. J., D. G. Wenny, and R. J. Marquis. 2008. Ecosystem services provided by birds. Annals of the New York Academy of Sciences 1134:25–60.
76. Whitman, R. L., M. B. Nevers, G. C. Korinek, and M. N. Byappanahalli. 2004. Solar and temporal effects on Escherichia coli concentration at a Lake Michigan swimming beach. Applied and Environmental Microbiology 70(7):4276–4285.
77. Westphal, L. M. 1993. Why trees? Urban forestry volunteers values and motivations. In P. H. Gobster, editor. Managing urban and high-use recreation settings. General Technical Report NC-163. U.S. Department of Agriculture Forest Service, North Central Forest Experiment Station, St. Paul, Minnesota, USA.
78. Wilson, M., and S. R. Carpenter. 1999. Economic valuation of freshwater ecosystem services in the United States: 1971-1997. Ecological Applications 93(3):772–783.

AUTHOR NOTES

CHAPTER 1

Acknowledgments

Funding for the Ecological Landscaping conference was provided by The Ohio State University and its Urban Landscape Ecology Program. Special thanks to Lisa Miller, Kevin Power and other members of the conference committee for their help in planning and executing the conference. We thank Eric Strauss, Anne Cumming, Jessica Schmierer, the authors of contributed papers and anonymous reviewers for their help in bringing this special issue to fruition.

CHAPTER 3

Acknowledgments

This work was supported by EPSRC Sustainable Urban Environments Thematic Grants EP/F007604/1 and EP/I002154/1. Infoterra provided access to LandBase; MasterMap data were supplied by Ordnance Survey. Soil type data were provided by Soils Data © Cranfield University (NSRI). We thank Sarah McCormack and Jonathan Potter for technical assistance and Mike and Sally Edmondson for advice on allotment management. We gratefully acknowledge Leicester City Council, the households, allotment holders and farmers for access to their land.

CHAPTER 4

Acknowledgments

The authors wish to thank Yolanda Williams, Matthew Warren and members of the Sacramento community for aiding in the collection of samples and removing debris from potential garden plots.

CHAPTER 5

Acknowledgments
The authors thank the Community Greening Resource Network for their partnership on the project and access to the Baltimore urban gardening community, and Rufus Chaney of the U.S. Department of Agriculture's Agricultural Research Service for analyzing soil samples from participating gardens.

Author Contributions
Conceived and designed the experiments: JM KD AP KN. Performed the experiments: BK MP JM KD AP KN. Analyzed the data: BK MP AP. Wrote the paper: BK MP JM KD AP KN. Acquired funding for the study: KN.

Competing Interests
The authors have declared that no competing interests exist.

Funding
This work was funded by a Faculty-Community grant from the Johns Hopkins Urban Health Institute (http://www.urbanhealth.jhu.edu/). The Johns Hopkins Center for a Livable Future is supported by a grant from the GRACE Communications Foundation (but did not provide funding specific to this project). The funders had no role in study design, data collection and analysis, decision to publish, or preparation of the manuscript.

CHAPTER 6

Acknowledgments
Authors greatly acknowledge the key contribution of WA Water Corporation who provided relevant data and the fund to undertake this study. We thank Satterley Property Group for their financial contribution; Centre for Planning at Edith Cowan University for the operational management of the study. We are also grateful for Mr. Tim Perkins (Centre for Planning, ECU) and Dr. Bishnu Devkota (Infra Tech Pacific/WorleyParson, past-WA Water Corporation) for their generous comments on this paper.

CHAPTER 7

Acknowledgments

We would like to thank Mark Pavett, John Deeming, Brian Levey, Mike Wilson, Ray Barnett, Roger Ball and Stuart Morris for taxonomic expertise, along with land owners and managers for access to sites. We thank Daniel Montoya, Ian Cleasby and Beth Atkinson for statistical advice and the following field assistants: Sally Donaldson, Peter Harris, Joe Hicks, Jasmine King, Olivia Norfolk, Mark Otieno, Despoina Roumpeka and Juan Carlos Ruiz-Guajardo. This work is based on data provided through the NERC (Centre for Ecology and Hydrology), Ordnance Survey, Office for National Statistics, UK Data Service (EDINA UKBORDERS, and Casweb MIMAS), Natural England, Countryside Council for Wales and Scottish Natural Heritage, and uses boundary material which is copyright of the Crown.

Author Contributions

The study was designed and carried out by K.C.R.B., M.A.G., D.M.H., W.E.K. N.M., L.M.O., S.G.P., K.M.R., A.V.S., G.N.S. and J.M. K.C.R.B. and I.P.V. carried out the statistical analyses. All authors contributed to drafts of the manuscript and gave final approval for publication.

Competing Interests

We have no competing interests.

Funding

This research was funded jointly by a grant from BBSRC, Defra, NERC, the Scottish Government and the Wellcome Trust, under the Insect Pollinators Initiative (BB/I00047X/1).

CHAPTER 8

Acknowledgments

We thank Dr. Guy Robinson for his assistance and advice on acetolysis and pollen identification. In addition, we thank Rosaly Fernandez for assistance measuring garden parameters. This manuscript was improved by discussions with Drs. Amy Tuininga and James Lewis. The New York Restoration Project, the New York City Department of Housing Preservation and Development, New York City Parks, and the Trust for Public Land generously granted us permission to use their gardens for this study. We thank the many gardeners and local citizens in and around the garden communities for their courtesy and assistance in making this project possible. This document represents contribution 238 of the Louis Calder Biological Field Station.

CHAPTER 9

Acknowledgments
We are grateful to the gardeners for their support and to Eden Matteson, Caitlin Bell and Christian Escobar for help capturing and marking bees in the field. This work was partially supported by funds from a Lindbergh Foundation Grant to G.A.L and represents contribution 241 of the Louis Calder Biological Field Station of Fordham University. The manuscript was greatly improved by comments from two anonymous reviewers.

CHAPTER 10

Acknowledgments
We would like to thank the University of California and the Agricultural Experiment Station for support of this project. This work in the Emerson Park Community Garden could not have been possible without the dedicated cooperation of lead gardener, Barbara Smith. She was essential in maintaining communication with the gardeners and also distributing and collecting questionnaire surveys. We would also like to thank the gardeners at Emerson Park who allowed us space in their plots and that actively participated in the survey. Misha Leong and Jennifer Hernandez kindly read an early draft of the paper and offered helpful comments.

CHAPTER 12

Acknowledgments

The authors wish to thank Stephanie Thompson, Bruce Lewenstein, Rebekah Doyle, and Alexey Kudryavtsev for their contributions to the Garden Mosaics evaluation, and Gretchen Ferenz, Alan Berkowitz, and the many Garden Mosaics educators for collaboration in creating and implementing the program. Funding for Garden Mosaics and related work was contributed by the National Science Foundation Informal Science Education Program (ESI 0125582), from the U.S. Department of Agriculture Sustainable Agriculture Research and Education and Federal Formula Funds programs, and from the Weed Science Society of America.

INDEX

A

abiotic xvi, 6–7, 11, 13–14, 267
acetolysis xx, 178–180, 293
African American xxii, 243–261
agriculture v, x, xv, xvii, xix, 42, 55–58, 63, 65, 67, 70–74, 81, 105–106, 129–131, 133, 137, 143, 145, 150, 193, 241–242, 270, 292, 295
Alabama 246, 252
alien species 36, 71
allotments xvii, 55–58, 60, 63, 65, 67, 70–74
Andropogon Associates 39
anemia 88
animals xvi, 13, 18, 34, 43, 85, 108, 149–150, 173, 197, 199–201, 278
ants 153, 156
apple 200
aquifer 131, 137, 143
Arkansas 246
asbestos 104, 114
Asclepias tuberosa 42
Australia x, xix, 130–131, 144–145

B

Baltimore xviii, 104–107, 121, 125, 292
bees x, xix–xxii, 149–150, 153, 157–158, 160, 163–164, 167–168, 177–178, 186–187, 193–207, 211–215, 221–236, 294
 carpenter 227
 cuckoo 228, 231, 234
 leaf-cutter 207
 sweat 187, 221, 227–228

biochar(s) 73
biodiversity xvi, xxii–xxiii, 16, 18–19, 22, 24, 34, 43–44, 49, 51, 71, 73, 129–130, 137, 149, 167, 212, 255, 261, 270
Biodiversity in Urban Gardens Study (BUGS) 43–44, 153
biomass xvii, 44, 55, 63, 71
biotic 6, 11, 14, 36, 41, 267
birds xxii, 8, 15, 18–19, 44, 212, 235, 252
bodegas 188
bonfires 73
Boston 79, 282
brain 86
Britain (British Isles) 33, 35–44, 47, 156
Bronx, the 175, 195–196, 198, 201, 206, 272
bumblebees xxi, 149–150, 153, 157, 187, 193–202, 204–206, 221
Bureau of Land Management 236
burrows 206
butterflies xxii, 44, 167, 207

C

cadmium 84–85, 104
California xxii, 44, 79, 90, 211–213, 221, 223–224, 228–229, 232–235, 294
 Farm Academy 79
 Polytechnic State University (Cal Poly Arboretum) 221, 228–229, 234
 poppy 221
 State Fair 79

Calluna vulgaris 156
Canada 235, 281
Capra, Fritjof 7–8, 25
carbon (C) xvii, 12, 42, 45, 55–59, 62–63, 65–73, 85, 95, 134, 137–138, 140, 158, 165, 175–176, 178, 180, 202, 274, 281, 286, 293
  dioxide (CO_2) 56
cardiovascular disease 88
Center for Land-Based Learning 79, 81–82
cereal crops 56
chemicals xviii, xxii–xxiii, 8–9, 15, 57, 85–86, 104, 107–108, 121–122, 125, 242, 258
Chicago xxii, 44, 79, 241–249, 253–254, 257, 259–263, 273, 276
children 22, 25, 85–86, 88, 90, 95, 104, 108, 121, 123–124, 212, 246, 248, 261, 271, 285
China 247–248
Chinese xxii, 243–249, 251, 253–256, 258–262
civic ecology 272, 274, 284–286
Clean Air Act 88
Cleveland Ecological Landscaping 9
Cleveland, OH 9
climate regulation 55
climatic models 42
Coleoptera 156
collards 199–200, 202, 214, 251–252, 256
Colorado 41–42
Community Greening Resource Network (CGRN) 105, 118, 292
compost xxiii, 58, 63, 71, 73, 108, 177, 258–260, 262, 282
conflict 284
copper 85, 124
corn 95, 97, 214, 250, 252, 254
Cornell 269–270, 272, 278
  Cooperative Extension 270

  University 269–270
Cornwall 47–48
cosmos 214–215, 223, 225–227
Creative Conservation Agenda 38
crops x, xxi–xxii, 56–59, 61, 72, 74, 108, 112, 116, 123, 130, 134, 149, 151, 188, 193–197, 199–202, 204–207, 243, 245, 248, 250, 252–258, 260–263, 271
  genetically modified 57
cucumber x, xx–xxi, 174–178, 180–187
Cues to Care 16, 21, 38

D

daffodils 214
Davis, California xviii, 44, 81, 90, 131, 221, 223, 235
decomposers 36
Detroit, IL 79
developing world 56
Diboll, Neil 39
Dig for Victory 57
Diptera 153, 156, 202, 207
Dorchester, Massachusetts 124

E

earthworm(s) 11
East Harlem 175, 177, 188, 195–196, 198–199, 201
Ecological Landscaping Association 4, 9, 23
ecological niche 36
Eden Project 47–48
Edinburgh 151
educators 270, 277–280, 282–283, 285, 295
eggplants 194, 197, 252
energy efficiency 20
EPA 94, 121, 260–261
erosion 33, 48, 56, 259–260

Europe(an) v, 34, 36, 42, 50, 56, 150, 194, 204
eutrophication 41, 56
evaporation 15, 134

F

farmland xix–xx, 56, 150–151, 153–154, 156–164, 167–168
farms xxii, 56, 79, 81, 112–113, 151, 157, 242, 250, 252
  city 56
feces 108
fences 16, 38, 248, 278
fertilizer(s) xvii, xxiii, 13, 15, 19, 55, 58, 62–63, 73, 107, 177, 258–259, 262
  synthetic xxiii, 55, 73, 258–259, 262
fill 108, 116, 124, 174
flood(s) 55
  mitigation 55
flora 36–37, 41–43, 259
floral cover x, xx, 173, 176, 178, 180–184, 186–187
flower(s) xix–xxi, 16, 36–37, 149–162, 164–165, 167, 173, 175–181, 183–188, 194–195, 197, 200, 202, 205–207, 212, 214–215, 221, 223–228, 233, 278
flower-visitor xix, 150–155, 157–161, 164, 167
food v, xv, xvii–xviii, xxi–xxiii, 11, 16, 18, 44, 55–57, 71, 73, 103, 105, 112, 129–130, 134, 145, 150, 163–164, 168, 178, 188, 193, 195–196, 211–212, 234, 241–257, 259–263, 268, 271, 278, 281–282, 284–286
  preserving 250
  prices 57
  production xvii, 56–57, 71, 129–130, 134, 145, 178, 188, 195–196, 242, 248, 260, 263, 268

security xvii, xxi, xxiii, 56, 73, 193, 242–243, 281, 284–285
web(s) 11, 16, 234
foraging x, xxi, 187, 205–206, 221, 227
forbs xvi, 34, 36–37, 39, 41–42, 45, 50, 152
forestry 130, 133, 137, 274, 285
  community 274, 285
fossil fuel 15
4-H 269
France 42
Franklin, Carol 39
Fruit x, xix–xxii, 57–59, 61, 63, 71–73, 129, 133, 173–176, 186–188, 193–194, 197, 200–202, 242, 254

G

Garden Inventory 270–271, 279
Garden Mosaics xxiii, 269–272, 276–284, 286, 295
garden(s) x, xv, xvii–xxiii, 6, 16, 19, 33, 37, 39–40, 42–45, 47, 50, 56–59, 61–62, 65, 67, 69, 71, 79–81, 83–84, 86–88, 93–95, 97–98, 103–108, 111–116, 120–125, 129–131, 133–134, 136–139, 141, 145, 150–151, 173, 175–178, 180–188, 193–207, 211–216, 221–229, 231, 233–236, 241–263, 267–274, 276–286, 291–295
  community x, xv, xviii–xxiii, 56, 80–81, 83, 98, 103, 105–107, 113, 125, 129, 133, 137, 173, 175, 177, 182, 186–188, 193–207, 211, 213–214, 221, 224, 226, 235, 241–243, 248–249, 260–261, 267–269, 271–274, 279, 281, 284–285, 294
  domestic xv, xvii, 58–59, 61–62, 65, 67, 69
  residential 137, 151, 211, 221

rooftop 193
suburban 43–44
Gardener Story 270–272
gardeners ix, xviii–xix, xxii–xxiii, 43–44, 73, 95, 103–116, 118, 120–125, 177, 186–188, 196–197, 200, 204, 206, 213–214, 222, 224–225, 231, 233, 235–236, 241–248, 250–252, 254, 256–263, 268–272, 276–279, 281–286, 294
garlic 252
gasoline 85–86, 88
geophytes xvi, 34
Grand Mesa 41
grass(es) xvi, 33–34, 38–39, 41, 44, 47–48, 152, 278
grassland(s) 44, 70, 204
green beans 214
green space x, xvii, xxii, 20, 33, 40, 44–45, 47, 57–59, 61–62, 65, 67–68, 70–72, 103, 125, 193, 196, 205–207, 212
groundwater xix, 15, 130–131, 133–134, 139, 141–144, 260
Guelph 235

H

halictids 226
Harlow Carr 47, 50
health ix, xviii, xxi, xxiii, 7–8, 12–13, 16, 73, 85–86, 103–104, 106, 108, 110–111, 119, 122, 125, 134, 260–262, 285, 292
  hazard 86, 134
Healthy Towns Initiative 57
heat island 130
hedgerow 151
hedges 38, 63
Hemiptera 153, 156
herbaceous 33–34, 37–40, 45, 47, 51, 58, 61–62, 65, 68–69
herbicides 233, 258

herbivores 36
herbs 199–200, 211, 214, 242, 251, 254
hollyhocks 214
honeybees 149, 153, 157, 187, 194, 204, 221, 225–228, 232, 234–235
hoverfly xx, 150, 157, 163, 167–168
Hymenoptera 153, 156

I

ice age 36
Indiana 104
infertility 88
insect(s) xix, xxii, 149–150, 152–153, 156, 162–163, 168, 174, 176, 180, 186, 204–205, 207, 235–236, 255, 272, 284, 293
invertebrates 43–44, 49, 73, 212
iron 85
irrigation ix, xix, 6, 13, 18, 129–131, 133–135, 137, 139, 141–145

K

kale 199–200, 202
Kansas 104

L

LandBase 61, 291
Landlife/National Wildflower Centre 38
landscape ix, xv–xvi, xix, 3–20, 24–27, 34–36, 38, 42, 47, 51, 152–161, 164–165, 167, 205–207, 236, 245, 256–257, 291
  architecture 9, 35
  design ix, xv, 4–5, 12, 17, 27
  parcels xvi, 3–4, 6–7, 9–13, 15–20, 24, 26
landscaping xv–xvi, xix, 3–25, 27, 40, 129–131, 133, 137, 140, 144–145, 291

chemicals 9
ecological xv–xvi, 3–5, 8–12, 14–25, 27, 40, 291
    industry 14–15
    recreational xix, 129–131, 133, 137, 140, 144–145
    social-ecological 9
Latino 243–244
lavender 214–215
lawn(s) 3–4, 6, 14–16, 18–19, 21, 25, 38, 41–42, 45, 51, 134, 137, 141, 242, 255
    management 16, 21
leaching 56, 260
lead xviii, xxii, 11, 17, 19–20, 27, 41, 79, 84–91, 93–95, 97–98, 104, 108, 121–124, 236, 258, 260–262, 275, 294
    poisoning 85–86, 88, 121
Lead-Based Paint Poisoning Prevention Act 88
leaf 15, 71, 207, 227
    blowers 15
    litter 71
learning x, xxiii, 21, 79, 81–82, 112, 212–213, 224–225, 262, 267–277, 279, 281–286
leaves 15, 63, 193, 200, 254
    edible 200
Leicester 43, 59–60, 62, 70–71, 291
Lepidoptera 156
lettuce 214
Los Angeles 213
lowland(s) 70

M

manure xvii, 58, 63, 71, 73, 258–259
marketing 25
Massachusetts 9, 124, 206
Master Gardener 116, 258
MasterMap 61, 291
Mawson Lake 131

meadow 35, 41, 50, 164, 206
Mediterranean 43
megachilids 226
melon 248, 254, 256, 258
mentoring 270, 273
metal(s) xviii, 81, 84–86, 90, 104, 114, 125, 246, 260
    alloys 85
    heavy xviii, 84–85, 104, 125, 246, 260
Mexican xxii, 214–215, 243–244, 246–251, 253–256, 258–259, 261
Mexico 247, 254
minority 63, 245, 263, 271, 275, 277, 285
    groups 245
mints 199
Mississippi 246, 252
mowing 6, 11
mulch(es) 11, 13, 46, 48, 71, 123, 134, 260
munitions 85

N

nasturtium 214
National xvii–xviii, xx, 4, 9–10, 25, 38, 40, 42, 47, 59, 70, 73, 151, 157, 236, 270–271, 285, 293, 295
    Botanical Garden of Wales 47
    Forum on Children and Nature 285
    Gardening Association 9, 40, 42
    Park Service 236
    Science Foundation (NSF) 270, 277, 295
    Soil Map 59
    Wildlife Federation 4, 10, 25, 236
Resources Conservation Service (NRCS) 236
nature xix–xx, 12, 22, 39–40, 43, 45–46, 51, 104, 119, 150–151, 153–154, 156–164, 167–168, 196, 212, 214, 224, 285–286

reserve(s) xix–xx, 150–151, 153–154, 156–164, 167–168
nature-deficit disorder 22
nectar 164, 176–177, 194, 206, 212, 216, 221, 223, 233
Neighborhood Inventory 270
nervous system 86
nesting 18, 150, 164, 206
neurotoxicity 86–87
New Jersey 41
New York xx–xxi, 79, 175, 182, 193–196, 201, 203–204, 206–207, 277, 282, 294
nitrogen (N) xvii, 19, 56, 58–59, 61, 63, 65–70, 72, 176–177, 194, 199–200, 216, 248, 260, 280, 283, 293
North America 35, 37
North American Pollinator Protection Campaign 236
nuclear 85
  imaging 85
  reactors 85
nutrient(s) xxiii, 11, 14–15, 19, 55–56, 58, 71–74, 115, 130, 137, 246, 250, 258–260, 262–263
  holding capacity 56, 58, 72

O

O'Hare Airport 44
Ohio 36, 40, 291
  Ecological Landscaping Conference xv, 9, 17, 40, 291
okra 95, 252
open spaces xix, 129, 131, 137, 139, 141
organic matter (OM) xxiii, 56, 58, 62, 67, 73–74, 90, 93, 179, 246, 258–260, 262
ornamental xv, 3, 6–7, 130, 175, 200, 206, 214, 255, 257
Owen, Jennifer 43–44, 205, 212, 234, 236

P

paint(s) 85–86, 88–89, 93, 198
parasites 36
parthenocarpy 176
Pasadena 235
pavement(s) 137, 151–152
peach 200
peanuts 252
peas 95, 252
Pennsylvania 277
pepperbush 206
peppers 95, 194, 199–200, 204, 252
percolation 15
Perth xix, 129–131, 133, 139, 141–142, 145
pest(s) 8, 11, 13, 16, 18, 42, 107, 263
pesticide ix, 8, 11, 17, 258, 284
petrochemicals 73
Philadelphia 79, 282
Phoenix, Arizona 17
phosphorous 19
pigment 85–86
Pingree Potato Patches 79
plant(s) x, xv–xvi, xix–xxiii, 3, 6–9, 11–14, 18, 20–21, 25, 33–37, 39–47, 49, 51, 56, 63, 71–72, 85, 95, 104, 116, 120–121, 124, 129–130, 134, 140, 149–152, 155–156, 159–160, 162, 164–165, 167–168, 173–178, 180, 184–188, 193–196, 200, 206–207, 212–216, 221–230, 232–236, 243, 245, 250, 252, 254–259, 261–263, 269, 271–272, 277–279, 281, 284
  native xix, 21, 34–36, 39–44, 134, 140, 156, 160, 164, 212, 221, 229, 243
plastics 85, 254
plums 200
pokeweed 254

pollen x, xx–xxii, 153, 156, 163–164, 167, 173–188, 194, 202, 205–207, 212, 216, 221, 223, 233, 293
  beetles 153, 156
  transfer 174–175
pollination xv, xxi, 149, 176, 180, 194, 196–197, 199–201, 204–205, 207, 212, 255, 284, 286
pollution 9, 16, 19, 24, 104, 259, 262, 274
polycyclic aromatic hydrocarbons 124
potassium 259
potatoes 250, 252
poverty 193, 244
prairie 4, 38–39, 41, 47–50, 276
Prairie Nursery 39
pre-urbanization 41, 71
predators 36, 255
pumpkins xx, 200, 228
Pyrenees 258

R

railroad ties 124
rare earths 84
raspberries 194, 200
remodeling 88
rhizomes 37
riverbank 273
Robinson, G. 34, 55–56, 178, 293
rodent 206
Roggeveld Plateau 41
roofs 20–21, 34–36, 41–42
  brown 34
  green 20–21, 36, 41
  impervious 20
rosemary 214–215
Royal Horticultural Society 47, 72
run-off xxiii, 13, 15, 19–20

S

Sacramento xviii, 79–82, 92, 235, 272, 291

San Francisco 213, 222, 235
San Luis Obispo xxii, 211, 213–214, 221–222, 228–229, 234–235
Scotland 152
scrub 35
seedlings 37, 45–46, 51, 177
seeds xxi–xxii, 13, 15, 37, 45–48, 51, 173–174, 177, 187, 193, 197, 200–202, 254, 256, 258, 262, 278
semi-metals 84
Sheffield Botanic Gardens 47
shrubs 8, 16, 33, 38, 61–63, 65, 69, 71
slug 37, 47
snail(s) 37
social x, xv–xvi, xviii, xxiii, 3–6, 9–12, 14, 16–17, 19–21, 23, 25, 35, 39, 103, 119, 122, 125, 144, 188, 198, 242, 244, 246, 257–258, 263, 267–269, 272–277, 281–286
  capital 16, 257, 283–284, 286
  networks 244, 246, 258
sociology 8
soil ix, xv, xvii–xix, xxiii, 6, 11, 16, 19, 41, 46, 55–56, 58–59, 61–63, 65–70, 72–74, 80–81, 85, 88, 90–91, 93–96, 103–108, 110–116, 118–125, 133–135, 164, 177, 242, 246, 258–262, 278, 282, 291–292
  contaminants ix, xviii, xxiii, 103–104, 107–108, 110, 112, 121–122, 125
  fertility 107–108, 115
  organic carbon (SOC) xvii, 56, 58, 62–63, 65–69, 70–73
  remediation 104, 116
  testing 104, 106, 111, 114, 118, 122, 258
soup kitchens 107
South Africa 41, 270, 281
Spain 258
spiders 8

spring 36, 47, 49–50, 91, 160, 221–224, 227, 229, 258
sprinklers 130, 133–134, 137
squash 200, 228, 252
stewardship xxiii, 267–268, 273–274, 276, 281–285
stormwater xxiii, 19–20, 58, 259–260, 262
  infiltration xxiii, 58, 259
strawberries 199–200, 204
students xviii, 21, 33, 35, 81, 267, 272–278, 284
sulfur 87–88
summer 36–37, 41, 49, 141, 214–215, 221, 223, 243, 246, 250, 269, 272, 277–278
sunflowers 116, 202, 206, 214–215
sunlight 13, 198
Surrey 47, 49
sustainability xvi, 5, 14, 16–17, 20–22, 40–42, 56, 73, 255, 257, 262–263, 286
Sustainable Sites Initiative 4, 10, 23
Sustainable Urban Drainage (SUDS) 34–35
systems thinking 7–8, 22, 24

T

Technical Review Workgroup of the Environmental Protection Agency 91
thrips 152
thyme 214
tomatillos 199
tomatoes 194, 199, 202, 204–205, 214, 251–252, 257
topsoil 46, 58, 61
Toronto 257
trees 3, 8, 33, 38, 43–44, 58–59, 61–63, 65, 69, 71, 93, 129, 137, 140, 164, 200, 202, 206, 242, 278
  fruit 71, 129, 202
Tremont Community Garden 182, 187–188, 198

turf 134
turnip 252

U

United Kingdom (UK) xvi–xvii, 36, 38–39, 42–43, 46, 48–50, 57–59, 61, 70–72, 149–153, 167, 204, 293
United States (U.S., USA) v, xxii, 33, 35–41, 45, 57, 243, 269, 281
  Department of Agriculture (USDA) 105, 107, 236
  Fish and Wildlife Service 236
  Forest Service 236
University of California 90, 221, 223, 233, 235, 294
University of Sheffield xvi, 43
uranium 85
urban v, ix–x, xv–xxiii, 3–10, 12, 14–17, 20–23, 25, 33–47, 51, 55–59, 61–62, 65–74, 79–82, 85, 88, 97, 103–106, 110, 112–113, 116, 118, 120–122, 124–125, 129–131, 133–134, 137, 143–145, 149–151, 153–154, 156–164, 167–168, 173, 175, 181, 186–188, 193–196, 204–207, 211–213, 221, 236, 241–243, 256–259, 261–263, 269, 271, 274, 277, 281, 286, 291–292
  cooling 137
  desert 71
  ecology 8, 10, 17, 34, 44, 160, 204
  forest xix, 129, 133
  home food garden (UHFG) xxii–xxiii, 242, 256–257, 260, 262
  park 33
urbanization 3–4, 41–42, 56, 71, 149–150, 154, 162–163, 168

V

Victory Gardens xviii, 103

W

Wales 47, 59, 152, 293
walls 7, 11, 38, 164
Washington 104
wastes 14–15, 24, 46, 63, 73–74, 93–94, 258, 262
  household 73
water ix–x, xix, 6, 9, 13, 15–20, 55–56, 58, 61, 71–72, 85–86, 90, 108, 123, 129–131, 133–134, 137, 139, 141–145, 179, 234, 246, 258–260, 262, 278, 292
  consumption 137, 139, 141–142
  drinking 131, 137, 139, 141, 144
  filtration 56
  fresh 55
  purification 55
  storm xxiii, 19–20, 58 259–260, 262
  tap 123
watermelon 194
watershed 274
  restoration 274

waterways 8
weather xix, 20, 88, 133, 224, 256–257, 278
Weed Watch 270–272, 279
weed(s) 14–15, 38, 46–48, 63, 214, 260, 270–272, 279, 295
weeding 6, 11, 204
Wild Ones 10
wildlife xxii, 4, 10, 18, 23, 25, 49, 212, 236–237
Wisconsin 39
woodland 35, 38, 50, 70, 151, 153–156, 164
World War II 103

X

Xerces Society 212, 236

Z

zinc 85, 87–88
zucchini 200, 204, 252